BETRAYAL

BETRAYAL

The Story of Aldrich Ames,
an American Spy

TIM WEINER,

DAVID JOHNSTON,

AND NEIL A. LEWIS

RANDOM HOUSE

NEW YORK

"When a man's partner is killed he's supposed to do something about it. It doesn't make any difference what you thought of him. He was your partner and you're supposed to do something about it. Then it happens we were in the detective business. Well, when one of your organization gets killed, it's bad business to let the killer get away with it. It's bad business all around. Bad for that one organization, bad for every detective everywhere."

—Sam Spade to Brigid O'Shaughnessy
in *The Maltese Falcon* by Dashiell Hammett

Contents

BETRAYAL

1

"You Must Have the Wrong Man!"

Les Wiser snapped awake in a rush of adrenaline. His watch—the one he'd bought in Berlin, with the red star and the letters "CCCP" on the dial—said three A.M.

He showered quickly, dressed in a pale gray suit, left his wife and two sleeping kids in bed, and drove swiftly from his home in the Maryland suburbs toward Washington. The roads were empty on this Monday, Presidents' Day, February 21, 1994. The federal government was closed, and most of the people who made it run were still asleep.

He steered his 1991 black Ford Taurus through the deserted side streets of the capital and into the garage of the Federal Bureau of Investigation's Washington Metropolitan Field Office. The ugly high-rise building, wreathed in the deathly orange glow of mercury vapor streetlights, stood in Buzzard Point, a grim and isolated backwater of the city. It housed the FBI's street humps, the agents who worked in the District of Columbia and its surrounding suburbs.

Wiser was a tall man of thirty-nine, low-key, bespectacled, his mustache flecked with gray. At first glance he could be taken for an ordinary government bureaucrat, but the nine-millimeter Sig Sauer semiautomatic pistol on his left hip gave him away. Wiser was an FBI supervisory special agent, a squad leader, who had joined the Bureau in 1983 after working as a Navy lawyer. He had started at the bottom, working wiretaps, fugitive cases, and graveyard shifts.

He rode the elevator to the eleventh floor, letting himself in through the secured doors, and walked down a corridor with beige walls and threadbare carpeting. He stopped at an unmarked door just a few yards from his boss's office, pressed the buttons on a coded lock, and entered a windowless interior room, the squad bay for his case.

For nine months, Wiser had worked out of this cramped cocoon of an office twelve hours a day, sometimes longer. Everyone working on his case—Wiser, his agents, the surveillance teams—had had to take lie-detector tests and abandon the idea of time off. Wiser himself had spent Christmas Day with headphones on in a tiny downstairs office jammed with blinking electronic gear, listening to wiretaps. Everybody knew Wiser hunted spies, but he waved off anyone who asked what he was up to, telling them he was working on a case from *The X Files,* a television show about FBI agents investigating paranormal phenomena.

In fact, he was working the biggest case of his life. It was an espionage case, code-named "Nightmover."

He and his squad had found a mole inside the Central Intelligence Agency. The mole had burned almost every Soviet agent who was secretly working for the United States. At least ten of them had been arrested and executed. It had been a disaster without parallel for the CIA. But the Agency had refused to believe it harbored a traitor, and it had surrounded the disaster in a shield of secrecy. It had not called in the FBI until 1991.

Once the Bureau knew the facts, in 1993, it had opened a full-fledged criminal investigation. Wiser and his agents—the listeners who tapped telephones and planted bugs in the mole's house, the accountants who sifted his American Express bills, the watchers who trailed him around the clock, the black-bag agents who stole his trash and surreptitiously searched his house, the pilots who flew the light plane that secretly trailed his car—had amassed a mountain of circumstantial evidence against their target. They had come to be on intimate terms with him, calling him by his first name, listening to the chatter and babble of his telephone conversations with his wife, and picking up clues that she was entangled in his espionage. They shadowed him when he took his five-year-old son to the movies, reacted with disgust when he paid $9,000 in cash one day at the Neiman-Marcus department store to settle his bills, surveilled him in airport bars as he drank vodka and smoked cigarettes like a man bent on giving himself a heart attack.

More than that, they knew his mind. He was arrogant. He was book-smart but not streetwise. And he was one of the sloppiest, most brazen, and least savvy spies imaginable.

But Wiser had been careful not to underestimate him. The man was, after all, a trained intelligence officer, schooled in the art of spotting somebody on his tail. And though the FBI knew their man was in touch with the Russians, and though they had tracked more than $1.5 million he had mysteriously deposited into his bank accounts, they never had caught him in the act of slipping CIA documents into a cache or pocketing a payoff from Moscow.

Six o'clock. Wiser waited in the dismal squad bay as the day dawned gray and dreary over the capital. His surveillance crew had spent the night at checkpoints throughout the mole's neighborhood across the Potomac River in Arlington,

Virginia—a fancy suburb, a lot fancier than Wiser or the rest
of his squad could afford. The lookouts had the mole's half-
million-dollar split-level house surrounded.

Downstairs at the field office, the listeners sat in a tiny
cubicle before a blinking circuit board tuned to the telephone
taps and hidden microphones in the house on North Randolph Street. Wiser checked the surveillance. Nothing stirring. The mole was unaware that an intricate web of
electronic and physical surveillance was about to snare him.
Still, Wiser felt a lump tightening in his gut, the fear that the
slightest mistake would make his quarry bolt. The mole was
scheduled to leave tomorrow on an official trip that would
take him to Moscow. The idea that he might defect was on
everyone's mind, and no one cared to contemplate the consequences.

Six-thirty. The Special Surveillance Group, the FBI employees who tailed the target night and day, reported that all
remained calm. They knew their man's habits by heart. He
would have left the house by now if he were going to send a
clandestine message to his Russian controllers, a chalk mark
on a mailbox signifying he was ready to deliver a computer
disk of classified documents covertly copied at CIA headquarters. If he went out early to leave a signal, they would
postpone the arrest to see what he was up to. But if he did
nothing, they would arrest him.

A few minutes after seven, Wiser gave the order to proceed
as planned. Nearly a hundred FBI agents, technicians, and
support personnel quietly converged on the neighborhood.
The men who were going to arrest the target drove directly to
their forward staging base, the parking lot of an Italian deli-
catessen a quarter mile from the house on North Randolph
Street. They had gone there a lot during the investigation.
Great sandwiches.

Wiser waited until nearly eight o'clock to drive across the Potomac River to the U.S. attorney's office on King Street in Alexandria, Virginia. Wiser met Mark J. Hulkower, the federal prosecutor whom he had asked to handle the case in court. The two men drove to the tidy red-brick office building in Alexandria that housed the courtrooms of the federal magistrates. Wiser carried a sheaf of papers, including a thirty-five-page affidavit he had written outlining the evidence amassed from electronic eavesdropping, break-ins, and thefts.

The day before, the prosecutor had asked Barry R. Poretz, the U.S. magistrate-judge, if he could be available on Monday morning. Wiser handed Poretz the papers, then left the magistrate alone in his chambers. The agent and the prosecutor waited in an outer office of the deserted building. As the clock crawled past nine and toward midmorning, Wiser grew more nervous with each passing minute. He visualized Poretz slowly reading every word of the dense, single-spaced affidavit while the complicated machinery Wiser had set into motion was put on hold. After what seemed like an eternity, Poretz summoned the government men to his chambers, asked a few questions, and at five minutes to ten began signing warrants for the arrest of the mole and his wife, the postarrest search of his house and safety deposit box at First Union Bank, and the seizure of his 1992 Jaguar and her 1989 Honda.

Armed with the warrants, Wiser called his immediate superior, John F. Lewis, Jr., at the command post in the FBI's Tyson's Corner, Virginia, satellite office. The office corridors were crowded with agents and bristling with the nervous energy and bravado that always accompanies a takedown in a big case. There was no fancy code word. Wiser just said, "Okay. Go ahead."

The trap was baited. One of the FBI agents telephoned the CIA's headquarters in Langley, Virginia, and talked to the target's boss. The CIA official then called the target at home and gave him a carefully scripted message.

"Rick," he said, "something important has just turned up. It has a direct bearing on the Moscow trip. You better come into the office. I think you need to see it now."

Rick Ames put down the phone and told his wife, Rosario, that he was going over to the CIA for an hour or so. Whatever this was, he needed to get it out of the way. He had been looking forward to this trip for months.

Ames was tall and thin and wore wire-rimmed aviator glasses. He combed his receding hair straight back and kept his mustache neatly trimmed. In his plainness, he bore a passing resemblance to Wiser. It was as if mole and mole hunter alike had chosen a bland exterior as camouflage.

Wearing brown slacks and a dark green shirt with a tiny sailboat embroidered on the chest, he walked out of the gray brick house with red shutters and double dormers at 2512 North Randolph Street, leaving Rosario inside with their son, Paul, and Rosario's mother, Cecilia. The morning was chilly, and he wore a windbreaker. In his wallet were nine crisp $100 bills with sequential serial numbers. He got into his 1992 Jaguar and rolled it down the hardtop driveway. He turned right on North Randolph and right again on Quebec, pressing the cigarette lighter with his right hand and firing up a Benson & Hedges.

Then he saw two pairs of taillights directly ahead of him, two cars side by side, blocking the two-lane street where Quebec intersected Nellie Custis Drive, his usual route to the office. Ames braked to a stop, waiting for the car in the right-hand lane to turn.

It didn't move.

Two more cars swung up Quebec behind Ames. Mike Donner, a hulking SWAT team agent who along with Wiser had designed the arrest scenario, pulled up close behind the Jaguar and stopped. Donner placed a red flasher light on his dashboard and switched it on along with a siren. Ames, good citizen that he was, pulled toward the curb. Donner pressed the front bumper of his car against the rear of the Jaguar. Eight FBI agents jumped from the four cars surrounding Ames.

Back on North Randolph Street, Yolanda Larson, a pregnant, Spanish-speaking FBI agent, rang the doorbell. A housekeeper answered. Rosario, dressed in a bathrobe, looked down the staircase. She hurried to the door. "Mrs. Ames?" Larson said. The agent told her her husband was being arrested for espionage and that she should come with them. Rosario stared and went slack with shock.

On Quebec Street, Donner and a fellow agent, Dell Spry, stood at the window of the Jaguar. Ames looked up, bewildered. Spry ordered him to keep his hands in sight and step out of the car. "What?" Ames said, lowering the electric window.

Donner reached in, pulled the cigarette from Ames's lips, and tossed it aside. "Get out of the car," he growled. Donner flung open the car door and pulled Ames to his feet. "Put your hands on the car," he said. "You're under arrest for espionage."

Ames gasped and sputtered, the blood draining from his face and his expression turning from confusion to terror. Spry told Ames to put his hands behind his head. The agent yanked his arms down one at a time and handcuffed him, palms out.

"What's all this about?" Ames shouted as the cuffs clicked shut around his wrists. "You're making a big mistake! You must have the wrong man!"

2

Cul-de-sac

Aldrich Hazen Ames was a child of the Central Intelligence Agency. For forty years, spying had shaped his thoughts and his speech and his sense of who he was. The son of a CIA man, he had worked for the Agency all his life, starting as a teenage handyman and file clerk in the summer of 1957 and rising to become a full-fledged spy in the clandestine service of his country ten years later.

Back then, the men of the CIA had a sense that anything was possible. They had bottomless purses, they had endless opportunities, they had a world to gain. They could make presidents and break prime ministers, and their work would never be questioned, for they were members of a great secret brotherhood. They were *different*. They had unique powers and responsibilities. They played by their own rules, and they broke them if needed.

Colin Thompson, a veteran CIA officer who worked with Ames in the Soviet division of the Agency's Directorate of Operations—the D.O.—put it this way: "There was a mysticism, some special thing that only exists in the D.O. And no one else can understand it. Everything's shrouded in secrecy. It's a mist you dip into and hide behind. You believe you have become an elite person in the world of American government, and the Agency encourages that belief from the moment you come in. They make you a believer."

The CIA had sent Rick Ames to exotic and exciting places—Ankara, the capital of Turkey, the crossroads of Europe, Russia, and Asia; Mexico City, the most popular outpost in the Western Hemisphere for Soviet spies; New York, where hundreds of Moscow's espionage officers gathered under diplomatic cover at the United Nations. But he had accomplished little. And along the way, things had gone wrong for the CIA, as well as for Ames himself.

Nineteen seventy-five was a particularly bad year. Ames was thirty-four years old and trying to claw his way up the greasy pole of the CIA when Saigon fell to the Communists. In the following months, the Agency's secret history of spying on Americans, overthrowing governments, and trying to kill foreign leaders was exposed. The year left permanent scars on the Agency. Before the war was lost and the secrets spilled out, the CIA had seen itself as a force for saving nations— saving the world—from communism. Afterward, many people at the Agency saw the world differently, and some of them, perhaps unconsciously, took on some of the attributes of the people they once had fought against.

Ames was aghast when, in 1981, President Ronald Reagan announced he was rebuilding the world's most famous intelligence service by appointing his campaign chairman, William J. Casey, as the director of Central Intelligence. Casey had been an operative in London for the Office of Strategic Services, the World War II predecessor of the CIA, and still retained some of that old OSS style—fighting rear-guard actions against his opponents in the U.S. government almost as hard as he had fought the Nazis. Casey wanted badly to restore the image of the CIA as the avenging angel of U.S. foreign policy. There were those in the Agency who doubted that the CIA could take on a hundred new global responsibilities. Even if it could, they felt, Casey was hardly the man to do it. It smacked of bringing in an old vaudevillian to reshape a television network. Many of the Agency's more buttoned-down managers sneered at Casey and despaired of his strange ways. He was often unintelligible—they nicknamed him "Mumbles," after the Dick Tracy character who couldn't utter a coherent word—and his suit coat often displayed evidence of his last meal.

Casey's admirers among the Agency's top brass—the barons, as they were called—saw him as the last great buccaneer from the good old days of the OSS. He succeeded in making the Agency's heart, the Directorate of Operations, jump as it had not done for a long time. He had the complete confidence of President Reagan and $3 billion a year to spend more or less as he pleased. He hired nearly two thousand new gung-ho covert-action officers. And he had a world full of Communists to take on. The White House and Casey had no goal more important than stopping the leftists of El Salvador, Nicaragua, and Guatemala. And they had no bigger secret than the intertwined covert operations they were running: an effort to ship weapons to the rebels in Nicaragua in defiance of a congressional ban and a murky conspiracy to buy the freedom of U.S. hostages held in Lebanon by selling weapons to the Islamic Republic of Iran.

Though he saw the Soviet Union as the inspiration of those who worked evil in places like Central America, Casey paid little attention to Moscow itself as an intelligence target. The aspect of the Agency that interested him the least was counterintelligence—the complex business of analyzing the operations the Russians were running against the United States, trying to figure out which CIA operations against Moscow might be vulnerable to penetration by Soviet intelligence, and working with the Federal Bureau of Investigation to catch spies.

"Casey and his people at the Agency didn't think much about counterintelligence, and when they did think about it, they didn't think anything was broken," Robert C. McFarlane, President Reagan's national security adviser from 1983 to 1985, said in an interview years later. "Their attitude was 'We're doing very well, thank you. Now get out of here.' They didn't want outsiders from the White House or anywhere else examining what they were doing." Given Casey's attitude toward counterintelligence, the territory became a backwater. It was not the path to power at the CIA, where careers were made by recruiting foreign agents, not by pointing out problems and potential penetrations by a mole or a machine tapping into the Agency's secrets. Counterintelligence did not always attract the best and the brightest, and it was sometimes used as a dumping ground for vaguely talented misfits who did not have what it takes to make it in the secret world.

And so it came to pass that in September 1983, Rick Ames, in the seventeenth year of his career as a spy, was appointed the head of the counterintelligence branch of the CIA's Soviet division. He was by then a gray, bland government bureaucrat, forty-two years old, possessed of an impressive title, a serious drinking problem, and a major midlife crisis. He spent long hours sitting at his desk and brooding, studying the past and thinking dark thoughts about the future.

He went to work each morning from a rented apartment in Falls Church, Virginia, through the crawl of commuter traffic on Dolley Madison Boulevard. He turned left into the main entrance of the CIA, rolled down his window, and flashed an identity card with his photograph and a number on it. He pulled into an immense parking lot behind the main building of the CIA's headquarters, a gray seven-story structure dedicated in 1962. He entered through a beautifully polished marble lobby. On the left was a gilded inscription from the Gospel of John: "And ye shall know the truth, and the truth shall make you free." On the right were fifty stars embedded in the wall, one for each CIA officer killed in the line of duty.

He inserted his coded identity card into a turnstile and took the elevator to the fourth floor, wending his way through a maze of pastel corridors that smelled faintly of Lysol and were decorated with good-enough-for-government-work art reproductions and posters promoting the gospel of secrecy. Ames's office was the last on the right in the corridor of the 4D wing. The door to his office was mounted the wrong way on its hinges, and it opened out into the corridor, creating a barrier to anyone seeking to enter his little world. You had to stop and squeeze between the open door and the wall of the corridor. Those who ventured down to the last corner of the maze and negotiated the cul-de-sac created by the backward door would find Ames resting comfortably with his feet up on his desk, classified files pulled from his little safe piled everywhere and a case study open in his lap.

Though Ames's position as the Soviet division's counterintelligence branch chief sounded important, it was not nearly prominent enough to his way of thinking. He had envisioned a career without limits, befitting his self-image as a brilliant man possessed with vision and insight into the nature of the

Soviets and their intelligence services. He deserved to be a station chief, the senior CIA officer in a foreign posting. That was the great goal, for the money was excellent and the power of the station chief abroad often surpassed that of the U.S. ambassador.

Ames's appreciation of his own talents clashed with his reputation as a deadbeat and a drunkard. Though he had a fading feather in his cap from his handling of a prominent Soviet defector in the 1970s, his record at the CIA was mostly a lamentable chronicle of mediocrity. When he left his office to wander the hallways of the fourth floor, he played the role of the office goof-off, getting in everyone's way with his aimless chitchat. People came to dread his time-killing visits. Those who liked Ames thought he was smart but lazy. Many others could not stand him.

He was well aware of the effect he had on his colleagues. Ames did not fit into Casey's CIA. He despised what he saw as its archconservative attitudes. And he did not hesitate to share those opinions. "I was perceived as a controversial person," Ames remembered. "And a lot of people didn't like me. I attributed it to rumors about my drinking. I attributed it to the fact that I had not engaged the sympathies of a lot of people making the decisions and that I was viewed as a person who thought too highly of himself and who had a lot of unsound opinions."

The stories about Ames were not rumors. Like everyone else at the Agency, Ames received annual report cards, based on the firsthand observations of his bosses. They showed that he had been inept at recruiting foreign agents while he had worked overseas, incapable of filing reports on time, in the grip of a sour and skeptical attitude toward his assignments, and increasingly unable to perform routine work after drinking his lunch. There was even a humiliating notation in the files about his inattention to matters of personal hygiene, especially his rotting teeth and his slovenly clothes.

Running the counterintelligence branch of the Soviet division was a far better assignment than Ames deserved. Looking back, people found his promotion to the post appalling, given his record. But Casey had hired so many new young people that the plodders in middle management had to be promoted. Besides, Ames spoke some Russian, he was a fairly intelligent fellow, and he could write well when he put his mind to it. The CIA almost never fired or demoted anybody, and the way the Agency usually handled a personnel problem like Rick Ames was to keep him out of sight: stick him into an office far down the corridor and give him a nice, complicated, time-consuming task.

Being out of the way suited him nicely. Besides, the job gave him a certain kind of power: access to secret information. He was required to know everything possible about the Agency's worldwide operations aimed at the Soviet Union. It gave him the ability to dig into the most sensitive files inside the CIA.

In the mid-1980s, CIA counterintelligence was divided into two sections. There was a counterintelligence staff under the direction of a patrician officer named Gardner Rugg Hathaway, eighty officers focused on the workings of all foreign intelligence agencies. Then there was Ames's shop, the counterintelligence branch within the Soviet division, a score of people focused solely on the intricacies of the struggle of the CIA against the KGB.

The branch itself was divided into two sections. One section dealt with analyzing covert operations aimed at targets outside the Soviet Union—in particular, the CIA's attempts to understand and foil the workings of the main Soviet intelligence service, the KGB, in foreign embassies around the world. The other section, which Ames supervised, oversaw

CIA operations aimed directly at Moscow. In 1984, the officer in charge of the first section became gravely ill and Ames found himself in charge. His most important tasks were to think through CIA operations that utilized Soviet agents secretly working for the United States, to determine if those agents were really on our side, to help recruit new Soviet sources, and to counter efforts by the Soviets to recruit informers—a simple way to describe the fantastically complicated world of counterintelligence.

During Ames's tenure as chief of the counterintelligence branch, Washington and Moscow saw each other as hell-bent on provoking nuclear tensions, escalating the arms race, and fighting shadow wars throughout the Third World. Each side sought advantage by espionage, by recruiting the other side's spies, by deceiving the enemy with disinformation, and by executing military and diplomatic feints and bluffs. But Ames tried to stay aloof from all that. He spent most of his time doing what he liked best—combing through the counterintelligence files from the Agency's archives, choosing the most celebrated and most intriguing cases.

He was especially interested in learning everything he could about the Soviets who secretly worked for the CIA.

3

A Seminar in Treason

Ames became a scholar in the field of double crosses. He called for the files on every important case involving Soviet officers who had sold out their motherland to work in secret for the CIA. He was particularly fascinated by the Agency's history of doubting the defectors and double agents who had offered themselves up as moles.

The cases had a common theme: betrayal and its detection.

He looked back over the decades of destructive introspection that had ripped the Agency apart as it agonized over whether it had been penetrated by a false defector. He would come to understand as well as anyone how the CIA could tie itself in knots just by thinking about the possibility of a traitor in its midst. His coworkers thought he was simply entranced by the past and indulging his taste for cerebral intrigue by dipping into the world's greatest espionage library. In fact, Ames was taking a self-taught seminar in treason and its consequences. All the while he tended his smoldering resentments about his colleagues and his career.

Ames had failed miserably in his stints as a case officer overseas, which was why he had been moved into counterintelligence. The CIA officer working abroad is supposed to be an outlaw, a criminal. He is a man apart from both his own country and the country where he works undercover. He exploits what is useful from both societies and disdains the rest. He abuses the law of the land where he works and subverts its social and diplomatic codes. Not only must he be a dissembler, a cheat, and a fraud, he is required to encourage these characteristics in others—the people he tries to recruit to work for the CIA and against their homelands. The best covert operators suborn foreigners to be agents for the CIA, and the agents do the dirty work while the CIA officer manipulates them. For this is the way that he can come into possession of secret information, and secret information is the one universal currency in the world of intelligence.

The nitty-gritty of operations work—recruiting and running agents—is high-stakes poker at three in the morning. Counterintelligence is chess.

The first principle of counterintelligence is to know your enemy, to learn what he knows without his knowing it. A higher goal is to know the enemy well enough that your knowledge surpasses what he knows about you. The way to achieve that goal is to win the secret allegiance of a Soviet intelligence officer, military officer, diplomat, or scientist. There are several ways to turn such a man into a spy for the United States. He volunteers. You use friendly persuasion. Or you trap and blackmail him. Turning someone can be a very tricky business. For he may turn again—against you—without your knowing.

In the golden age of the CIA, the 1950s and 1960s, the finest and rarest achievement was to have a spy in the enemy's camp. But then the computer age brought highly sophisticated, fantastically expensive satellites and other devices that could listen in on the enemy. Their proponents argued that technology was far more dependable than quirky human beings; machines did not require the subtle care and feeding that spies did, and they assuredly did not turn traitor. Traditionalists said the presence of a spy in the sanctum of the enemy could provide information unmatched by any satellite's. The battle over priorities went on and on, like an argument over religion or politics. The fact was that a good intelligence service needed both.

By 1984, the CIA had a small network of Soviet spies, carefully cultivated and nurtured over the past twenty years. They worked in Moscow, London, Athens, Lisbon, Bonn, Vienna, San Francisco, New York, and Washington. There were barely a dozen of them, all told, placed inside Soviet embassies and Soviet society, and they were the jewels in the Soviet division's crown. Most of them had firsthand information about what the Soviet intelligence services were doing, for they were highly ranked and deeply trusted officers of the KGB and the GRU, the Soviet military intelligence agency. Ames read all about these living agents and some who were long gone. He also studied the CIA officers who ran the agents and evaluated their work.

The principal actor in the CIA's cast of characters was James Jesus Angleton, chief of counterintelligence from 1954 until 1974. Angleton was brilliant in often indecipherable ways, like the modern poetry he championed while a student at Yale in the 1930s. Arguing with him was a philosophical exercise on the order of disproving the existence of God.

Angleton's way of seeing the world had begun with a diabolical Soviet operation of the 1920s known in counterintelligence lore as The Trust, a case the CIA was still struggling to understand sixty years later. A man named Aleksandr Yaku-shev had come out of the chaos of the Bolshevik Revolution in 1921 with the news that the Soviet experiment was a failure. Yakushev had said he was part of an anti-Soviet underground operating in Moscow, and he had helped organize resistance groups of exiles throughout Europe. He had fed information to eleven Western intelligence services, and they had given him money, men, and machine guns in return. Then the exiles' leaders had begun disappearing. Dissident newspapers had vanished. Documents obtained through The Trust had been revealed as clever forgeries. The Trust, it had turned out, was a gigantic sting, and the West had unwittingly financed it. The Soviets had demonstrated their capacity to dispatch false defectors, to orchestrate deceptions, and to use double agents in a grand scheme to dupe the West with disinformation.

Therefore, Angleton argued, nothing was what it seemed to be. Every ardent defector could be a double agent, every appearance deceptive, every accepted fact a fiction. When people questioned his conclusions, Angleton could cock an eyebrow and say there were files they had not been cleared to see, things they could not possibly know; the intricacy and ingenuity of Soviet deception was so deep that only Angleton could fully understand it.

He had become possessed by the idea that the Soviets had penetrated the CIA with a mole and had then sent double agents to the United States in the guise of defectors to delude the Agency into thinking it remained secure. It was part of a diabolical plan of immense complexity and depthless intrigue, designed to sap the Agency's strength, blur its vision, befog its thinking. The mystery gradually consumed Angleton's mind.

Angleton's detractors believed that his pursuit of the mole had led him to the brink of madness. They traced his long

slide into obsession back to the three-martini lunches Angleton had regularly enjoyed with his counterpart in British
counterintelligence, Kim Philby, in 1949 and 1950. Philby
had been recruited by the Soviets in his youth and assigned to
infiltrate British counterintelligence, no matter how long it
might take. By the end of World War II, Philby had been running all British counterintelligence operations against the
Soviets and betraying British and U.S. secrets to Moscow.
The revelation in 1951 that his colleague and confidant was
working for Moscow had enraged Angleton and fueled his
search for a traitor inside the CIA.

There was no question that Moscow had infiltrated the German, French, and British espionage agencies, and it was therefore impossible, Angleton thought, that the CIA was intact. A
quarantine was the only cure for the disease. Angleton isolated
the Soviet division from the rest of the CIA. On no account
could the Soviet division see the files he maintained about
Soviet intelligence operations. He began to transfer officers he
suspected of disloyalty out of the division. Angleton's suspicions destroyed some of the Agency's best people, including the
first CIA station chief in Moscow, Paul Garbler.

Angleton trusted one man: Anatoly Golitsin, a KGB officer
who defected in 1961. Golitsin convinced the counterintelligence chief that every defector who followed him was part of
the immense Soviet scheme. They were "dangles"—still
faithful to the Soviets, masquerading as defectors.

For example, there was "Top Hat," a Soviet military intelligence official who began secretly working for the United
States a few months after Golitsin did. Initially recruited in
New York by the FBI, Top Hat began handing over invaluable information at clandestine meetings arranged through
cryptic classified ads in *The New York Times*. The fact that
Top Hat's reporting seemed impeccable did not dissuade

Angleton. After all, it was a proven technique of spy agencies to use truthful information to enhance a dangle's credibility.

Top Hat's true name was Dmitri F. Polyakov, and he had been a general in the Soviet Air Defense Command. For two decades, Top Hat had provided some of the best inside information on the Soviet Union the CIA had ever had. When on foreign assignments, he had met with the CIA at out-of-the-way rendezvous in Burma and India. In the 1960s, he had given the United States hard evidence that Moscow and Beijing were going their separate ways, refuting Angleton's long-held belief that Russia and China were a monolithic threat. He had given up information on Soviet weapons systems; he had identified a mole inside the National Security Agency, the United States' electronic eavesdropping organization; he had told the CIA precisely which secrets Moscow sought to steal from the Pentagon. And when Rick Ames came across his case, Polyakov was alive and well and living in the Soviet Union, enshrined in the counterintelligence annals as one of the greatest spies the CIA had ever known.

By the early 1970s, almost no one outside Angleton's tight circle of acolytes could follow his byzantine thinking. A schism became inevitable. William Colby, the Director of Central Intelligence from 1973 to 1975 and himself the subject of Angleton's suspicions, concluded that the man's paranoia had crippled the Agency's ability to run operations against the Soviet Union. How could the CIA ever recruit Soviet spies if it was always mortally afraid it would be betrayed? At the end of December 1974, Colby fired Angleton. The counterintelligence staff was purged and rebuilt. The Soviet division began to take in defectors and agents without the fear that its recruits would be committed to purgatory.

As Rick Ames studied the counterintelligence files in 1983 and 1984, Angleton was dying of lung cancer, the result of his chain-smoking endlessly as he pored over the same old papers in his curtained office, searching and searching for the traitor poisoning the Agency he loved.

Though Angleton never found the mole he sought, two cases of treason at the Agency had come to light in the years since his excommunication. Ames reviewed them with intense interest.

One was the matter of David Barnett, who had joined the Agency as a twenty-five-year-old recruit in 1958, worked for twelve years in the Directorate of Operations, and retired in 1970 after a stint in Indonesia. In 1976, Barnett had contacted the Soviet cultural attaché in Indonesia and offered to sell his services to the KGB for $80,000. He had met a high-ranking KGB officer, Oleg Kalugin, at the Soviet trade mission in Vienna, disclosed the true identities of thirty CIA officers and agents, and received four thousand $20 bills. Kalugin had assigned him to infiltrate the Agency. He had returned to the CIA in January 1979 as an outside contractor, conducting training programs for new Agency officers in Washington and Indonesia. He had been arrested in October 1980, had pled guilty, and had been sentenced to eighteen years in prison. Barnett had been betrayed by a Soviet source secretly working for the CIA—a lieutenant colonel in the KGB code-named JOGGER.

There was also an intriguing new case that no one had quite sorted out: Karl Koecher, who had been arrested by the FBI's counterintelligence squad in November 1984. Born in Czechoslovakia, Koecher had come to the United States in 1965 after two years' training as an intelligence officer and infiltrator by the Czech spy service, an outfit owned and operated by the KGB. He had become a U.S. citizen, won a set of security clearances, and begun working for the CIA as a translator and analyst in 1973, first as a full-time employee, then as an outside contractor. He had worked on his translations out of an office building leased by the CIA in Rosslyn, Virginia, called the Ames Building. Everything Koecher learned went straight back to Prague.

Barnett and Koecher were, so far as anyone knew, the first CIA employees who had worked for the KGB. They were not the moles Angleton had feared; they were analysts and outside contractors, low-level people. They had not wandered through the sanctum sanctorum of operations against the Soviets and their allies, stealing secrets to sell. Still, they belied the idea that the Agency had never, ever been penetrated.

And in the fall of 1984, as Ames spent his days delving into the past, there was an uneasy feeling growing in the Soviet division, a sense that all was not well in the Agency's Moscow station, a tingling sensation that something, somewhere, had gone wrong. In Moscow, the CIA's case officers had the distinct sense that the KGB was on their trail, watching over them as they tried to make contact with their agents. They reported that "the KGB was looking at them in funny ways," said Milt Bearden, then a rising star in the CIA's Soviet division.

No one knew that there was a traitor from within the division: Edward Lee Howard. He had worked right across the hall from Rick Ames, he had been fired a year earlier, just as Ames had been joining the counterintelligence branch, and he was selling some of the secrets of the CIA's operations in Moscow to the Soviets. In a year's time, he would be regarded as the greatest traitor in the history of the Agency.

But Ames knew nothing of the Soviet division's fears or the workings of the fired officer. He was focused on a new and intriguing assignment: recruiting a Soviet diplomat to work for the CIA.

4

COURTSHIP

The CIA and the FBI had a joint effort under way to find Soviets based in the United States who would be willing to become traitors. The program was code-named COURT-SHIP. It was the brainchild of George Kalaris, who had replaced Angleton as the CIA's counterintelligence chief, and James Nolan, a top FBI counterintelligence official. COURT-SHIP began in 1980, after much hand-wringing and many meetings on the subject of the failure of the Bureau and the Agency to coordinate their counterintelligence work. "It was four FBI guys, three CIA guys, with an FBI guy in charge and a CIA guy as deputy," recalled Colin Thompson, Ames's colleague in the counterintelligence branch. "Their job was specifically to recruit Soviet intelligence officers. Each member of the unit was assigned his own target. Any information we had, or the FBI had, on a Soviet intelligence officer in the United States was supposed to go through COURTSHIP."

Whenever a Soviet citizen landed in the United States, the unit was supposed to decide whether the man was a KGB officer. CIA psychologists tried to assess the man, to make an educated guess as to whether he might become a turncoat. FBI agents tailed him to learn if he had personal weaknesses or professional shortcomings that could be exploited. Once chosen as a target, the Soviet would be courted through flirtation and enticements. Or he could be forced to cooperate through blackmail.

The main target of COURTSHIP was the Soviet Embassy on Sixteenth Street in Washington. There were more than two hundred officially accredited Soviet diplomats in Washington, half of them based full time at the embassy, and the FBI believed at least a third of them were KGB officers. Washington was a city awash with secrets, and the Soviets worked overtime trying to steal them. They maintained apartments across the Potomac River in Virginia, where they used electronic eavesdropping equipment to intercept communications of the U.S. government and other nations' embassies. The Soviets also were building a huge new diplomatic compound on Mount Alto, one of the highest parts of the city, about a mile up Wisconsin Avenue from the bustle of Georgetown's bars and boutiques. Mount Alto's height made it ideal for intercepting microwave communications, which travel in a straight line from antenna to antenna. Properly wired by Soviet intelligence, Mount Alto would serve as one big ear for the KGB.

In 1984, as the new Soviet compound was being built, the senior Soviet delegation in Washington was undergoing its own renovation. Most of the diplomats—including the KGB officers under diplomatic cover—were no longer clunky, charmless officials who looked as though their wardrobe came from People's Clothing Factory Number Four. They were now smoother, more cultured, fashionably dressed, almost able to blend into American society. One official, named Boris Davydov, liked to give speeches to American groups that were liberally laced with references to American pop culture. He bragged to his colleagues that he was becoming a kind of Russian Johnny Carson.

The embassy on Sixteenth Street became more festive. Diplomats held luncheons for businessmen, political figures, and journalists. The Soviets typically served wretched Georgian wine, but they also provided excellent Russian caviar and salmon, though they served them, with earnest clumsiness, on untoasted Thomas's English muffins. The embassy itself was the former mansion of the Pullman family, whose fortune had come from building luxurious sleeping railcars as well as carriages for the common folk. The Soviets maintained the embassy in its original grand capitalist style, ensuring that the profusion of gilt paint in the large public rooms was always shining.

More than thirty KGB officers worked at the embassy. Two of them were traitors.

Lieutenant Colonel Valery F. Martinov and Major Sergei M. Motorin had arrived in Washington in 1981. Both held the innocuous rank of third secretary, and they were assigned, respectively, to the Cultural Affairs and Information sections of the Soviet Embassy. Martinov's real job was to seek out secret scientific and technical information; Motorin's was to gather political intelligence to help Moscow understand Washington's plans for fighting the cold war. Within two years they had been recruited by the COURTSHIP unit. Martinov volunteered his services to the FBI in 1982. According to one of his handlers, the FBI's Jim Holt, Martinov worked for the United States for ideological reasons, not for the money. Such spies were rare in the 1980s.

But Motorin's recruitment was a more telling tale of how COURTSHIP worked. It was not a romantic story.

Motorin found life in the nation's capital exceedingly pleasant. He traveled freely and made a nice home for himself, slowly filling it with the material goods—clothes, furniture, televisions—that came pouring out of the great capitalist cornucopia. He wanted to grab as much as he could while the getting was good.

There was a discount electronics store on a grubby block of F Street in downtown Washington that Motorin favored, and one day in 1983 he walked in with two cases of vodka he'd purchased at a diplomatic discount at the Soviet residential compound on Wisconsin Avenue to see if he could barter the twenty-four bottles, which would cost more than $300 in a liquor store, for a decent stereo system. Across the street, an FBI surveillance team recorded the deal, and a few days later an FBI agent approached Motorin and showed him the pictures. If they were sent to the Soviet Embassy, they would constitute a firing offense; at best, Motorin might spend the rest of his life as a file clerk back in Moscow. Motorin told the FBI man what he could do with his pictures, but the man kept approaching him on the street, and these meetings, too, were surreptitiously photographed.

The ante was now immeasurably higher. The FBI man showed Motorin nine clear snapshots of their meetings. That was not a firing offense, it was a firing squad. So Motorin began working for the United States, and over the next two years he burned many of his KGB colleagues in the Soviet Embassy and fed reams of disinformation composed by U.S. intelligence back to Moscow. Everybody on the COURTSHIP team was thrilled. Recruiting an agent inside the Soviet Embassy was a major triumph. That was how you won promotions and got ahead.

In August 1984, Rick Ames took on the task of trying to recruit a Soviet. His telephone rang one morning at his office at the CIA, and Bill Phillips, the chief of the CIA's Washington station, was on the other end of the line. The Washington station, which operated outside the Agency's headquarters in four rented offices in Bethesda, Maryland, worked with COURTSHIP trying to recruit Soviets. Phillips was calling to ask Ames if he could spare someone to help out with a promising operation. He told Ames that the Washington station had found itself short of bodies and needed someone who could meet with a promising potential recruit: Sergei Divukulsky, a diplomat from the Soviet Embassy. Could Ames provide someone?

Sure thing, Ames said. I'll handle it myself. The conversation planted the seed of an idea in his head.

Ames went operational. He assumed an alias, Rick Wells, and a false identity as a member of the intelligence community staff, a group of about two hundred people who served as free-floating experts on everything from spy satellites to nuclear weapons. He began courting the Soviet diplomat Divukulsky over convivial lunches, trying to convince him that he was talking to a well-placed bureaucrat authorized to discuss the intricacies of U.S. foreign policy. The game Ames was playing was uncomplicated—feel the Soviet out, glean information from him, and, if he gave the slightest indication that he might want to work for the United States, seduce him. Things never got that far, because Divukulsky was called home at the end of 1984.

But before he left for Moscow, he did Ames a favor. He arranged an introduction to a colleague, Sergei Dmitriyevich Chuvakhin, an arms control expert with the Soviet Ministry of Foreign Affairs.

Though Soviets and Americans met one another in Washington all the time under the banner of diplomacy, Chuvakhin was reluctant to meet at first. But by the end of the winter of 1985, after a series of telephone calls from Ames and consultations with his superiors, Chuvakhin came to believe that this persistent American might be making a legitimate attempt to thaw relations between Washington and Moscow, an idea that became increasingly appealing after a new Soviet leader with a reputation for innovative thinking, Mikhail Gorbachev, took power on March 11, 1985. Finally convinced that the get-together would be nothing more than a constructive chat about the full range of issues that bedeviled the White House and the Kremlin, Chuvakhin agreed to make a date for mid-April.

As Sergei Chuvakhin was making up his mind about the nature and importance of the meeting, so was Rick Ames.

5

A Quick Killing

Rick Ames regarded the pastel walls in his cubicle at the end of the fourth-floor corridor at the Central Intelligence Agency. He felt them closing in. This was as high as he would ever go at the CIA—these walls, this little room, his old files. Waiting for noon to have the first drink. Returning at two in a daze. Waiting for the energy and clarity to write another paper on another unresolvable case. Waiting to retire at fifty-five.

Ames passed the winter of 1985 stirring his resentments like the coals of a fire. He says he was seething with anger at the CIA and sick of the great game of fighting the KGB. The whole thing was corrupt, he thought, an empty pursuit. Spies recruited spies who revealed information about more spies, not real intelligence about how things worked in the Soviet Union. The files piled up on his desk, and locked in his safe were treasures beyond value to the CIA. He knew better. He knew what they were really worth.

Ames had devoted his life to the CIA. Now that devotion started draining away. As he put it, he began "to distance myself from the Agency as an institution and to place my own interests—and, in a sense, my own judgment—above that of the institution, the organization, the loyalties that I had to the Agency."

His interests included money. He was in the middle of a complicated, costly divorce from his wife, Nancy Jane Segebarth, a former CIA officer. Their childless twelve-year marriage had come apart in 1981, when Ames had been sent to Mexico City for a two-year stint. Now he was preparing to be married again, to a Colombian woman named María del Rosario Casas Dupuy, whom he had met while he was stationed in Mexico and she, a cultural attaché, was a recruited agent helping out the CIA with a few favors.

Rosario had expensive tastes—so did he, for that matter—and they planned to have a child, but they had no house and next to nothing in the bank. Ames regarded the one-bedroom apartment where he lived in Falls Church, Virginia, as unworthy of him and utterly unsuitable for a woman of Rosario's taste and breeding.

"I felt embarrassed and potentially humiliated to be in a situation in which I had lost control of the household budget, and getting from one paycheck to the next was getting increasingly difficult," he said. Ames was making more than $60,000 a year at the CIA, but the divorce settlement, which was nearly sealed, would obligate him to pay his first wife $300 a month for the next four years, on top of paying off their outstanding common debts, which all told came to about $33,500. He had no house, a new car that was only partially paid off, and he and Rosario were accumulating thousands of dollars of bills. The financial pressure hurt him. And all around him he saw people who were rich, or getting rich, and displaying their wealth ostentatiously in the spirit of the times.

He wanted "a new life," he said. And it occurred to him that he knew how to get it.

He spent February and March 1985 contemplating those files. They *did* possess a certain value. He began regarding himself as if he were a stockbroker with inside information and the knowledge of how to trade upon it. But the information needed to be handled delicately, an elaborate groundwork laid, so that he could get into and out of the marketplace of stolen secrets. If it worked, he could make a quick killing.

He began to devise a plan he thought brilliant in its complexity and daring. He was going to play a gigantic trick on the world's two great intelligence agencies. He said he decided to sell "useless information" to the Soviets: information the CIA thought was bogus but the KGB would find valuable.

His coming contact with Sergei Chuvakhin would be the opening.

In late March, Ames cleared the meeting with the COURTSHIP unit. "I had an opportunity," Ames said. "I had an overt, covered relationship with a trusted Soviet Embassy official, through which I felt I could pass a message to the KGB securely, without detection or suspicion, since I was operating with the FBI's knowledge."

The date with Chuvakhin was set for the elegant bar of the Mayflower Hotel, two blocks from the Soviet Embassy, at four P.M. on April 16, 1985. Ames left the CIA an hour early and drove into Washington. He parked his car at a garage on K Street and ducked into the bar of an empty Chinese restaurant. He had two quick drinks for courage. He walked up Connecticut Avenue to the Mayflower, went to the bar, and ordered a vodka. Fifteen minutes went by. No Chuvakhin. Another vodka. Another. Sometime before five P.M., Ames decided to force the issue.

He walked a few hundred feet east and crossed Sixteenth Street. Three FBI field agents who kept the Soviet Embassy under constant surveillance saw him. A fourth pair of eyes was across the street: a set of concealed cameras perched on the façade of a trade union's headquarters. They all watched as Ames walked by the budding trees that graced and obscured the embassy's driveway. They lost him as he disappeared through the ornate doorway and into the gilded reception hall.

Ames handed a sealed envelope to the duty officer seated at the reception desk. It held three documents. The first was addressed to top-ranking KGB officer in the embassy Colonel Viktor Cherkashin. It described two Soviet intelligence officers who had secretly offered to work with the CIA. On its face, the note appeared to be an effort to expose the betrayals to Moscow. But Ames believed the men were frauds. Based on his sense of his own counterintelligence skills, his insight into the way things really worked, he had concluded that the Soviets remained loyal to the KGB. They were dangles, agents of deception. The intelligence they offered was worthless, or worse, so their exposure could not harm the CIA.

Ames thought he had conceived an ingenious double cross, a confidence game within a confidence game. The KGB had no idea that the CIA suspected the two men were double agents. Therefore the information Ames was giving them would be seen as a genuine offer of stolen secrets from someone inside the CIA. And that would be worth something to Moscow.

To make sure the Soviets realized that they were being presented with a unique opportunity, Ames said, he took a huge risk: "I identified myself by true name."

That was the purpose of the second document: a page from a personnel directory for the CIA's Soviet division. One line was highlighted with a yellow felt pen: *Aldrich H. Ames, chief, counterintelligence branch.* "That was an especially unusual step," Ames said. "I calculated that this would guarantee a positive response."

The third document was a request for $50,000. "Fifty thousand dollars was an appropriate sum," Ames said. "It was a sum they had frequently offered Agency officers in recruitment approaches over the past five, ten years. I was sure they would respond positively. And they did."

Three weeks later, Sergei Chuvakhin called and invited him to return to the embassy. Ames contacted the COURTSHIP unit and cleared a series of appointments to meet the Soviet. He won permission to see the man where and when he chose, as long as he reported the meetings after the fact. He told them he had a date with Chuvakhin in mid-May and that he had high hopes that he had a recruitment in the works.

So did the Soviets.

The embassy had a standard operating procedure for handling a walk-in. The duty officer had taken Ames's offer of information, and his request for money, directly to Viktor Cherkashin. Cherkashin had then sent an urgent message to Moscow, seeking approval from the KGB's First Chief Directorate, the division responsible for foreign intelligence. The message went out in a densely encoded "burst" transmission, an electronic explosion of 9,600 characters a second, designed to lessen the likelihood that U.S. intelligence could intercept it. Moscow had to sign off on the deal. The KGB did not improvise these arrangements. They would much sooner spit out someone they thought a provocateur than take the chance of swallowing him whole.

On May 15, 1985, Ames returned to the Soviet Embassy. This time, the same duty officer escorted him to a windowless conference room. A man walked in; Ames didn't know him by sight, but he had a good idea of who he was: Colonel Viktor Cherkashin. No words were exchanged. The man passed Ames a note saying: We agree. We would like you to use Chuvakhin as the cutout, the go-between for our discussions. Everyone understood that a deal had been sealed.

Two days later, over a long, boozy lunch, Chuvakhin slipped Ames a small package containing five hundred $100 bills.

At first Ames felt secure in the knowledge that no one else would ever know what he had done. The KGB never shared sensitive information with those who did not need to know. Things were compartmented, locked away within a small circle of people. Everything the CIA had taught him about the other side suggested there would be no heavy-handed demands by the Soviets for more secrets. Ames was confident that "they would not try and twist my arm. They wouldn't try and blackmail me. They would sit back. They would be accommodating, and they would hope that this would eventually turn into something of permanent value. . . . I had no fear that the KGB would try to pressure me."

But a different kind of pressure rose inside Ames a few weeks later. "It came home to me, after the middle of May, the enormity of what I had done," Ames said. "I had crossed a line. I could never step back. Between the middle of May and the middle of June, it was as if I were sleepwalking. It was as if I were in almost a state of shock—the realization of what I had done."

Something began to churn inside him. It was fear. He had begun to realize there were ways in which he could be betrayed.

To begin with, there was the problem of Martinov and Motorin, the FBI's recruits inside the Soviet Embassy. And as far as Ames knew, at least ten other Soviet intelligence officers around the world secretly worked for the United States. Any one of them could conceivably find out what he had done.

"I didn't assume they would ever be involved or become knowledgeable," he said, "but accidents happen."

The decision Ames arrived at—"and it was a very sudden decision," he said—was simple and brutal. If all the Soviets working for the CIA and the FBI could be . . . compromised . . . that is to say, rendered ineffective . . . in other words, removed from operational status . . . then they would pose no threat. When he thought out loud about this decision, years later, his sentences broke down into fragments of speech; listening to him talk about it was like watching a car crash in slow motion. He was talking not only about his life in the CIA—the power of secrecy, that mist you slipped into—but about his decision to betray it.

"It's really hard to talk to an outsider about it," he said. "There is a mystique—and it has nothing to do with facile things, like falling in love with an agent—but there is an old tradition in the Agency—maybe it's still around. You get older, you tend to think it's faded by now. But I was a strong believer in the kind of bond, in addition to the overriding duties that you had as a case officer toward an agent, and your responsibilities to the Agency and all that—you also had a kind of professional, personal obligation. I think many, many people certainly felt that way and probably still do. The process that enabled me to just suddenly justify turning my back on the whole complex, not to mention just the normal sense of human responsibility—I panicked a little bit." In his panic, his fear and weakness, he decided that "only by all of a sudden giving them everyone" would he be saved.

There was another, stronger motivation: greed.

If the Soviets would pay fifty thousand dollars for useless information, what would they pay to learn something real? What would they pay to know what Ames knew—the fact that there were a dozen of their own secretly working for the United States? Ames had something they wanted more than anything: living, breathing, up-to-the-minute information on the KGB's traitors.

"My knowledge of the KGB was as extensive, at the time, I guess, as anyone's," he said. If he gave up what he knew, he would be rich: "There was as much money as I could ever use, if I chose to do that."

In the last week of May and the first week of June 1985, Ames set to work inside his office, assembling a unique set of documents—originals, copies, it did not matter. At the CIA, "paper is unaccountable," he said. "Every time they would inventory top secret documents, hundreds and thousands would turn up missing. You would go and look for a file on a Soviet official or a project, and it would just have disappeared from the face of the earth. And everybody would religiously search and look, and it might turn up years later, or it might not." No one ever did much about it, due to "bureaucratic inertia and friction."

He began with copies of classified cables from overseas. He added internal memoranda and reports, the weightiest of the flotsam and jetsam from the tide of paper that washed over his desk in the normal course of business. And then he put together dossiers on the most important Soviets working secretly for the United States and its allies, men with whom he felt well acquainted, though all existed for him only on paper. In most cases, he never even knew their names—only the cryptonyms attached to their case files.

When Ames was done, he had hundreds of pages in a six-pound stack. Every piece of paper in it held information powerful enough to kill. It was an espionage encyclopedia, a who's who that revealed the identities of every important Soviet intelligence officer working for the United States.

There was a file on Dmitri Polyakov, the man known by his FBI code name, Top Hat, who had devoted two decades of his life to spying for the Bureau and the Agency.

A second was on Oleg Gordievsky, the KGB chief in London, whom the CIA had code-named TICKLE, a frivolous alias for the greatest Russian spy ever recruited by British intelligence.

A third dossier betrayed the spy in the Soviets' Washington embassy with a fatal love for stereo equipment, Sergei Motorin, whose CIA code name was GAUZE.

A fourth doomed his colleague, Valery Martinov, code-named GENTILE.

A fifth would mean five years in a prison camp for Boris Yuzhin, code-named TWINE, a KGB lieutenant colonel who worked undercover as a journalist for the TASS news agency in San Francisco—a dedicated if bumbling operator who kept doing things like leaving a camera concealed in a cigarette lighter in the auditorium of the Soviet Embassy in San Francisco.

A sixth murdered MILLION—KGB Colonel Viktor Smetanin, based in Lisbon.

A seventh killed JOGGER, the KGB lieutenant colonel who had served in Jakarta and had returned to Moscow.

An eighth would be the death of a KGB officer in Moscow code-named COWL.

A ninth slew FITNESS, KGB Lieutenant Colonel Gennady G. Varennik, who had fed the CIA information from his posts in Vienna and Bonn.

A tenth condemned ACCORD, an angry colonel of the Soviet military intelligence service, the GRU, who was based in Budapest. This was Vladimir M. Vassiliev, who was furious at the Soviet Union and its endless foreign policy fallacies and betrayed his nation with zeal.

The eleventh was a death warrant for WEIGH, a KGB officer named Leonid Polishchuk, one of the Agency's best inside sources in Moscow, whose courage and daring at stealing secrets awed the CIA's Moscow station and whose tendency to drink too much while doing his spying always terrified his handlers.

Ames's sworn account of this list, the recollection of a man whose memory has been blunted by alcohol and shaped by self-interest, is flawed on two points. He has sworn that the two Soviets he gave up in April were dangles and that he betrayed no one else until June. But it is indisputable that he also sold out two men who were recalled on pain of death by the KGB in May 1985—Oleg Gordievsky and Sergei Bokhan, a colonel in Soviet military intelligence based in Athens and code-named BLIZZARD. Both men escaped with their lives by defecting to the West. Whether Ames's recollections are flawed or his account is bent in some self-serving direction or he merely confirmed the KGB's previous suspicions of Gordievsky and Bokhan is impossible to tell. As best he can recall, there were a few other minor figures in his files and his memory: three people who worked for the Soviet mission at the United Nations in New York and had cooperated with the CIA in the 1970s: a bookkeeper and a Latvian husband and wife, all low-level employees without any true power or access to deep secrets. No one knows what became of them.

On June 13, 1985, Ames scribbled a note to the KGB, describing this six-pound stack of documents and added a postscript saying: I would like to continue this relationship. He stuck the papers into plastic bags, stuffed the bags into his briefcase, gripped his briefcase in his hand, walked to the elevator, took the elevator down to the lobby, and walked right out the door of the Central Intelligence Agency. He was carrying the biggest stack of secret documents ever smuggled out of the CIA. There wasn't a chance of his being caught, for the CIA had stopped searching its employees a few years back. Trust was the watchword of the day.

Ames walked out to the parking lot, got into his car, transferred the documents to a plastic shopping bag, and drove to a luncheon appointment in Washington with his new friend Sergei Chuvakhin. As they dined, the shopping bag sat under the table. It held nothing but the documents—and the soul of a burned-out CIA man.

"In a sense, I was delivering myself along with them," Ames said. "I was saying: Over to you, KGB. You guys take care of me now. I've done this. I've demonstrated that I'm holding nothing back. You guys take care of me."

At the very same hour, six thousand miles away, a team of KGB security men was stalking one of Rick Ames's colleagues. They were armed with information handed over by the cashiered CIA officer who once had worked down the hall from Ames.

At nightfall in Moscow, they made a strong-arm arrest of an American loitering in a city park: Paul Stombaugh, a CIA officer posing as a second secretary of the U.S. Embassy. The official KGB report on the arrest said Stombaugh had been awaiting the arrival of "a Soviet citizen" and had been carrying "CIA instructions printed on miniature sheets of paper that dissolve rapidly in water, five minicameras, maps of the region where the meeting took place, and so forth."

The KGB threw Stombaugh into its own private prison, down in the basement of its headquarters in Dzerzhinsky Square, the Lubyanka. Word of his arrest reached the CIA's

Soviet division at about the same time Ames sat down to lunch with Chuvakhin. Stombaugh would doubtless be released. But his prize agent—Adolf G. Tolkachev, a Soviet scientist working on secret military technology—was doomed.

"That was a shattering blow," said Milt Bearden, who was about to be appointed deputy chief of the CIA's Soviet division. "Tolkachev was one of the biggest things that ever happened. Paul went into Lubyanka—the KGB general who worked the case has pictures of the arrest—and we went to general quarters," meaning everyone went on high alert. No one knew why this disaster had struck.

There were theories galore in the summer of 1985, for a wave of treason cases was beginning to sweep the nation. The FBI was starting to grab turncoats all over the country. A series of spectacular arrests had started three weeks earlier, at the end of May, when the Bureau had arrested John Walker, a retired Navy man who had used his family and friends in a crude but effective spy ring that had stolen secrets for nearly two decades. By the time Walker and his coconspirators were behind bars, their work was deemed by the Pentagon the worst espionage case in U.S. history. On June 20, galvanized by the arrests, the Senate intelligence committee vowed to overhaul U.S. counterintelligence. In a letter to President Reagan sent that day, the committee said the espionage epidemic presented the nation with "an historic opportunity . . . to dramatically improve U.S. counterintelligence and security."

Twelve days later, on July 2, the Central Intelligence Agency gave Rick Ames the only official scolding for violating security regulations that he would ever receive in the course of three decades: a written reprimand for leaving his office safe open when he went home at night. He promised it would never happen again.

6

A Turn of the Wheel

Colin Thompson trudged from the parking lot to CIA headquarters on the morning of Thursday, August 1, 1985, antic-
ipating nothing more than another day at the office.
Thompson worked side-by-side with Rick Ames in the Soviet
division's counterintelligence branch, handling cases out of
Eastern Europe. He paid no mind to the swampy heat that
made a miasma of midsummer Washington; he was a veteran
of the CIA's secret wars in Laos, Cambodia, and Vietnam,
and he'd been through harder days in hotter jungles. It wasn't
the humidity that was wilting his spirit, it was the work—
actually, the lack of it. It had been the dullest stretch anyone
could remember. Nobody had anything to do.

"Summer seemed endless," Thompson recalled. "Then—
bam! Here comes Yurchenko."

That morning in Rome, long before dawn in Washington,
Vitaly Sergeyevich Yurchenko, a forty-nine-year-old colonel in
the KGB, had gone for a stroll. Wary that he might be followed
by his KGB colleagues, he disappeared into the bustle of the

city's biggest railway station, the Stazione Termini, and resurfaced a half mile away at the Ambasciatore Palace Hotel on the Via Veneto, across the street from the palatial U.S. Embassy. He picked up a pay telephone and called the embassy.

By the time the sun was above the trees at Langley, the Russian had been whisked into the U.S. Embassy and debriefed by the CIA's Rome station. A few hours later, he was smuggled out of the embassy and driven to a U.S. Navy base in Naples, where a jet flew him to the Rhein-Mein air base outside Frankfurt. At Rhein-Mein, a U.S. Air Force C-5A, the biggest airplane in the U.S. military, was ready to take him to Washington.

Yurchenko was the highest-ranking KGB officer ever to defect to the United States. The electrifying news from Rome first flashed down that morning from a CIA satellite to the Agency's communications center outside Warrenton, Virginia, where it was relayed to CIA headquarters and up to the fifth-floor office of Burton Gerber, the chief of the Soviet division.

It was the purest manna from heaven for Gerber. His great goal in life was recruiting KGB officers. Gerber had been the CIA's station chief in Moscow in the early 1980s, and he saw himself as the Agency's preeminent officer in Soviet affairs— not only the most powerful but the most knowledgeable. He was held in high esteem by his fellow barons at the Agency. But to many of his underlings, he was a hard boss, humorless, quick to anger, and slow to forgive. He was distinguished by a fancy for show dogs; a fascination with wolves, acquired in the Soviet Union; by his weirdly clashing combinations of clothes; and by his garrulousness at staff meetings, where in the view of some of his subordinates he spent too much time talking about too many secret operations to too many people.

Gerber immediately relayed the news about Yurchenko up to the director's office on the seventh floor of the CIA. Bill Casey was beside himself with pleasure.

At noon, in the private dining room adjacent to his office, Casey shared the good news with some of the grandees of U.S. intelligence and law enforcement, the top brass of the Agency and the Bureau, who were gathered for a formal luncheon. CIA security officers served drinks to the assembled guests. William Webster, the former federal judge from St. Louis who ran the FBI, was there, along with his top counterintelligence chief, Edward O'Malley, who had coordinated the work of the COURTSHIP unit and approved Rick Ames's visits to the Soviet Embassy. There was Clair George, who by dint of brains and cunning had come up the ranks of the Agency from chief of station in Bamako, Mali, to director of covert operations, the top spy at the CIA. And there was Gardner "Gus" Hathaway, the chief of CIA counterintelligence.

The occasion was a retirement party for O'Malley, but it turned into a celebration of a coup against the KGB. Glasses clinked as Casey and his party welcomed the imminent arrival of Vitaly Yurchenko.

By two o'clock, the news spread through the CIA's hierarchy down to the end of the 4D corridor. Rick Ames picked up his telephone and heard Gerber summon him upstairs. He walked up one flight and entered Gerber's office, a somewhat unnerving room with its huge oak desk and the wolves and dogs staring down from the walls.

Gerber made it as brief as he could: Vitaly Yurchenko of the KGB would be arriving at Andrews Air Force Base outside Washington the next morning. "You take care of him, Rick," Gerber said. He was assigning Ames to be Yurchenko's handler, the man in charge of debriefing the defector. The choice was inevitable. Ames was not only the head of the Soviet division's counterintelligence branch, he was also the only person in the group who spoke passable Russian.

Gerber had a new cable from the Rome station on his desk, the result of the station's preliminary debriefing of Yurchenko. It poisoned his exultation with rage. He told Ames that Yurchenko had revealed the existence of a mole at the CIA. Yurchenko knew the man as "Robert," a code name assigned by the KGB. He said that Robert had been assigned to go to the CIA's Moscow station, but before the assignment had come through, there had been some kind of trouble, something about drink or drugs, and the man had been fired in 1983. Taking revenge, the man had dredged up from his memory the detailed instructions about his assignment—the names of the CIA officers he would have been working with, their methodology in dealing with Soviet sources, and, worst of all, the identities of a few of those sources—and he had sold them to the KGB.

Gerber knew instantly exactly who Yurchenko was talking about. This was the man who had worked down the corridor from Ames. It was Edward Lee Howard. There was going to be hell to pay for this, he said.

Ames tried to clear his head. He had met with his Soviet contact, Sergei Chuvakhin, the night before, and he had had a lot to drink. He had never heard of this Howard character. He found the fact that there had been a mole in the Soviet division intriguing. But he was alarmed by the fact that a Soviet defector who knew about that mole—and perhaps others—was arriving on a morning plane.

He returned to his office, called up a copy of the CIA's thin dossier on Yurchenko from the file room on the ground floor, and spent the rest of the day trying to focus on it. Yurchenko's main job for the past five years had been monitoring the hiring of foreign agents and investigating suspected espionage by KGB officers. He'd held that post from September 1980 to March 1985. So there was no way Yurchenko could have found out about him in that job, because Ames hadn't walked into the Soviet Embassy in Washington to sell his secrets until April. A close call.

From March 1985 until his defection, however, Yurchenko had been deputy chief of the First Department of the KGB's First Chief Directorate. His main job had been coordinating Moscow's recruitment of agents in the United States and Canada, overseeing the KGB's five stations within the Soviet embassies in New York, San Francisco, Montreal, Ottawa—and Washington. But the files on Yurchenko also showed—and this was the straw Ames grasped at and clung to harder and harder—that the Russian had probably focused on operations in Canada, rather than on the KGB residencies in the United States.

Ames went home to his one-bedroom apartment in Falls Church late that night. On top of everything else, his divorce had become final that day. He started drinking and did not stop for a long time. When he finally awoke Friday morning, badly hung over, he realized with a start that he had slept through the alarm and had missed the early-morning rendezvous he had scheduled with the security detail at CIA headquarters. He'd have to drive himself out to Andrews Air Force Base. As Ames struggled through the morning traffic, he tried to cut through the fog of alcohol, to calm himself by thinking things through. That did not help: the more he thought, the worse he felt.

What promised to be a godsend for U.S. intelligence was a potential disaster for Ames. Would Yurchenko betray him? Did he know there was a new high-level mole within the CIA? Ames says he kept running through a mental checklist of the details from the defector's dossier, trying to convince

himself that Yurchenko could not know about him. He told
himself that the KGB's passion for secrecy and compartmen-
tation would save him. Yurchenko would not have been
entrusted with a secret of this magnitude. Only three or four
people inside the KGB were aware of Ames's existence.
Yurchenko could not be one of them.

And yet he couldn't help playing the mind games that were
the curse of his profession. There was a chance that the secret
could have been shared. There was always the problem of
corridor gossip, the favorite sport of every intelligence
agency. If Yurchenko knew, he already might have told the
Rome station during the few hours he had spent there. And if
he had told the Rome station, the last person to know might
well be Ames, in the split second before he was arrested by
the FBI.

The FBI was waiting at Andrews Air Force Base when
Ames showed up, twenty minutes late. "He looked awful,"
Colin Thompson remembered. "He said he'd overslept. But
he was still drunk." The top Soviet specialists from the
Bureau were on the scene, and a CIA security team was
scouting the area, looking out for Soviets who might be looking for Yurchenko. Then the plane from Frankfurt arrived, a
little behind schedule, and there he was: a redheaded man
with a handlebar mustache and a serious case of jet lag.

Surrounded by an escort of security men, Yurchenko
walked across the tarmac and was greeted by a cluster of CIA
and FBI men. Ames and Yurchenko shook hands, the American offering greetings in his rough but recognizable Russian,
the Russian speaking in his far more fluent English.

Ames introduced himself as "Art." Tradecraft always
demanded false names. Yurchenko was called "Alex." Colin
Thompson was "Charlie." Sometimes it was hard for Ames
to keep them all straight.

More protocol: a convoy of four government cars was to take Yurchenko to a CIA safe house for a full debriefing. A lead car and a tail car would provide security, the second car would carry the defector, and a third would transport the FBI agents who would join Ames and Colin Thompson at the debriefing.

Into the second car went Yurchenko, Ames, and Rod Leffler, a straight-arrow Nebraska farm boy who was the acting chief of the FBI's Soviet unit. Leffler sat in the front with the driver, a security officer, while Ames and Yurchenko took the rear seats.

Ames regarded the back of Leffler's head, wondering what was in it. He briefly but bitterly regretted the fact that he had coordinated his earlier meetings with Sergei Chuvakhin with the FBI. Leffler knew as much about the ins and outs of the Soviet Embassy as anyone in the Bureau. He certainly knew about Ames's meetings with Chuvakhin. And if the FBI had any inkling that its prize recruits, Martinov and Motorin, the Soviet Embassy officers whom Ames had betrayed in June, were now in the KGB's crosshairs, Leffler would be the chief custodian of those suspicions.

Ames silently ricocheted between calm and terror as they weaved through the traffic on the Capital Beltway, the grueling eight-lane loop that surrounds Washington. He decided he had to do something to settle his fears. He pulled out a notebook, scrawled a message in Russian, and slipped it to Yurchenko. "It said, 'If you have any information that you would like to tell only to the director of Central Intelligence or some other senior U.S. government official, tell me, and I'll take you to him,' " Ames remembered. It was the only way he could think of to find out for himself if Yurchenko knew his secret.

The Russian defector looked at the note and then looked at Ames. He had no idea what the man was talking about. Ames sent up a silent prayer of thanksgiving as the government car drove on.

The lead and tail cars pulled away as the convoy arrived at a nicely appointed seven-room suburban town house with a brick façade—2709 Shawn Leigh Drive in Vienna, Virginia, about twenty minutes from CIA headquarters. Its brown wall-to-wall carpet filled three bedrooms, a living room, a den with a fireplace and a bar, a kitchen, and a storeroom. This was one of many safe houses maintained in and around Washington by the CIA. The neighbors never knew.

Ames, Yurchenko, Leffler, Colin Thompson, and two FBI men, Special Agents Robert Wade and Reid Broce, gathered in the living room. Yurchenko wanted a cup of tea to settle his churning stomach, but the safe house had none, and one of the FBI agents gave him a cup of hot water instead. They settled back as the debriefing, led by Ames, got under way.

"The drill for the first question," Thompson said, "is clear and established for over three decades: ask the defector immediately if the Soviets are preparing an imminent attack. It's quite ingrained in every CIA counterintelligence officer—ask that question first!"

Yurchenko replied that, as far as he knew, World War III was a long way off. The second question was almost as urgent to the CIA.

So, Ames asked, who are the spies?

Yurchenko knew a few. Elaborating on his brief interview with the Rome station, he told Ames details about the man code-named "Robert." He'd never met the man, but he understood that the KGB had been working with him for more than a year. The man had sold many secrets to Moscow, including the names of at least two Soviet agents secretly working for the United States, and he had been paid handsomely.

"Robert"—Edward Lee Howard—had joined the CIA in 1981, the first year of Bill Casey's leadership and a time of enormous expansion in the Agency's clandestine service. Hundreds of new officers were being hired, and standards had sometimes slipped. Howard had had a serious drinking problem, a history of using cocaine, and a dangerously exaggerated sense of self-esteem. He was, in short, a head case. Nonetheless, he had received more than a year of highly specialized training for handling the Soviets who were on the CIA's payroll in Moscow: their names, the dead drops where messages and information could be secreted and picked up, the whole routine of running agents in a forbidding city. Finally, just before his scheduled departure for Moscow in 1983, lie-detector tests had turned up a pointless petty theft—and that, on top of the alcohol and drug abuse, had tipped the scale. Howard had been forced out, and that was when the real trouble had begun. Over the next two years, officials in the Soviet division had become aware that Howard was slipping over the line. From his home in Santa Fe, New Mexico, he had made bizarre, stone-drunk phone calls to the CIA station chief in Moscow. He had confessed to two CIA officers that he had seriously considered spying for Moscow, had approached the Soviet Consulate in Washington, and had almost walked in the door. The CIA knew all this. Nobody had done anything. Nobody had told the FBI.

As a consequence, no one was aware that Howard had met in secret with some very inappropriate people. On April 29, 1985—only days after Ames's first approach to the Soviets—Howard had had a get-together with the KGB in Vienna. By the time it was over, he had told them everything he had learned while the CIA had prepared him to go to the Moscow station, including the identity of the man the Agency had sent in his place, as well as the man's most important Soviet contact. Six weeks later, the KGB had arrested those men: Paul Stombaugh, the CIA case officer in Moscow, and Adolf G. Tolkachev, the Soviet scientist working on secret military technology. Yurchenko's revelation made it clear—at least, it was clear to the CIA—that Howard had betrayed one of the Agency's best sources.

The FBI, however, could not reach this conclusion. The Bureau had no idea who Robert was.

FBI special agents Wade and Broce drove back to headquarters after Yurchenko's first debriefing that Friday afternoon, August 2. The Bureau's ranking intelligence and counterespionage officials knew immediately that the Agency had a serious problem involving this man Robert. But the Bureau knew nothing beyond that. The CIA did not share its knowledge that Robert was Edward Lee Howard of Santa Fe, New Mexico, for five long days. Only then did the Agency confess the nature of its problem and the identity of the dangerous malcontent it had fired.

The delay proved crucial to Howard's getaway. On Saturday, August 3, he flew from Santa Fe to Vienna, where he met again with his Soviet handlers. Upon his return, he became a sober, cunning man who knew he was under suspicion. Later that month, the FBI put a heavy-handed surveillance on him, using a fleet of cars, light planes, phone taps, and photoreconnaissance. Howard was quick to detect it.

In September, utilizing the training in "drycleaning"— evading surveillance—that he'd received from the CIA, Howard fashioned a dummy, had his wife take him for a drive, and jumped out at a bend in the road, while she pushed the dummy up into his place. The FBI agent who was tailing Howard fell for the trick; he later offered the lame excuse that the sun had been in his eyes. He is no longer with the FBI. But Howard is alive and well and living in Russia, and the agent he burned, Adolf Tolkachev, is dead. Within days of Howard's escape, the Soviets announced that Tolkachev had been arrested. He was executed by the KGB a year later. It was hard to conceive how the Agency and the Bureau could have handled the matter more clumsily, and the cost of their carelessness was measured in lives.

A subsequent report by a presidential panel concluded that the Howard case had exposed fundamental problems at the Agency. "Senior CIA officers continued to misread or ignore signs that Howard was a major CIA problem," it said. This myopia resulted from "a fundamental inability of anyone in the Soviet division to think the unthinkable—that a Directorate of Operations employee could engage in espionage."

Yurchenko revealed the existence of another spy that first weekend in August—Ronald W. Pelton, who had worked for the National Security Agency, the enormous electronic eavesdropping engine of U.S. intelligence based at Fort Meade, Maryland, twenty miles north of Washington. In 1979, a few months before his first act of treason, Pelton had declared bankruptcy and quit the National Security Agency after a fifteen-year career. He had first become a spy by strolling into the Soviet Embassy in Washington and volunteering to sell whatever he knew. In 1983, he'd spent four days in Vienna at the invitation of the KGB. He had sold the Soviets sufficient information to foil several hundred million dollars' worth of U.S. eavesdropping hardware. By 1985, Pelton was a pathetic figure, hard in the grip of a personal breakdown, estranged from his wife, drinking heavily, and using drugs. After the Howard fiasco, the FBI carefully stalked and seized Pelton, who received a life sentence in prison.

The Howard and Pelton cases fell into a dimly understood pattern of behavior that was all too common among military and intelligence officers who betrayed their country. A team of counterintelligence analysts who interviewed imprisoned traitors in the late 1980s found several common denominators among them. Intelligence agencies were inept in dealing with troubled employees who exhibited obvious signs of financial distress, emotional instability, or excessive drinking. They shut their eyes to behavior that was blatantly out of line and ignored remarks that with hindsight were understood to have been inarticulate confessions.

Almost no one at the CIA imagined that anyone on active duty could be a mole—especially not the man just selected to handle the highest-ranking KGB defector in the history of the cold war. No matter that Rick Ames drank prodigiously and showed a certain contempt for his work. He did not stand out among his colleagues in those respects. And in any case, as Ames let it be known to his few friends at the CIA, he was sobering up, getting his act together, turning his life around.

One milestone in the reformation of Rick Ames came on August 10, 1985, when he married María del Rosario Casas Dupuy.

Nine days after his divorce, the dour CIA man wed the demure Colombian professor in a hastily planned and somewhat desultory ceremony at the Unitarian church in Arlington, Virginia. Rosario had been raised a Catholic, and Ames was an atheist; after her initial resistance, they had compromised on the Unitarians. They were attended by fewer than twenty people—Rosario's mother, Cecilia; a cousin and his wife; Rick's mother, Rachel Aldrich Ames; her mother, Mabel LaBrash; and Rick's sisters, Nancy and Alison, along with their husbands and children. Nancy's husband, Hugh Everly, served as best man. Colin Thompson and a woman he was dating at the time came, as did a handful of Ames's colleagues and Rosario's friends.

The whole occasion took only half an hour. A hired photographer snapped the obligatory pictures of the smiling couple flanked by their well-wishers. There was no reception. And there would be no honeymoon. Over the next six weeks, Ames spent more time talking with Yurchenko than with his new wife.

An endless outpouring of questions and answers marked the days with Yurchenko. "Upon arrival, all defectors want to establish their bona fides and they talk, talk, talk," said Colin Thompson. "It took us two weeks to get him to stop talking all day." And when Yurchenko finally stopped to take a breath, Ames and Thompson had questions whose answers opened up more lines of inquiry. At the CIA's Research and Analysis division, Thompson said, there were "little old ladies running computers to generate questions, endless computer-generated questions" created by microchips that collated and cross-indexed the CIA's files—thousands of names, dates, places, operations, and double crosses in their infinite variety and detail. It was a method designed to strip-mine the man's memory.

And once the most important life-and-death issues of war and peace and betrayal were done, Yurchenko talked about the most fascinating thing in the world—himself. He took Ames on a long journey back to Stalin's Russia.

He paced the brown shag carpet as he recited the story. It had begun on May 2, 1936, in a Russian village called Bolshoye Shkundino. His father had been a factory hand, killed in World War II during the siege of Leningrad. He and his mother had settled in the half-ruined, half-starved city after the war. He had gone to a naval academy and became a submariner based in the eastern port of Vladivostok, north of Japan. He had married in 1958, just past his eighteenth birthday; the marriage had gone rotten long ago.

In 1959, he had been recruited by the KGB. During the 1960s, he had worked on counterintelligence in the Black Sea Fleet, searching for spies in submarine crews, in a naval aircraft unit, and in an engineering school. From 1968 to 1972, he served at the Soviet Embassy in Cairo, working to recruit Egyptian soldiers as Soviet agents. His career took a leap in May 1972, when he joined a new section of the KGB's Third Directorate whose aim was to penetrate Western military intelligence services, run double agents, and recruit new spies.

In 1975, Yurchenko began a five-year posting as the senior security officer at the Soviet Embassy in Washington. Despite the heavy FBI surveillance endured by Soviet intelligence officers, despite the restrictions on travel imposed by the United States, it was a heady pleasure to breathe the air of America. Some of the Soviets posted in Washington wanted more than just a whiff of the forbidden fruits of Western freedom. Yurchenko's duties included keeping an eye on them. He kept the building locked down, stayed on the lookout for leaks— and on rare occasions confronted an American offering his services as a spy.

But for a turn of the wheel of time and chance, it could have been Yurchenko who handled Ames when he walked into the embassy offering to share his secrets. The wheel had come around, and it was Ames who had to handle Yurchenko.

Ames's assessment of the Soviet was crucial to the CIA's verdict on the man: genuine defector or deceiver? Lives depended on the correct answer. The truth could be determined only through calculations of immense complexity. To embrace a deceitful defector was to allow him intimate contact with one's own secrets; to reject a real one was akin to letting a drowning man die.

This was the many-chambered heart of counterintelligence. For decades, debates about the true nature of defectors and the false footings of deception had tied the CIA in knots and driven experienced intelligence officers to drink and despair. Though Angleton's ornate theories of Soviet deception had been debunked by his doubters, the primal fear always lingered when dealing with a defector: Who is this stranger? Is he telling the truth? The situation in the safe house was a little like the old Greek riddle in which a traveler comes to a village. The headman comes to greet him. "All men in this village are liars," he says to the traveler. Is he telling the truth?

Ames had orders to determine whether Yurchenko could be trusted. It mattered on two levels—for the CIA, insofar as Ames still cared, and for his own safety. He had to calibrate the bearings of Yurchenko's mind. He wanted to know everything the man was thinking so he could sell more secrets to the Soviets. He had to judge the true motives of his mirror image, the man who'd made the same trip in the opposite direction.

7

Out of Sight

Throughout August 1985, Rick Ames and Vitaly Yurchenko spent their days staring at each other, two mustachioed men in their mid-forties sitting in an air-conditioned office, calling each other by their phony names, talking about the cold war's intrigues and betrayals.

The Agency moved the daily debriefings from the safe house in Vienna to an anonymous three-room suite in a small shopping center in Great Falls, Virginia, about five miles up the Potomac from the Agency's headquarters. Four days a week, the CIA and the FBI would take Yurchenko on a deliberately indirect route from the safe house, zigzagging through a maze of development tracts, turning into dead-end streets and doubling back, parking across the street at the Safeway supermarket one day, in front of the insurance office or the hairstylist at the shopping center on another. It was a strange commute to a stranger job.

Ames fidgeted through the day, pacing the room, playing with the Mr. Coffee machine, because Yurchenko asked him not to smoke. Yurchenko was nervous, too, on the verge of neurotic, saying he was convinced that his growling gut was a sure sign that he was dying of stomach cancer. He drank weak tea or hot water to ease his dyspepsia. The two men forced themselves to remain seated around a plain rectangular table in a room devoid of charm, with a tape recorder running and all the time in the world to reminisce.

They met twenty times, occasionally one on one, sometimes with other CIA and FBI men participating, during August and early September, and they formed a superficial bond, like a driver and a hitchhiker, based on the sharing of stories. "I have always believed that Yurchenko liked and respected me above the others," Ames said years later.

Yurchenko's knowledge was in large part historical: who had done what to whom in the past. But he knew enough about operations against the U.S., Canadian, and European intelligence services to fill up quite a few CIA files.

As they talked through the summer days, Ames grew comfortable with his initial instinct that Yurchenko would not and could not have exposed him. In the debriefings, the KGB man said he had indeed focused on Soviet intelligence operations in Canada, not in the United States, in his most recent posting.

Yurchenko also had been responsible for coordinating the KGB's Special Reserve agents—the sleepers. These were intelligence officers working in the United States under diplomatic cover who were assigned to doff their sheep's clothing if the KGB officers in their city were all expelled—or if World War III erupted. The defector named them; Ames took notes.

The question of double agents arose. In the early 1980s, the FBI had worked closely with the Army, the Navy, and the Air Force to create a small team of military officers who pretended to sell out their country to the Soviets stationed in the United States, the goal being to learn as much as possible about the people inside the Soviet embassies who were spies. There had also been a handful of CIA officers and military men who played that role overseas. Yurchenko revealed that the KGB was on to some of these American double agents and was feeding them false information to confound the United States.

Sometimes counterintelligence was like an existential detective novel: a puzzle without a solution. Sometimes it was like a joke without a punchline. But Yurchenko's information was good enough to give the CIA many sighs of satisfaction and a few bitter chuckles as well. Ames was amused to learn that Yurchenko's duties in Moscow, in the early 1980s, had included baby-sitting Kim Philby, the most famous traitor in the history of the cold war. Philby's epigraph for himself was: "To betray, you must first belong. I never belonged."

To whom did Yurchenko belong? The CIA's assessment of Yurchenko, based in part on Ames's reports, was that the man was genuine. If he was acting, the chiefs of the Soviet division said, he deserved every Oscar ever invented. Ames still says—and most of his old colleagues in the Soviet division still agree—that Yurchenko was for real. "The Angletonian thesis of false defectors has no credibility," he said. "Anyone who says they believe in that kind of stuff is immediately discredited in my eyes."

Others had their doubts, and they still have them. In intelligence, there are secrets and there are mysteries. Secrets can be unraveled. Mysteries may never be.

If Yurchenko had been dispatched by the Soviets to deceive the CIA, it was a masterstroke. It was the stuff of Jim Angleton's nightmares. Yurchenko could offer up a couple of U.S. spies who'd outlived their usefulness—and in doing so distract the Agency from a much bigger traitor. Both Howard and Pelton were long gone from their posts inside U.S. intelligence. They could sell no new secrets.

But in the summer of 1985 the KGB had something far more precious: an agent in place at the CIA, and a well-placed one at that. No mole could ask for a more perfect burrow.

If the KGB had weighed the six-pound satchel of secrets it had obtained in June and found it valuable beyond measure, surely the sacrifice of less-precious sources was worth protecting its prize. The calculation grows still more sophisticated when one considers who debriefed Yurchenko. That provided a flawless feedback loop on the course of the operation. Finally, there was a fail-safe mechanism: the defector could redefect.

Hold the case up to the light at a certain angle, and it is what it appears to be. Turn it a few degrees, and it turns into its opposite: the classic counterintelligence conundrum. The question has been argued both ways for a decade, and no one has arrived at the truth.

If Yurchenko was for real, as the conventional wisdom holds, then by September he was beginning to go through the internal ordeal that sooner or later confronts most defectors. He had broken with his country, his culture, his career, his compatriots, his friends, and his family for the privilege of sharing his life with strangers in a suburban living room.

The handling of defectors was not one of the CIA's great strengths. The Agency lacked people with the psychological and social skills required to deal with them; for that matter, it did not even have enough people who spoke Russian. Take the case of Viktor Gundarev, who defected from the KGB a few months after Yurchenko did. He was grilled endlessly, his genuineness questioned over and over, and he became profoundly alienated from the men into whose arms he had run. He came to believe, as he wrote to the CIA, "that those people who would like to defect with the help of CIA should think twice."

In the 1980s, most Soviet defectors, once their talk ceased, were dumped into the strangeness of American society to fend for themselves. Few fared well. It was like giving a man who has spent his adult life behind bars nothing but a bus ticket and a hearty handshake upon his release. There was no equivalent of the federal witness protection program, no new life at the government's expense. Highly skilled, intelligent people wound up as busboys and motel managers on lonesome state highways.

In early September, Ames noticed that Yurchenko was beginning to behave erratically. This time it wasn't his stomach. He'd been having a love affair with the wife of a Soviet diplomat in Canada. His twenty-seven-year marriage—his wife was an engineer at a dismal state planning institute in Moscow who helped to crank out phony economic reports—was a sham. Later in September, Yurchenko demanded to be driven across the border to Montreal for a secret rendezvous with her. Colin Thompson went along for the ride. Yurchenko failed to convince her to join him in the United States.

The defector was not the only one who was unhappy. For six weeks, ever since Yurchenko had arrived, Paul Redmond, the chief of the CIA's Yurchenko task force, had been seething about Rick Ames. Redmond couldn't believe that Ames—that goddamned lazy good-for-nothing bastard—had been put on the case.

Redmond was a Harvard man, thickening around the waist at forty-four, proficient in Serbo-Croatian and profanity. He had steeped himself in the culture of the Serbs, and he had taken on some of their attributes: a certain hardheadedness, an instinct to fight battles to the finish. He rarely won the bureaucratic wars he fought, because people didn't always listen to him. They didn't listen because they weren't afraid of him: he was a short, squat man whose voice and demeanor had a hint of the cartoon character Elmer Fudd, the one who was always hunting the trickster Bugs Bunny but never catching him. Still, Redmond had been in the CIA's Soviet division long enough to know whom he trusted and whom he did not. There were more than a few people in the latter category, and Rick Ames was at the top of the list.

"Redmond didn't like Ames," Colin Thompson said. "He saw right off that he was a layabout, that he did not want to work hard. Paul was full of opinions, and his opinion was that Ames was no good." That opinion did not carry the day when Burton Gerber assigned Ames to be Yurchenko's chief debriefer.

Redmond consoled himself with the knowledge that Ames would soon be out of sight.

Ames was set to leave the task force in mid-September to prepare for a new overseas assignment. Despite the fact that his work was judged way below average by his bosses—he was ranked just above the bottom 25 percent of his grade of officers in his 1985 evaluations—he was being transferred to a fine new job. Ames was going to go to Italy in the summer of 1986, to handle covert operations and counterintelligence work out of the Rome station. It was a plum assignment at a glamorous post. For the next nine months, all Ames had to do was read up on the operations being run out of Rome—many of which took place in Eastern Europe—and attend the CIA's language school to pick up some Italian. Redmond was livid that Ames had won a fine new posting, but then he himself was about to be promoted. He was taking over as chief of the counterintelligence branch. Colin Thompson, a man Redmond trusted, would run the Yurchenko task force.

The team had doubled in size; eleven CIA and FBI counter-intelligence officers were now on the case. Yurchenko was talked out, he had told his story, but the questions never ceased. The task force had turned into a truth squad. New and occasionally skeptical interrogators kept going over and over the same ground and then probing into areas he knew nothing about or delving into things he didn't want to talk about. In the beginning, there had been something resembling human relationships between Yurchenko and his handlers. Now the human factor was fading. The unending computer-generated questions, the facelessness of the interrogations—he was facing a hundred-headed bureaucracy that was treating him less and less like a man and more and more like a data bank, a source of information to be downloaded, sorted, and locked away in a vault. Yurchenko's knowledge of the KGB was nearly exhausted, and when that was done, so was his usefulness. Unless he was different from most other Soviet defectors of the 1980s, he began to experience deep doubts about his decision. By October, Yurchenko was miserable.

As for Ames, these were the strangest days he had ever experienced. He felt as though he were sleepwalking through life. To call it a life was to misconstrue it; everything about his daily existence was suffused with lies and subterfuges. It was hard to keep track of things. He had his new marriage. He would go to debrief Yurchenko every second or third day. Then he would go to the CIA to keep up with his work, gathering, collating, and memorizing his files and cables as a mole for Moscow. And when the time was ripe, every two or three weeks, there were those long lunches with Sergei Chuvakhin.

The talks with Chuvakhin were, as diplomats might say, mutually beneficial. Ames handed over a running account of everything that took place during the debriefing of Vitaly Yurchenko, down to the telephone numbers of the safe house in Vienna and the office hideaway in Great Falls. He gave up choice gleanings from the classified cables he saw every day and selected highlights from the files he reviewed. From his memory came written memoranda on the CIA's missions, its structure, its secret budget. Ames and Chuvakhin never so much as winked at each other. Not a word about what was going on beneath the surface passed between them, only the shopping bags they exchanged under the table. Ames's bags contained hundreds of secrets. And each one of Chuvakhin's bags held a packet of money, a slim green brick containing tens of thousands of dollars.

At first Ames tried to convince his bosses at the CIA and his counterparts at the FBI's counterintelligence office that Chuvakhin was a pretty good source and a potential recruit, and he filed regular reports on their lunches. He was walking a very fine line.

"Rick was trying to play a funny game," Paul Redmond told his colleagues. "He wanted to make it look good enough so that everybody would want to continue the operation, but on the other hand not to make it look so good that people would start to focus on it."

Then Ames stopped reporting the meetings. It was breath-takingly foolish of him. A CIA officer looking for rewards and promotions would file reports on the meetings as a matter of course; they would prove he was out there doing his job, trying to cultivate a potential turncoat. But Ames's conduct was part of a perverse pattern, maintained throughout his career, of failing to perform elemental tasks, even if it meant putting himself in danger.

His decision should have created deep suspicion among the CIA and FBI officials monitoring the meetings: either the man was hopelessly lazy, or he had something to hide. But it only created confusion.

"Ames had cleared with us, coordinated with us, that he was going to be in contact with this guy," said John F. Lewis, Jr., who in 1985 ran the FBI's Special Operations Squad, which focused on the KGB in Washington. "They have to let us know that they're in contact. The reason we do that—and it's a very simple reason, really—is so that we don't expend manpower to try to identify an unknown contact. I personally have spent at least a week following a guy around one time, and finally I identified him by following him into CIA headquarters."

When Ames stopped filing the reports, Lewis said, the FBI asked him what was going on. No reply. "Then we sent a message to the CIA to ask him to explain some of these contacts, which was ignored," he said. "That was a real bone of contention. . . . Back in those days, the relations were not that good" between the Agency and the Bureau. They did not improve soon enough.

Lewis and his colleagues asked their CIA counterparts at least three times, both face to face and in writing, why they were not receiving any reports on Ames's meetings with Chuvakhin. But they never received a response. Because the paper stopped flowing, Ames had at least a dozen unreported meetings with his cutout. Nobody from the CIA or the FBI followed up on the matter. They simply lost sight of Rick Ames.

8

Reckless Abandon

The KGB, however, never lost track of Ames. In September, after thoroughly assaying the purity and the strength of the secrets he had smuggled out of the CIA, the Soviet intelligence service came to a momentous conclusion. Its chairman, Viktor Mikhailovich Chebrikov, took his findings to the highest level of the Soviet leadership: the Politburo.

"The Politburo said, in the case of Ames, the guy has presented information of such value that he should be paid as much as possible," said Oleg Kalugin, the KGB major general and former counterintelligence chief who broke with his old service in 1990. "Ames was the top spy ever."

In late October, Sergei Chuvakhin delivered a startling message to Ames at their regular lunch date. "He passed me a note, a package with money and a note," Ames said. "And in the note, the KGB said that they had set aside two million dollars for me."

It was the biggest payoff the notoriously stingy Soviet intelligence service had ever made to an American spy. It reflected a deliberate decision made by the KGB to raise the ante in its poker game with the CIA. The Soviets knew that greed, not ideology, motivated most American spies. That being the case, the supply of money had to meet the demand for secret intelligence—a free-market phenomenon even the most devout Communist could understand.

The chief of the KGB's foreign intelligence directorate, Vladimir Aleksandrovich Kryuchkov, had realized that one of his problems with recruiting and keeping agents was the KGB's reputation for parsimony. In 1982, he sent a memorandum to all his residents abroad, ordering a "bolder use of material incentives" for rewarding spies. If the CIA offered million-dollar payoffs—and Kryuchkov knew they did—so would the KGB.

Ames was ecstatic, though he could share his joy with no one. He informed his new employers in a note passed through Chuvakhin that he would be able to slip away from Washington at year's end. He could hardly wait to meet the man appointed by the KGB to be his handler.

On November 2, a few days after Ames received the promise of a fortune, Vitaly Yurchenko and a twenty-six-year-old CIA security officer named Tom Hannah went for supper at Au Pied de Cochon, a brasserie in the Georgetown neighborhood of Washington. They ordered the poached salmon. Yurchenko fell silent for a few minutes; he had grown tired of speaking English to his security guards, and of course Hannah spoke no Russian.

Suddenly Yurchenko stood up and threw his napkin down on the table. "I'm going for a walk," he told Hannah. "If I don't come back, it's not your fault."

Yurchenko disappeared.

Rick Ames's biggest case had ended in an unmitigated disaster. Everyone agrees how it happened; there are endless arguments about its meaning. It called into question everything Yurchenko had said in the past three months—not to mention the professionalism of U.S. counterintelligence. Losing a man like Yurchenko was something like the Secret Service losing the president in an uncontrollable crowd.

It got worse: two days later, Yurchenko called a press conference at the Soviet Embassy. It ran live on television. Surrounded by grinning diplomats and KGB men, speaking in his slightly off-kilter English and through a translator, he described "three horrible months" in the hands of CIA kidnappers: "In early August 1985, while on a business trip in Italy, I was forcibly abducted in Rome by some unknown persons. Unconscious, I was brought from Italy to the U.S.A." The story quickly grew more lurid. "Here, I was kept in isolation, forced to take some drugs, and denied the possibility to get in touch with official Soviet representatives. Only on November 2, due to the momentary lapse of attention on the part of the persons watching me, I was able to break out to freedom."

Excuse me, Mr. Yurchenko, an American reporter asked, but aren't you a KGB officer who told all to the CIA? "When I was drugged with the use of some special drugs, I don't know what I was saying or what I was doing," Yurchenko said. "I was threatened. When I was conscious and when they were talking with me, they were telling me that, well, you see, everyone thinks you're a traitor. . . . And they, I think, were hoping that eventually I will start to believe that I have indeed passed some information of secret nature. Please, ask CIA officials what kind secret information I gave them."

Yurchenko suggested he had been thinking about fleeing from the CIA throughout October. "They tried to lure me for the past three weeks. And they were telling me that, anyway, they are regarding you as a traitor. You see that there were things written about you in the newspapers. If you flee and return to the Soviet Union anyway, a prison and death is awaiting you. We'll send the KGB all the materials we got from you, and you will be jailed there. And here that man three times brought to me a contract" offering him a million dollars up front and a healthy salary.

Upon reflection, Yurchenko said, there had been one positive thing about his experience: it had been a great education in the ways of the CIA. "I know your side," he said. "It's better than reading a thousand books."

It was a fantastically audacious performance, letter-perfect propaganda, a combination of pure lies mixed with palpable truth: the classic formula for deception. And it touched off years of angry arguments, finger-pointing, and infighting in the U.S. intelligence establishment.

The FBI, the White House, and Congress turned the intelligence community into a sniper's alley, with their bullets aimed at the CIA. Either the Agency had let a million-dollar defector slip through its hands or it had been seduced, abandoned, and left naked by its principal adversary. After taking the heat for the escape of Edward Lee Howard, the FBI shot back at the CIA: How exactly had the Agency managed to let Yurchenko escape—and then let him hold a press conference? More than one harrumphing senator took aim at Bill Casey. The director had taken plenty of fire from Capitol Hill over the past four years, but largely over questions concerning his political judgment, his mumbling but unmistakable contempt for Congress, and his sometimes strained relationship with the truth. Now Casey's competence, and the CIA's, were being questioned.

Open warfare broke out between the CIA's Soviet division and the National Security Council over Yurchenko's story. The Agency swore he was for real. The hawkish Kremlinologists of the National Security Council said the whole thing smacked of theater. And they had the ear of the president of the United States. Ronald Reagan ventured that perhaps the whole thing was a KGB trick to disrupt his first scheduled meeting with the new Soviet leader, Mikhail Gorbachev. With his usual charming blend of fact and fable, Reagan told reporters that Yurchenko's information was "not anything new or sensational. It was pretty much information already known to the CIA. You can't rule out the possibility that this might have been a deliberate ploy, a maneuver. We just have to live with it because there is no way we can prove or disprove it." Not exactly: Yurchenko had unmasked Howard, fingered Pelton, and provided a wealth of inside detail on Soviet counterintelligence techniques. But Reagan was indisputably right on one point: there was no way to rule out the chance that the whole thing had been a charade. There never would be. And the CIA was going to have to live with that.

But how was the KGB going to live with Yurchenko? Could anyone in the Soviet intelligence service deny that he was a traitor? Could they swallow his ridiculous story? They had to, explained Oleg Kalugin. His reasoning was rooted in his experience of Soviet society and in the universal and infinite capacity for self-deception that is part of the human condition.

"When Yurchenko defected, he was genuine," said Kalugin. "Can you imagine the reaction? The outrage? Soviets are very touchy about defections. Then he redefects, and he concocts this story of having been drugged and kidnapped—and that story was his superiors' salvation. They knew it was false, but they pretended to believe. If it had been accepted that they had allowed him to defect, that they were sloppy and inattentive, it would have ruined them. It's a human trait. People want to keep their jobs, and they want to save their necks. This is also one of the complexities of counterintelligence work. It's very hard to believe that one of your compatriots in this closed, elite company could betray the company and his country. So of course he was welcomed back with open arms. 'Vitaly Sergeyevich! Comrade! So good to see you!' " Kalugin smiled a wry half smile, the corners of his mouth turning downward, a smirk at the folly of intelligence services everywhere.

Yurchenko received a hero's send-off on November 6. An Aeroflot jet was dispatched from Moscow to meet Yurchenko at Dulles Airport outside Washington. He walked across the tarmac, surrounded by Soviet diplomats and KGB officers, two of whom carried bouquets of red roses, and as he leaped up the stairs to the jet, he turned and waved for the cameras. He looked like a card sharp who could not restrain his pleasure at having just filled an inside straight.

In the delegation escorting Yurchenko back home was Valery Martinov, the cultural affairs secretary from the Soviet Embassy who had two lives: KGB officer and secret agent stealing Soviet diplomatic and intelligence secrets for the United States. Martinov's return to Moscow deeply confused both the CIA and the FBI. They thought perhaps all was well. Maybe Martinov wasn't under suspicion. Maybe this was simply another act in the continuing tragicomedy of the Yurchenko case. Maybe he was being reassigned. Maybe he would find a way to continue to report from Moscow.

But Martinov disappeared like a plummeting plane vanishing from a radar screen.

There were other clues—many others—in the fall of 1985. But no one saw them as they happened, and when they were seen, no one put them together as part of a larger pattern. Slowly, one by one, some of the CIA's moles inside Soviet intelligence began disappearing from their posts around the world. Not all of the spies were immediately ordered home to Moscow. They were called back over the months, each for a seemingly plausible reason. Some were reassigned to other countries from which they could be unobtrusively snatched and taken to the KGB's headquarters in Dzerzhinsky Square, there to be marched down to the basement and interrogated over the course of months. The CIA did not notice anything until it was too late, which was exactly what the KGB wanted.

First there had been the betrayal and near death of the KGB's resident in London, Oleg Gordievsky. The British intelligence service learned that he was recalled to Moscow in June, and it claimed to have engineered a spectacular secret rescue mission, stealing Gordievsky out from under the KGB's nose in Moscow in July. That had been a huge relief, but the rest of the story was unrelievedly grim.

The CIA learned that one of its best new double agents in Moscow, an intelligence officer code-named WEIGH, had been arrested in September. This was KGB man Leonid Polishchuk, a young man on the rise, much admired by the two CIA case officers who had met him.

Another prized Soviet source, the lieutenant colonel in the KGB code-named JOGGER, the man who had helped catch the traitor David Barnett, had vanished in Moscow in October.

Then a fourth man disappeared: Vladimir Vassiliev, the angry colonel in the Soviet military intelligence service, based in Hungary and code-named ACCORD. He had been arrested at his post in Budapest and dragged back to KGB headquarters.

In December, the CIA lost touch with MILLION, KGB Colonel Viktor Smetatin, and FITNESS, Lieutenant Colonel Gennady Varennik. And Valery Martinov's colleague and fellow spy at the Soviet Embassy in Washington, Sergei Motorin, was soon recalled to Moscow, never to return.

Perhaps Valery Martinov thought he would receive a hero's welcome upon his return for his role in helping to handle

Yurchenko's about-face. But he and the other traitors underwent the shock of arrest, the loneliness of imprisonment, the terror of interrogations, and finally the executioner.

In all, five of the CIA's Soviet agents disappeared in the fall of 1985. Paul Redmond, the newly appointed chief of Soviet counterintelligence, began trying to focus as hard as he could on the fact that, as he put it, the Soviets "were wrapping up our cases with reckless abandon." As year's end approached, Redmond and the very small group of people within the CIA who knew the facts were beginning to come to a terrible, if tentative, conclusion.

There was no way Edward Lee Howard could have betrayed all the men who were missing and presumed doomed.

That knowledge left the CIA precisely nowhere. In mid-December, a handful of the barons—Clair George, the chief of covert operations; Gus Hathaway, the head of counterintelligence; Soviet division chief Burton Gerber, and his deputy, Milt Bearden—hurriedly convened a meeting with Bill Casey up in the director's office on the seventh floor to talk things over. Things were a good deal grimmer than they had been four months before, when they had been clinking their wine glasses over lunch and crowing about Yurchenko.

Clair George laid out the facts: our people are dying and we don't know why. Casey was fascinated. For once, he didn't mumble. He looked hard at his chief spymaster and spoke loud and clear.

"So, Clair," he said, "what are you going to do about it?"

9

To the Moscow Station

Clair George sent Milt Bearden off on the next plane to Moscow to brainstorm with the Agency's station chief in the Soviet Union, Murat Natirboff. Perhaps they could find a way to stop the killing.

Bearden contemplated Moscow in its December cloak, and the gray day and the grim city did nothing for his mood. A foreboding that more men would die in the basement of the KGB's Lubyanka prison weighed heavily on his mind. He walked down Tchaikovsky Street, stomped the snow from his shoes, and strode into the U.S. Embassy, an ugly rococo building that time and soot had tinted a dismal shade of yellow. Bearden rode the elevator up to the embassy's seventh floor, checked in with a Marine guard, and entered the redoubt of the CIA's Moscow station.

The station chief was waiting for him. Murat Natirboff was sixty-four years old and weary to his bones. His spindly build and haunted eyes gave him a faint resemblance to Boris Karloff. He had been born in 1921, the son of Islam-Girey

Natirboff, a princely captain of a Circassian cavalry regiment. The Circassians were Sunni Moslems who had lived on the northeast shore of the Black Sea, and they had resisted the Russian Revolution until they were driven into Turkey. Murat had been born while his family was on the run; in his childhood his father had made his living as a stunt rider in a traveling circus. They had made their way to New York City in the 1930s. Moved by a spirit of adventure and a deep hatred of the Soviet Union, Murat had spent most of his adult life fighting communism for the CIA. He had chosen Moscow for his final tour of duty, but his last hurrah was becoming a horror show. He was dying inside, watching helplessly as his network of Soviet agents disappeared.

Natirboff led Bearden up two flights to the ninth floor and past another Marine sentry. He punched in the entry codes that let them through a double-locked, lead-lined door, and they entered the "bubble," the specially shielded room of the embassy. Resembling a tiny suspended indoor tennis arena, with a constant hum of white noise, the bubble was designed to defeat every electronic eavesdropping technique known.

Even inside the sealed room, Natirboff was nervous. Things had been going wrong for too long for him to behave otherwise. Under the best conditions, U.S. intelligence operatives working in Moscow faced immense difficulties. The Agency had been unable to set up a proper station in the Soviet capital until 1961, and ever since then the simplest operations had been a struggle. Natirboff, his deputy, and ten case officers were surrounded by the world's biggest and most hostile intelligence service. Making contact with an agent in Moscow required weeks of planning and hours of evasive action for a few stolen minutes when money and information might be exchanged. The threat of arrest was always near. The Moscow station's tradecraft had improved over the years to the point that it could provide its agents with dead drops, concealed hiding places for secreting documents. Under extraordinary circumstances the station could steal an endangered agent out of the country. While most of the Soviet intelligence officers working for the CIA lived in other capitals, several continued to work from inside the KGB's headquarters. They all were in mortal danger.

Only a year earlier, Natirboff learned that the KGB had found its way into the Moscow station. In December 1984, acting on a tip from the French intelligence service, the CIA had discovered that the Soviets had bugged some of the IBM Selectric typewriters in the station with ingenious little devices that recorded and transmitted every stroke of the machines. Then, in June 1985, the KGB had grabbed Paul Stombaugh, thrown him into prison, and seized his agent, Adolf Tolkachev. And now these deaths and disappearances.

Motioning to Bearden to be silent, Natirboff settled into his seat and pulled out a notepad and a pen. Bearing down gently, he wrote a note. He tore off the page—then tore off the page beneath it, so that no one who might find the pad could trace the imprint of his writing—and pushed the message across the table to Bearden.

"Sometimes I feel like they are in here with me," it said.

The specter of the KGB floated in the bubble as the two men talked about the awful situation, trying to reach a common understanding of the crisis. Each of the Soviet agents who had died could have been betrayed by sloppy tradecraft—their own poor work, or the CIA's, in covering their tracks. It could be a technical penetration—some electronic eavesdropping device stealing information from the CIA's secure communications channels, the network of word processors, computers, satellites, and printers that connected the CIA's headquarters with its foreign stations. It could be human penetration—a mole. Or it could just be a run of very bad luck.

They decided that nobody's luck was that bad.

The CIA had been penetrated by machines or by men. Natirboff could feel the enemy's presence. But neither man thought the deaths and disappearances could have been the work of a mole. They felt that the likeliest cause of the catastrophe was a Soviet technical penetration in Moscow or back in Washington. Compromising details about the Soviet division's crown jewels had been flowing back and forth in encoded communiqués between the two cities for years. If the Soviets had found a chink in the technological armor that shielded those communications, the Agency had no secrets left.

Bearden left the bubble with the beginnings of a plan.

The order from Casey was to *do something* about the serial killings that were striking down the Soviet division's best sources, and Milt Bearden would do anything. A burly man with a sharp mind, an iconoclastic attitude, a slightly scarred tough-guy face, and a silver tongue, Bearden was the kind of covert operator Bill Casey and Clair George loved. He had distinguished himself while still in his thirties, running operations against the Soviets from Switzerland in the early 1970s. He had won Casey's attention with his work as station chief in Khartoum, the capital of Sudan, from 1983 to 1985. He had helped to foil some of the more flamboyant schemes of the Libyan dictator Muammar Qaddafi. And he had pulled off some tricks of his own. In late 1984, Israel had been secretly airlifting thousands of Falashas, the black Jews of Ethiopia, from refugee camps in Sudan to a new home in the Promised Land. The Israelis had worked covertly because the Islamic government of Sudan had barred them from entering the country to rescue the Falashas. The operation had been nearly complete when the Sudanese had found out about it and stopped it, stranding eight hundred Falashas. Bearden had taken over the operation and shipped the rest of the lost tribe to their spiritual homeland on U.S. C-130 transport planes.

Clair George had made him the Soviet division's deputy chief in the hope of stoking a fire in its belly. The Soviet division had grown weary and stale over the decades of the cold war. Its officers had been working, living, drinking, and sleeping with one another since the 1950s. No one ever really left the outfit. Bearden thought they had come to resemble the people of a remote Appalachian village—so far back in a hollow that they had become isolated and inbred and more than a little strange.

"The old-time Soviet division was a valley that had been snowed in for several generations," Bearden said. "It was a closed circuit within a closed circuit," the most secret part of a secret society. "The old-timers thought the engagement of the KGB by the CIA was the most important thing in the world. It was important, but not necessarily the most important part of what we were doing. The most important part is the part that *does things*—in support of American foreign policy, in support of the West, in support of Christendom."

A few days before Christmas, 1985, Milt Bearden said good-bye to Murat Natirboff, left Moscow, and returned to CIA headquarters, full of ideas for finding the penetration in the U.S. Embassy. That same week, Rick Ames flew to Bogotá, Colombia, to say hello to his KGB controller.

Ames told his superiors at the CIA that he was going to Bogotá with his wife to spend Christmas week with her mother and her family. That much was true. But he had another stop on his itinerary.

Things were tense in Bogotá that month. A few weeks earlier, the government had attacked the Palace of Justice, which was being held by an urban guerrilla group, the M-19 movement, and more than a hundred people, including most of the country's Supreme Court, had died in the assault. The smoke and bitterness from that debacle had barely cleared when one of the most deadly volcanoes in recorded history erupted 100 miles north of the city, obliterating entire villages and killing more than 20,000 people. A pall of ash still hung in the sky, leaving Bogotá in constant twilight.

Bogotá is normally an extraordinarily pleasant city once you get used to the altitude of 8,500 feet, which was never easy for Ames, with his smoke-scarred lungs. The Andes soared above the capital, the weather was eternally mild, flowers bloomed everywhere, and street vendors sold huge bundles of orchids for the equivalent of three dollars in the colonial part of the city, La Candelaria, amid old homes with whitewashed walls, wrought-iron balconies, and red-ceramic-tiled roofs. The city was conservative and cosmopolitan but also a little magical; at noon, illusionists, jugglers, musicians, and patent-medicine dealers set up shop on the street corners downtown.

In the late afternoon of December 20, 1985, Ames slipped away from the Casas household, telling his relatives he was going Christmas shopping. He took a taxi to the city's central business district and walked a circuitous route to the Soviet Embassy, a neocolonial mansion that had seen better days. He was met at the entryway and escorted through a reception hall to an inner office, where he was welcomed by a man who introduced himself as Vlad.

Vladimir Metchulayev was a senior member of the KGB's counterintelligence directorate. He had flown from Moscow to Bogotá to meet Ames, for he was going to be the American spy's case officer. They had only ninety minutes to talk, so after a few pleasantries they toasted each other with vodka and got down to the business of how best to handle the money and information that was going to flow between them.

Vlad told Ames that a Soviet Embassy official, a legitimate diplomat by the name of Aleksei Khrenkov, would be his regular contact after Ames arrived in Rome in the summer of 1986. Like Sergei Chuvakhin, Khrenkov was an officer of the Soviet Ministry of Foreign Affairs. As with Chuvakhin, Ames was to tell his superiors at the Rome station that he was trying to develop the man as a source, thus giving him a legitimate reason to meet with Khrenkov regularly. They would meet every six or eight weeks. For security's sake, Ames was to call him "Sam" in any direct communications with the KGB. Sam would be the cutout, collecting whatever information Ames could steal in his new assignment and passing him his money.

Ames was not happy with the financial arrangements. He did not want the money doled out piecemeal. He wanted his millions now. Ames had been doing some financial planning over the past two months, ever since he had learned that the Soviets had set $2 million aside for him. His idea, he told Vlad, was to have the KGB transfer most or all of it to a Swiss account.

"I was planning, rather vaguely, but planning to do some serious money laundering," Ames said. He thought he might set up a company in Colombia, a dummy corporation in his mother-in-law's name, and deposit a million or two into its account. Too risky, Vlad said. The CIA had ways of finding out about large-scale electronic transfers by international banks. Better to parcel the money out, hand to hand, $10,000 or $20,000 at a time. No thanks, Ames said, I want the money up front. They argued, but Vlad's insistence on caution held sway. The Soviets were worried that if they gave Ames the windfall he wanted, he would have been far easier to spot.

"There was no way, they felt, it was secure to transfer a large amount of money like that," Ames said. "I made all the arguments I could think of, and their constant reply was they could not trust the existing mechanisms."

Ames said the idea had occurred to him that perhaps the Soviets didn't trust him. Maybe it was because he had drunk so much during his meetings with Chuvakhin. Maybe they feared that in Rome he wouldn't have the access to the sort of material he once had had as chief of the counterintelligence branch. In any case, their wariness was characteristically Russian, Ames realized. It reminded him of the catchphrase the CIA's Soviet analysts used to use with the arms control negotiators: *Doveryai, no proveryai.* Trust, but verify.

The meeting broke up under the pressure of time, and Vlad told Ames that they would see each other in nine months in Rome. He warned him to be careful and wished him all the best before escorting him out of the embassy and sending him off into the ashen twilight.

10

Hard Targets

On the afternoon of Friday, February 28, 1986, Rick Ames stopped in at CIA headquarters to read up on the latest in the endless struggle between the CIA and the KGB. He came in only on Fridays these days; the rest of the week was reserved for his Italian lessons. An easy pace, and it suited him nicely.

He was brought up short by a startling report from Moscow. KGB Chairman Viktor Chebrikov had made an unusual appearance at a public meeting of the Communist Party congress in Moscow. Chebrikov's speech was a rare confirmation that the Soviet Union had arrested and executed some spies.

"A number of agents of imperialist intelligence services, renegades who sold important official secrets to foreign organizations, have been uncovered at some ministries and departments recently," he said. "These people received strict but just punishment in accordance with the law." Just punishment, in this case, meant death.

No one in the U.S. government outside the tight circle of top officials at the CIA understood the full meaning of what Chebrikov had said—no one except Rick Ames.

Within that tight circle, among the chosen few who knew what was happening—spymaster Clair George, counterintelligence czar Gus Hathaway, Soviet division chief Burton Gerber, and his deputy, Milt Bearden—a plan of attack took shape. It reflected the hubris of the men who conceived it. They assumed that no CIA officer would willingly betray his country. They had hand-picked the people who were granted access to the secret kingdom and chose to believe that the people they had promoted could never violate that trust.

The plan began with a severe crackdown on the flow of information inside the Soviet division. Data about operations against the Soviets were restricted to a very small circle inside the CIA, and full knowledge of the disaster was kept within an even smaller group of the Agency's senior officials. For the next few years, the Soviet division's operations would be planned and analyzed in the bureaucratic equivalent of a locked room guarded by armed men. If past operations had been blown, at least future activities could be protected from all outsiders.

Then the barons of the Soviet division began devising ways to test their communications links, the wiring that connected the CIA's headquarters with Moscow. They would pump the system full of bogus information and see if the system leaked. It was a procedure similar to doctors injecting radioactive barium into a patient's bloodstream so that X rays could detect flaws in the veins and arteries. If the trick worked, the Soviets would pick up on the false information and act upon it. That might reveal the location of a weak link in the CIA's chain of command and communications.

"But the dog didn't bark," Milt Bearden said. "So we wound up sitting around and saying: 'Either there's no weakness, or it's you, Clair. Or it's you, Milt.' "

Then Bill Casey ordered an in-house study of the situation by John Stein, the CIA's inspector general. Stein was a fifty-three-year-old Yale graduate who had joined the CIA in the 1960s, had served in Cambodia and Libya, and had risen through the ranks to become Casey's director of covert operations in July 1981. After three years, Casey decided Stein was too cautious and legalistic for his taste and replaced him with Clair George. Stein became the inspector general, the internal watchdog who growled on command and could be muzzled when the occasion called for silence.

Casey posed three questions for Stein: What went wrong? Why did it go wrong? Was there some kind of a pattern to the deaths of the agents? Stein took the better part of two months to produce a ten-page memo. He theorized and speculated, keeping with a long-standing Agency tradition of hedging bets on complex questions. The on-the-one-hand, on-the-other-hand approach allowed the CIA to say that it might not always be right, but it was never wrong.

Stein's best guess was that each case had contained the seeds of its own destruction. Each failure could be traced to sloppy work by the Soviet agents or their case officers. There was still an outside possibility that the problem might be a technological glitch, a bug, a wiretap, or some other diabolical method the Soviets had devised to intercept the CIA's communications. But there was no common denominator.

The CIA was a community of twenty thousand people, and something or someone was murdering some of its most valued citizens. Any other community confronting the evidence that a serial killer was in its midst would have sent for the FBI. The Agency did not.

The CIA has no domestic police powers; by law, it must rely on the FBI to catch spies within the United States. But a chasm of mutual suspicion separated the two agencies. It had always been that way, said Jim Nolan, the FBI counterintelligence chief who had helped set up the COURTSHIP unit. He had been through it twice, in cases that had led to the arrests of William Kampiles, a CIA technician convicted in 1978 of selling a manual on a secret spy satellite to the Soviets for $3,000, and Larry Wu-tai Chin, a low-level intelligence analyst and translator who had spied for China for thirty years and killed himself after his conviction in 1985.

Nolan said the CIA could not accept the evidence that there was a traitor in its ranks. "Their reaction is: 'It's not true!' " he said. "There is a personal reluctance and a bureaucratic reluctance to admit there's a problem. They think it's always something else: communications, technical means—but not people. And most of the time, of course, it is people."

In late April 1986, a scathing damage report on the Edward Lee Howard case landed on Bill Casey's desk. After reading it, he reprimanded Clair George and Burton Gerber, holding them personally responsible for the "organization and attitude that contributed to this catastrophe." Pouring salt onto the still-fresh wound that Howard had inflicted on the Directorate of Operations, Casey said he was appalled by the "unwillingness to accept even as a possibility a D.O. officer committing espionage for the Soviet Union." Casey warned that "the D.O. must be more alert to possible counterintelligence cases in the ranks."

That same month, however, George and Gerber relaxed their alert. The crisis seemed to be at an end. Whatever problem the Soviet division had suffered, it was only some sort of temporary snafu. Two new Soviet intelligence officers had volunteered their services in Europe. For the moment, the

KGB seemed unaware that this had happened. The tension that had gripped the Soviet division began to drain away. The collective wisdom at the CIA, Milt Bearden said, was that the catastrophe was over: "If we had a problem between Howard and now, it's not there anymore. Which also means maybe it was never there. Maybe there was no mole."

. . .

At the end of April, Rick Ames finished up his Italian-language classes—the Agency had thoughtfully invited Rosario to join him, and she had learned the language much more easily than he had—and began preparing for his new assignment in Rome. That meant a two-month stint on the Western Europe operations desk, studying up on the work of the CIA's Rome station. The station had influence far beyond Italy's borders: it coordinated cases and covert missions throughout the Mediterranean, the Middle East, Europe, and North Africa. Ames was "read into"—granted access to—information about hundreds of them.

One case in particular caught his eye: Oleg Agraniants, the Soviet Union's political consul in Tunis.

Tunis was North Africa's most interesting intelligence outpost. It served as the headquarters in exile for Yasser Arafat and the Palestine Liberation Organization, and Arafat had connections to the KGB dating to the early 1970s. The PLO had played both ends against the middle for years; some of its officers had CIA contacts as well. It was a challenging assignment for a young diplomat like Agraniants.

In September 1985, Agraniants had gone to the U.S. Embassy in Tunis and had a private conversation with the deputy chief of mission, G. Norman Anderson. Agraniants had told the American that he wanted to work for the United States. Anderson had conveyed the message to the CIA station chief. The CIA had immediately taken Agraniants under its wing. He had proved to be an outstanding source, an extremely intelligent and well-versed consul, and for the next eight months he had supplied the Agency with information about the Soviet Union's operations throughout North Africa and its contacts with Arafat and the PLO.

Ames betrayed him.

He slipped his cutout, Sergei Chuvakhin, a fresh dossier. A few weeks later, an urgent notice from Moscow arrived at the Soviet Embassy in Tunis, ordering Agraniants home. Agraniants called Anderson, who told the CIA station chief. There was only one course to take, and Agraniants knew it: he defected to the United States.

And then COWL disappeared. He had been one of the CIA's best new agents in Moscow, a KGB officer reporting to the Agency from inside the heart of Soviet intelligence headquarters. The CIA presumed—correctly—that he had been arrested and condemned to death. This disappearance shattered the conventional wisdom at the CIA. COWL had been recruited in early 1985—long after Edward Lee Howard had been kicked out of the Agency. So his betrayal could not be blamed on Howard, nor on some fleeting lapse in security. By now there had been at least eight suspected deaths among the CIA's network of Soviet spies. Combined with the betrayals of Gordievsky, Bokhan, and Agraniants, there was almost no one left to provide the CIA with firsthand accounts of what was going on inside Soviet intelligence, military, and diplomatic circles.

. . .

On May 2, 1986, not long before he was to leave for Rome, Rick Ames faced the biggest crisis yet in his short career as a spy. He had to take a polygraph, a lie-detector test. He was terrified at the prospect. Though employees were supposed to submit to the machine every five years, the

CIA's Office of Security had not been able to keep up with the tremendous expansion of the Agency's ranks under Casey, and the testing was running years behind schedule. It had been nearly a decade since Ames had last been strapped to the machine. But he vividly remembered the experience.

When he had learned a few weeks earlier that he was facing the test, he had passed a note to the KGB through Sergei Chuvakhin, urgently asking for advice on how to handle it. There had to be a way, he thought. Some combination of tranquilizers? Clenching your toes when asked your name to even out the stressfulness of your responses? Maybe visualizing an ocean or a clear blue sky?

Ames received a note back shortly before the test. "And my initial response was: This is all they have to tell me?" he recalled. "It said: Get a good night's sleep, and rest, and go into the test rested and relaxed. Be nice to the polygraph examiner, develop a rapport, and be cooperative and try to maintain your calm." Though disappointed at its simplicity, he took the advice all the same. "I did reflect on the fact that the KGB had invested a tremendous amount of time and effort and work in the polygraph, even though they didn't believe in it the way the Agency does," he said. "I also thought: There probably isn't anyone that the KGB wants to help pass a polygraph more than myself."

The test took place in a rented suite with an unmarked door at the Tysons II Corporate Office Centers, in Tyson's Corners, Virginia, a business park west of Washington, where Casey had relocated most of the CIA's Office of Security. The fact that the security unit was housed miles from Langley illustrated its second-tier status at the CIA.

The polygraph examiner was extremely chummy as he strapped Ames into the polygraph. A tube was fastened around Ames's chest to measure his breathing rate. Electrodes attached to his hands would record any sweating of the palms. Cuffs around the biceps would calculate his blood pressure and pulse. All were linked to sensors that would record these indicators of stress with ink lines on a moving cylinder of paper.

Ames knew what the key questions would be. They were always the same: Have you divulged any classified information to any unauthorized person? Have you had any unauthorized contact with foreigners? Have you gone to work for the other side? Have you been pitched—that is, approached—by a foreign intelligence service?

As Ames answered that last question, the needle quivered. The examiner told Ames that his responses indicated deception, and he asked about his reaction. Well, Ames replied, of course, all of us in the Soviet division are sensitive to that question. We know the Soviets are out there, and we worry about that. I myself have pitched the KGB's people in Washington. And the thing is, I spent some time in 1985 with that Soviet defector, Yurchenko, and I think I might be known to the Soviets as a result. And, you know, I'm going to Rome in July, and I have some concerns that I might be pitched there. Thank God, he thought, I'm telling the truth. He had not been approached by the KGB. It was the other way around.

"I was totally relieved," Ames remembered. The dreaded lie-detector test was a farce. The machine said he had been telling the truth when he had been lying and said he had been lying when he had been telling the truth. And the man controlling it was not much better as a judge of character. The polygraph operator deemed Ames forthcoming in all respects, and he called Ames's responses "bright" and "direct." Thanks to the helpful advice from Moscow, the incompetence of the polygraph operator, and the dubious value of the lie detector, Rick Ames had kept his secret.

Only one major event marred his mounting excitement and anticipation about going to Rome. On the morning of May 18, his mother, Rachel Aldrich Ames, was sleeping in Rick and Rosario's apartment in Falls Church, Virginia. She had come to celebrate the graduation of her grandson, Rick's nephew, from the U.S. Naval Academy in Annapolis, Maryland. Rick decided to let her sleep in that day. When he went to awaken her, he found her dead of a heart attack. "Rick had a lot of deaths in his family—all of a sudden everybody died," Rosario said. Within two years after their wedding in 1985, Rick's mother, grandmother Mabel, and sister Alison were all gone.

He dealt with the rituals of his mother's funeral and placed her obituary in *The Washington Post*. His name was in the obituary as well.

In July, he wrapped up his affairs in Washington, packed his bags, assumed the guise of a State Department officer, and flew with Rosario to Rome. The CIA offered few better postings. An operations man starting out would want small, tough Third World stations where he could prove himself, but the top jobs at the Rome station were supposed to be for people who had arrived or were about to—the most promising, industrious, and imaginative officers of the clandestine service. Ames's transfer to Rome had won the blessing of Dewey Clarridge, chief of the CIA's European division. Clarridge had been Ames's station chief in Turkey in 1971 and had written him off as worthless back then. His opinion of Ames had not changed, Clarridge said by way of explanation, it was just that the Agency didn't have a very deep bench.

The Ameses found a lovely three-bedroom apartment in a fine old building on the Via Bellini. It had high ceilings and huge windows, and it was a fifteen-minute walk through the

Borghese Gardens to the U.S. Embassy, where the CIA's station was hidden. The embassy itself was an elegant seventeenth-century villa on the Via Veneto, a boulevard that was a fading center of nightlife in Rome. The villa had been heavily fortified in the 1970s, when the Red Brigades terrorist group was active; barricades and Marine sentries guarded the entrances. At the time, the CIA station had been located in the oldest part of the building, a rear wing. But in the early 1980s, it had nearly doubled in size, expanding to fifty officers and support staff, and had outgrown its old offices. It now occupied most of the fifth and topmost floor of the main villa. It had become "a vastly overstaffed station with people trying to invent things to do and justify the few bogus things they were supposed to do," in the opinion of Mark Blanchard, a young case officer who served there with Rick Ames from 1986 to 1989.

Ames worked for Alan Wolfe, the station chief, a theatrical, egotistical, short, and portly man with a booming voice who combed his silvery hair straight back. This was Wolfe's farewell tour. He had served in CIA stations from Rawalpindi to Rome, and he was part of the clan of covert operators who had taken over at the Agency—Clair George, Dewey Clarridge, and their friends—the stars who had risen in the CIA's Near East division during the seventies.

Wolfe had divided his station into seven sections. Third World focused on the Middle East, Iran, Iraq, and North Africa. Internal dealt with Italy. Liaison swapped information with the intelligence services of friendly countries, an important business because it was profitable. The CIA's analysts back at headquarters poured out unceasing torrents of information, which could be traded for something better on the Libyans or the Iranians. There also were technology, commercial, and administrative desks. The most important of all was Hard Targets, the section that focused on the Communist threat.

The CIA put Rick Ames in charge of Hard Targets. "I had four or five officers working for me," Ames said. "And we had to go around and try to recruit Soviets, East Europeans, North Koreans, Chinese, Cubans, Laotians, whatnot. And also counterintelligence programs, getting some double-agent cases running."

Before arriving in Rome, Ames was unsure of how successfully he could lead a double life. As chief of the counter-intelligence branch back at headquarters, he was guaranteed access to the Agency's crown jewels. He was worried that the quality of the information he would be able to obtain for the KGB would fall off drastically in Rome. But shortly after he arrived, he saw quickly that whatever problem he might have with the quality of the secrets he could deliver would be counterbalanced by their immense quantity.

Two rivers of paper converged at the Rome station. One was directed to Ames. He received daily reports on a wide variety of CIA operations around the world. As an action officer, a person who was supposed to go out and do things, Ames received extra copies of these reports. The second river, even wider, flowed to the station at large: classified State Department reports, CIA papers on everything under the sun, cables from other stations—and all were available in duplicate. Taken together, a six-inch stack of secret papers piled up on his desk each day.

"I had access to a wide range of stuff," Ames said. "Not to sensitive Soviet operations, except little bits and pieces. But I had a wide range of other information that the KGB was eager to get and happy to get. Generally, operational stuff"— that is, what the Agency's covert operators were doing, as opposed to what its analysts were thinking.

The take included details of the Agency's operations throughout the Mediterranean and the Middle East; information about what the Agency was planning to do over the coming months and years; data on the Directorate of Operations' policies, budget, staff, and programs. Ames learned the code names and sometimes the real names of foreign agents working for the CIA, the details of what those agents did and said in their meetings with CIA case officers, the dates and places where those meetings were held. He coordinated double-agent operations that the U.S. Army and Navy were running against the Soviets—that is, American dangles pretending to cooperate with the KGB. He read through reams and reams of reports from headquarters about everything he was deemed to have a need to know.

The paper came in "from headquarters, from stations elsewhere in Europe and elsewhere around the world who for some reason thought to put Rome on the routing. You would find it hard to believe, probably—I know the KGB found it very hard to believe—that as much paper washes through our overseas stations as does. Just tremendous volumes of stuff," he said. It kept him going as the KGB's star spy.

Rick Ames and fledgling case officer Mark Blanchard worked together on matters concerning the KGB once a week within the Rome station. Blanchard grew accustomed to the way Ames spoke, thought, and acted. "It was all talk and contemplation, but no action," he said. "He would spin things out in slow motion, consider all the possible ramifications of everything . . . always double-thinking, triple-thinking, and quadruple-thinking everything . . . and never doing anything. People in the Soviet division always took the circumlocution approach, spinning ideas out so far that they could be killed, spinning out people forever and never terminating them, procrastinating, making things longer, padding the books. Ames was a real Soviet division man. He was a typical mediocre old officer, going nowhere."

Ames usually wandered in well after nine in the morning and left for a good long lunch at noon, returning too befogged to think straight three or four times a week. "Sure, he was a drunk, but I knew far bigger drunks at the station," Blanchard said. "Thirty percent of the station went out and got drunk at lunch. It was a drunken culture. A lot of people spent a lot of time drinking because they didn't have an awful lot to do. We had a lot of people who were worse disciplinary problems. We had NOCs"—Americans working under nonofficial cover, usually posing as businessmen, without the disguise of a State Department post—"that we knew were embezzling and ripping money off. We had people sleeping around with people they weren't supposed to be sleeping around with. Rick Ames certainly did not stand out."

The reality of everyday life at the CIA gave Ames a kind of protective camouflage. Espionage was not the glamorous life the movies make it out to be. In the real world, the CIA was a big bureaucracy, albeit a clandestine one with special tribal rites—a cross between Yale's secret Skull and Bones society and the Post Office. Most people at the CIA had ordinary talents and ordinary problems. They suffered from midlife crises, drank too much, sometimes shirked hard tasks, and silently nursed grudges against their superiors. Only on occasion did their work rise to the level of espionage fiction. More often it fell far short, as when Blanchard worked with Ames on a scheme aimed at recruiting Russians.

"We would arrange encounters where you could bump into the Soviets," Blanchard said. "The usual thing was to con them into getting together with us for volleyball games, basketball games, and a mini-Olympics. The Russians were carefully selected. Ames directed me in trying to set these things up, and he was always very careful in directing me who to talk to." No recruitments ever came of these sessions. As far as Blanchard was concerned, nothing of value came out of Rick Ames.

For his part, Ames saw Blanchard as an example of a cultural quirk of the CIA: its heavy recruitment of members of the Church of Jesus Christ of Latter-Day Saints. The Agency always had loved Mormons, and it was easy to see why. They had done missionary work overseas and spoke odd languages, and they had had the unusual experience of spending years trying to talk foreigners into giving up their deepest beliefs for something different, something better. But the Mormons did not always love the Agency. "A few of them had ethical problems," Ames said. "I think most people who had been brought up with a strongly religious background could easily have problems like that. And the hard drinking. All of that made it difficult for some of them."

In fact, Blanchard himself confronted an ethical problem during his stint in Italy, and it made him leave the CIA. "I happened to develop a contact within the Rome office of the African National Congress," he remembered. "This man was very cautious about contacting me, but I had gotten him to the point where he was ready to begin a dialogue. I wrote up our conversations, thinking I was working for the benefit of both our causes. Then, some months later, I got a visit from an officer from headquarters, a woman about ten years my senior. She took me aside and said, 'Between you and me, your reports on the ANC contact are wonderful, and everybody likes them. But I want you to know they go straight to our liaison with the South African intelligence service. You do what you think is necessary.' I torpedoed the relationship."

These kinds of betrayals were part of the game of espionage. They did not trouble Rick Ames.

Shortly after he arrived in Rome, Ames asked Wolfe, his station chief, for authorization to meet and try to recruit a Soviet Embassy official, just as he had done in Washington. Taking his cue from Vlad, his KGB controller, he told Wolfe that he thought he might be able to win over Aleksei Khrenkov, the diplomat at the Soviet Ministry of Foreign Affairs in Rome who was actually his go-between. Ames told Wolfe that "I was assessing the guy to see if he'd be of value as a target." He immediately won permission to meet the man whenever the time was ripe.

His first meeting with Khrenkov set the pattern for the next three years. Every six or eight weeks, Ames would throw together a stack of a hundred or more classified reports he had accumulated and stuff them into envelopes. By the time he was done the stack would be six inches thick. It added up to about a thousand documents a year.

Ames rarely bothered to use a copying machine. "I just took the originals," he said. "They were in my office, in my safe. Typically I would meet with my cutout in the early evening. And I would simply stay in my office until six or so, quickly gather up, review, and gather up information that I thought would be of value. Not by any means everything. And package it up and leave the station." He would slip the secret documents into a shopping bag filled with magazines and stroll out of the embassy, flagging a taxi for a restaurant rendezvous with his go-between. The exchange of shopping bags under the table was routine for Ames now. "He would give me usually a box of Cuban cigars," Ames said. "I don't know where he got the idea I was a cigar smoker. They weren't really high quality. And that box would contain some money." The box was usually lined with two hundred $100 bills smelling faintly of Communist tobacco.

By this point, Ames had transferred whatever loyalties he had left to the KGB. There was not much besides Moscow's millions to motivate him at work. Within weeks after he arrived in Rome, the strain of his double life began to show. "It was not much fun in Rome," Ames said. "I lost a lot of drive in Rome, and I think it was largely due to the relationship with the KGB." He said he felt "unconsciously shadowed" by guilt and fear. He obliterated that feeling whenever possible with most of a bottle of vodka. He would always be drunk when he met his clandestine contacts.

"The actual meetings I had with Soviets, I would—I usually had several drinks before a meeting," he said. "I would drink during the meeting. They would try and keep it very paced and everything, so I wouldn't be completely drunk, but I would definitely have had more than just enough to put an edge on."

In September 1986, at their second meeting, Khrenkov slipped Ames $20,000 and told him that Vlad, the controller, would be coming in late October. It was to be an important meeting, the most important of Ames's career as a spy. For he had a sense, a well-founded feeling, that he was in danger—not from the CIA, but from the KGB.

11

Searchlights

Nothing fundamental ever changed in the Soviet Union as long as the KGB held sway. Glasnost and perestroika may have sounded wonderful to the West, but openness and new thinking had no place in the Soviet intelligence service. Mikhail Gorbachev could tinker all he wanted to with the machinery of state, but he dared not change the KGB.

In 1986, Gorbachev turned to the KGB chairman, Viktor Chebrikov, again and again, seeking answers on how best to use espionage to advance the struggle against the West. The solution the KGB chief offered was the traditional one: dig deeper into the U.S. intelligence and military agencies, steal more secrets, recruit more spies in order to gain a better understanding of the United States' real motives. Three months after Gorbachev took power, the KGB succeeded beyond anyone's imagination. When Ames handed over his first shopping bag of secrets, the Soviets gained their first agent in place inside the CIA's operations directorate in the history of the cold war.

But if Ames represented an immense opportunity for the Soviets, he also created a terrible dilemma. When Ames revealed that Soviet intelligence was shot through with traitors, the KGB was compelled to ask the Politburo what to do about them. When the ruling council's shock and anger at the depth of the betrayal receded, the answer was clear: death to spies. Chebrikov had publicly proclaimed that decision back in February with his speech to the Party congress.

More men betrayed by Ames were tried and sentenced for treason in the summer of 1986. Two of their cases were discussed briefly at a Politburo meeting on September 25, 1986, in which Gorbachev, Chebrikov, and Foreign Minister Andrei Gromyko discussed the handling of political crimes against the Soviet state.

"What kind of crimes are the most dangerous, and what kind of punishment is meted out for them?" Gromyko asked the KGB chief.

"Espionage," Chebrikov replied. "Punishment is either execution or fifteen years in prison. Polishchuk has been shot for espionage. Yesterday Tolkachev's sentence was implemented." Leonid Polishchuk was the agent code-named WEIGH who had been double-crossed by Ames. Tolkachev was the Soviet scientist who had been exposed by the cashiered CIA man Edward Lee Howard.

Ames knew—from reading about Chebrikov's speech and from the CIA's grapevine of gossip and corridor chatter—that the Agency's Soviet spies were being killed at a ferocious rate. And that mortified him. He was sure the CIA would realize that someone in its ranks was a traitor.

"It was as if neon lights and searchlights lit up all over the Kremlin, shone all the way across the Atlantic Ocean, saying, 'There is a penetration,' " Ames recalled. "I knew this was turning into a potential, a tremendous danger. That the signals were lighting up. I mean, the KGB might as well have taken out an ad in *The New York Times* saying, 'We got a source.' "

For weeks, as he awaited his meeting with Vlad, who was coming to Rome in late October, Ames agonized over the stupidity and brutality of the KGB. He did not spend a moment mourning for the men he had helped murder. But he could not understand how the KGB could be so stupid and so brutal as to threaten the well-being of the best spy it had ever had.

But the CIA never saw the searchlights blazing from the Kremlin.

•   •   •

The Agency paid little attention when, on October 3, 1986, the Senate Select Committee on Intelligence completed a fifteen-month investigation into the failures of U.S. counterintelligence. Over the past two years, twenty-five people had been convicted of spying against the United States. A twenty-sixth—Edward Lee Howard—was sitting safely behind the iron curtain, thumbing his nose at the CIA. Incredibly, the report said "the nation's counterintelligence structure is fundamentally sound." It made two recommendations for strengthening that sound foundation. One, get the FBI involved early in espionage cases; when intelligence agencies kept the Bureau at bay, "events have often gotten out of control." Two, keep tabs on the finances, foreign travel, and foreign contacts of people with access to secrets.

As for the foreign counterintelligence specialists at the FBI, they were too preoccupied with trying to handle a disaster of their own. In early October, they picked up hints that the two Soviet Embassy officials who had been recruited by the Bureau through the COURTSHIP program—Valery Martinov, who had escorted Yurchenko back to Moscow, and his colleague Sergei Motorin, who had been recalled to a new assignment at KGB headquarters—were either dead or about to be executed.

Jim Holt of the FBI had spent hundreds of hours with Martinov. When he learned that the man was doomed, he said, his first thought was: My God, what did we do? How did the Bureau screw up? What allowed the Soviets to uncover Martinov's betrayal?

"The loss of those two men was devastating to us," said Robert "Bear" Bryant, the chief of the FBI's national security division.

So the FBI assigned six investigators to determine who or what had killed the Soviets. Tim Caruso, a tightly wound, up-and-coming FBI analyst who specialized in uncovering Soviet penetrations of U.S. intelligence, received the order to run the team from his boss, Tom DuHadway, the FBI's deputy assistant director for intelligence operations. Caruso selected a code name for the investigation at random from the dictionary: he chose ANLACE, an archaic word for a medieval dagger.

ANLACE, Caruso said, consisted of "six people sitting in a room . . . for ten months" with a twelve-foot-thick stack of files. They called their tiny windowless office at FBI headquarters "the Vault." But ANLACE was locked out of the case, not into it.

"It did not look at CIA personnel," Caruso said. "It did not look at tradecraft that was used by the CIA." Its conversations with the Agency about the case were stilted and cryptic. It had no idea of the scope of the present crisis at the Agency. No one there had seen fit to inform the FBI. All the Bureau knew was that something had gone wrong.

"We really couldn't put a finger on it," Bryant said. "We just didn't know what was happening."

The small circle of those in the know at the CIA had no inclination to talk to the FBI in early October 1986. After a brief hiatus, their own human sources inside the Soviet Union were again dying. Now almost all of their best Soviet agents had fallen silent—under arrest, under sentence of death, or dead and buried. Paul Redmond, the chief of the Soviet division's counterintelligence branch, sent a memorandum up the chain of command saying he thought that "45 Soviet and East European cases and two technical operations"—that is, electronic eavesdropping on the Soviets—"were known to have been compromised or were evidencing problems."

Instead of joining forces with the FBI, the Agency's counterintelligence chief, Gus Hathaway, formed his own committee to analyze the situation.

Four people, a special task force composed of two Soviet division officers and two retirees, were ordered to take a long look at the situation. The task force was headed by Jeanne Vertefeuille, a gray-haired woman in her late fifties. She was, in the eyes of her colleagues, a competent counterintelligence officer who would never set the world on fire. In the 1970s, she had served in the Netherlands, not exactly a hot spot in the cold war. Her overseas postings had been limited; very few women won prominent jobs within the Directorate of Operations in those days.

The special task force, to be blunt about it, was simply not that special. None of its members had any experience in investigative matters or financial analysis. It was kept small, on Clair George's orders, so that it would stay secret. It undertook a limited review of a few elemental questions about the deaths and disappearances. Who had handled these cases? How many of the losses could be blamed on Edward Lee Howard? How many could be blamed on shoddy work by the CIA?

The task force did not investigate anyone or compile a list of potential suspects. It sealed itself off in a room and began sending for files. It did not emerge for years. Redmond, who oversaw the task force, was blunt about its shortcomings: "We didn't make any progress," he said. "We didn't get any answers."

They got no answers because they never asked anybody any questions, much less the right questions. "They were not looking for an officer," Colin Thompson said. "They didn't want to admit it was an officer. They did not address the issue in 1986. And nothing changed."

. . .

Then, on October 5, 1986, the last chance for a coherent internal investigation at the CIA was destroyed.

That morning, a teenage militiaman in southern Nicaragua hoisted his Russian-built surface-to-air missile onto his shoulder and brought down a low-flying C-123 cargo aircraft with his first shot. The marksmanship of a skinny boy in a Central American jungle proved to be a fatal distraction for the CIA. Four days later, the sole survivor of the crash, an unemployed construction worker from Marinette, Wisconsin, named Eugene Hasenfus, appeared at a press conference held in the Interior Ministry in Managua. He said he had been helping to ferry military supplies to the contra rebels who were trying to topple Nicaragua's leftist Sandinista government. He said the flights had come from Ilopango, a military airfield in El Salvador, under the supervision of CIA officers—one of whom he identified as Max Gomez.

The CIA had been barred by law from providing military aid to the contra rebels, but its fingerprints were all over the mission. For one thing, "Max Gomez" was in reality Felix Rodriguez, a retired CIA officer recruited by the Agency to help run the contra resupply operation. He was a frequent visitor to the White House and had even met with Vice President George Bush.

President Reagan had been trying to overthrow the government of Nicaragua since 1981. He had authorized a covert-action program, proposed by Casey, to support the contras, a right-wing rebel force composed of disaffected

Sandinistas and former members of the National Guard. The operation had faltered in 1984, when Congress had cut off aid to the contras for two years and banned the Agency from providing them with military or intelligence assistance.

Reagan had told his national security team to do whatever was needed to keep the contras together. His aides, led by Lieutenant Colonel Oliver North, had created a gunrunning operation they called The Enterprise. They had helped the contras buy arms using surplus profits from another covert operation—the secret sale of arms to Iran, part of an effort to obtain the freedom of Western hostages held by Iranian-backed radicals in Lebanon. The CIA had been deeply involved in the weapons sales to Iran as well, and some of its top officers had heard rumors that North was diverting profits from those sales to arm the contras. Clair George and Dewey Clarridge had known the details of both operations, and they thought it was incomprehensibly stupid of North to have merged the two strands into a single tangled web. Now the unraveling of the Nicaraguan mission threatened to expose the Iran initiative.

So the Sandinista militiaman's missile was a bullet aimed at the Agency's heart—and another stupendous stroke of luck for Rick Ames. Most of the principal players who might have led the effort to hunt Ames down were suddenly diverted to what the Agency thought was a more immediate and serious threat. Bill Casey, Clair George, Dewey Clarridge, and a handful of others at the CIA quickly realized that congressional inquiries were inevitable.

Clair George, the man in charge of all the CIA's covert operations and ultimately responsible for tracking down the cause of the disaster in his Soviet division, felt the chill of fear strongest of all.

George was the consummate Agency man, with thirty-three years of service as a spy. As the CIA's chief of operations, he spent his days and many of his nights supervising the work of six thousand officers in the clandestine service. He had crossed paths a few times with Rick Ames, who remembered him as "a very smart guy who could be very, very abrasive."

In many ways Clair George was a conundrum. He lacked the elite breeding common to many officers of his generation but concealed it well. George had been raised in Beaver Falls, Pennsylvania, and after his father died while he was in high school he had been obliged to work the night shift at the local steel mill to help pay the family's bills. Not many senior CIA officers had ever carried their lunch to work in a pail. While many of the people George would work with at the Agency had gone to Yale or Harvard, he had graduated from Penn State. George compensated for this lack of social status by sprinkling his speech with Briticisms, phrases like "dear fellow" and "old chap."

George had become fluent in Mandarin Chinese in the Army's language school and had been recruited by the CIA to go to Hong Kong and debrief defectors from the Chinese mainland. He had married a young operations officer, Mary Atkinson, and after a stint in Paris had begun to work "the night-soil circuit," a series of backwater capitals fertile with opportunities. The young spy with bright red hair had excelled. Where better to recruit disaffected Soviets than in obscure posts where resentments festered? In 1971, the CIA had put George in charge of running all Soviet agents outside of the Soviet Union and the East Bloc. Barely past forty, he was now a commander in the secret war.

He won the admiration of his fellow spies for having taken on two of the most dangerous assignments in the world. He was station chief in Beirut when Lebanon was in the throes of a ferocious civil war. His next assignment was to take over in Athens after the station chief there, Richard Welch, was assassinated by masked gunmen. George chose to conceal his identity in Athens as the CIA's top man by hiding in plain sight. While the U.S. Ambassador rode in a heavily armored car guarded by an armed convoy, George rode to work in an old Volkswagen Beetle, gambling that the anti-American gunmen would never figure out who he was. In 1978, he had returned to headquarters to run the Africa division of the clandestine service; his State Department counterparts often thought he was running operations on them.

Casey loved him for his bravery, his charm, and his cunning and had made him chief of covert operations in 1984. What little leisure time George had in those years was spent playing tennis at the Chevy Chase Club and casually lying to new acquaintances about what he did for a living. He looked less like the nation's chief of spies than like a midlevel official at the Bureau of Weights and Measures.

George had two characteristics in equal measure: loyalty to the Agency and disdain for Congress. After the C-123 went down over Nicaragua, both emotions were in full play. George was summoned to Capitol Hill to answer questions about the affair in a closed-door session of the Senate Foreign Relations Committee. He chose to conceal much of what he knew, a decision that led to immense legal trouble.

In early November, Iranians intent on humiliating the United States began revealing the story of the arms-for-hostages affair in a Lebanese newspaper. That was the beginning of the end for the cover stories created by the White House and the CIA to conceal the operations and protect President Reagan. It was clear that careers and reputations were going to be ruined. And as the arms-for-Iran and cash-for-the-contras schemes began slipping out of control and into the public arena, Casey behaved like a man coming undone. In late November, he gave patently false testimony about the affair to Congress, and those who heard it said that Casey was lost and listless. He stumbled through the next three weeks, forgetting where he was and what he was saying, shifting in and out of focus like a man trying to awaken from a bad dream. He never did. On December 15, a seizure struck him down in his seventh-floor office at the CIA, and tests revealed a rare form of brain cancer. The disease robbed him of his speech and his thoughts at the height of the biggest intelligence scandal in a decade.

A six-alarm fire was consuming the CIA. Its chief was dying. Its top officers and foremost covert operators were entangled in the Iran-contra affair: not only George, the spymaster, but Gates, the acting director; Clarridge, the chief of the European division; a half-dozen station chiefs in the Middle East and Central America; and many more of the CIA's best minds, top investigators, and leading in-house lawyers. All would spend the next year giving sworn testimony and depositions, compiling dossiers for congressional and criminal investigators, or rearranging the Agency's personnel lists to replace those forced to quit. The government indicted Dewey Clarridge and Clair George, though both received presidential pardons in 1992.

For George, there was a professional tragedy on top of the personal disaster. He would never complete the life-or-death task Bill Casey had given him: doing something about the killings of the CIA's Soviet agents. Without him, no one at the CIA would.

12

The Art of Deception

On October 20, 1986, as the Central Intelligence Agency struggled to stop its secrets from spilling out in Teheran, San Salvador, Tel Aviv, and Washington, Rick Ames stood in a bar in Rome, steeling himself with shots of vodka.

The plan for the late-night meeting at the Soviet residential compound with his KGB case officer, Vlad, had been passed on to him in a note a few weeks earlier. "I would be picked up in the car, and they would drive around for about forty minutes, making sure there was no surveillance," he remembered. "I would have a jacket and a baseball cap on, take my glasses off, hunch down, and we'd go zooming in, and then they'd take me up to a little room they'd constructed up in the attic for me. And we'd sit there for about four or five hours."

Once inside the gates of the Soviet compound at the Villa Abamelek and safely up in the attic, Ames settled in for a long night among friends. He liked Vlad and the rest of the Soviets who handled his case. They showed him a kindness and a solicitude that no one in the Agency ever had, and they made him feel important. But his warm feelings were soon overwhelmed by anger. Ames took another drink, and another, as he talked about his fear that the KGB's killings of the traitors he had exposed would in turn reveal his own treason.

Vlad apologized. It was inexcusable, he told Ames. He said that Vladimir Kryuchkov, the longtime chief of the KGB's First Chief Directorate—the division responsible for foreign intelligence—had become "intimately involved" with the case and that Kryuchkov and his colleagues deeply regretted what had come to pass.

"You must know that we would never have chosen to do it the way we did it, but the decision went up to the highest levels, and it was decided it had to be done," he said, according to Ames. It was a political decision, Vlad implied, one that had been taken out of the KGB's hands by the Politburo. The Soviet leadership had been so angry about the betrayals that the spate of arrests and executions could not be stopped.

"We know the tremendous danger that this creates," Vlad said, "and we just wish it had been otherwise." Ames was stunned. The information he had given the KGB—proof that the all-powerful state security system of the Soviet Union was shot through with traitors—had compelled the Politburo, and thus Gorbachev himself, to order the executions.

There was more. "We're very concerned about where an investigation of all this is going," Vlad told him. The KGB was positive that the CIA knew it had been penetrated. But it was also confident that the Agency had no idea how the penetration had occurred or when or by whom. That uncertainty gave the KGB a magnificent opportunity.

Vlad promised Ames that the KGB would try "everything we can to divert, to mislead" the CIA with false and confusing clues. "He said, 'We're trying to find effective ways of diverting attention, and one of the ways is to create the impression that there's a commo problem.'" "Commo" was shorthand for communications. The KGB was going to try to convince the Agency that a breach in secure communications, a wiretap or a bug or the breaking of a code, was the cause of the disaster. The plan matched the CIA's assumptions perfectly.

That was all Ames remembered of the meeting with Vlad. "I had had a lot to drink," he said. "We were going to meet at the same place the next night, and he was going to bring money. Only I forgot about it. It washed out of my mind with the alcohol."

But the KGB kept its promise to Rick Ames. He knew it. And he loved them for it. "The KGB was trying its best to divert attention," he said proudly, "and it worked." For the next five years, Vladimir Kryuchkov and a team of Soviet counterintelligence officers masterminded a series of deceptions to protect their prize spy.

Kryuchkov was a hardheaded, humorless workaholic who was carefully consolidating his power under the new regime of Mikhail Gorbachev, waiting for the day when he would be named to take over the KGB. He had served thirteen years as the head of its First Chief Directorate, the most prestigious arm of the Soviet spy service, which was responsible for spying on the world outside the Soviet Union's borders. He presided over twelve thousand officers serving abroad, a force twice the size of his main adversary, the CIA's Directorate of Operations.

Like his old rival, Clair George, he had come from a poor family and started out in life as a factory worker. He had earned a law degree by night, trained to be a diplomat, and served for five years in the 1950s at the Soviet Embassy in Budapest, where he had attracted the attention of the ambassador, Yuri Andropov. In 1967, Andropov had taken over the KGB, and Kryuchkov had been there to serve as his right-hand man. By 1983, Andropov had been running the Soviet

Union, and his protégé was in a position to succeed him as the head of the world's biggest intelligence service.

Kryuchkov knew that the arrests and executions of the men Ames had betrayed could alert the CIA to the existence of a mole in its midst. It was one of the ironies of intelligence: a source provides great information, but if you use the information, you risk destroying the source. Kryuchkov had to convince the CIA that someone or something other than Ames was killing the Agency's Soviet spies.

Deception is as old as war. The two merge in the craft of intelligence, which seeks victory without weaponry. The tradition begins with Sun Tzu's *The Art of War,* the 2,600-year-old text that argues that "all warfare is based on deception." It runs through Niccolò Machiavelli, the Renaissance's greatest advocate of cunning and dishonesty, to Civil War general Thomas "Stonewall" Jackson, whose credo was "mystify, mislead, and surprise." The craft was deeply respected within the KGB, which had an entire branch devoted to *maskirovka,* or deception techniques. They took it extremely seriously, in the manner of a chess grand master who studies every game his opponent has ever played in preparation for a match.

For Kryuchkov's subterfuges to succeed, he first needed every scrap of available information from Ames. Questions and tasks from Kryuchkov and his staff were passed to Ames in Rome through the go-between, Aleksei Khrenkov. They sought the identities of Soviet and Eastern European intelligence officers and diplomats cooperating with the CIA and U.S. intelligence officers who had contact with Soviets abroad. All could serve as conduits for the deception plan. To hear that there was a new CIA source somewhere at the Soviet Embassy in Prague was good enough; the KGB would take it from there. Kryuchkov had to know the full cast of characters before staging his plays.

Over five years, the KGB ran at least five separate but intertwined deception operations to protect Ames, each with its own subplots. An opportunity for one of them arose in December 1986, only two months after Ames and Vlad met in Rome. The setting was the U.S. Embassy in Moscow.

U.S. Marines stood watch at the Moscow embassy, guarding the entryways, the CIA station, and the Communications Program Unit, which sent and received coded messages to and from CIA headquarters. The Marines were outnumbered by the Soviets who worked as cooks, chauffeurs, maintenance people, and receptionists at the embassy and reported regularly to the KGB. The Soviet employees provided a picture of how the embassy was run: who did what, who worked where, and, most important, who might be vulnerable to an approach. As it turned out, some of the Marines often fell for the oldest approach of all. The few, the proud, the brave, were also young, single, and lonely.

Sergeant Clayton J. Lonetree was more vulnerable than most. Though he was descended directly from celebrated Winnebago and Sioux warrior chiefs, as a Marine he was a misfit. Not long after arriving in Moscow in 1985, he had been confined to quarters for forty-five days for drunkenness. Upon his release, he ran into Violetta Seina, a Soviet employee at the U.S. Embassy, in a seemingly chance encounter at one of Moscow's magnificent subway stations. They had a spirited conversation. Soon he was sleeping with her, violating explicit regulations against fraternizing with Soviets. Violetta told Lonetree that her Uncle Sasha wanted to meet him. Uncle Sasha was, in reality, Aleksei Yefimov, a KGB officer. He made it clear to Lonetree that to keep on seeing Violetta he would have to answer some questions about how the embassy was run. Lonetree ended up turning over information about the layout of the building and his suspicions as to the identities of CIA officers operating under diplomatic cover. Then, in March 1986, Lonetree was reassigned to the U.S. Embassy in Vienna. Uncle Sasha said he would arrange for another new friend—a KGB officer, of course—to meet him there occasionally. Lonetree's transfer was no great loss, since Corporal Arnold Bracy, another Marine guard at the Moscow embassy, was having an affair with Galina Golotina, a cheerful, plump assistant cook at the embassy. She was also a KGB plant.

In December 1986, Lonetree, drinking heavily, decided to share his guilty feelings with someone he was sure would understand: the CIA station chief in Vienna. Lonetree implicated himself and Bracy, saying they had shared information on the embassy's layout and procedures with the Soviets. From the moment of Lonetree's heart-to-heart confession, the CIA saw the Marine guards as an answer to the mystery of the disappearing agents.

Over the next three months, Lonetree and Bracy faced fierce and sometimes unprofessional interrogation by the Naval Investigative Service. In March 1987, after a nonstop nine-hour grilling, the investigators pushed Bracy into a startling admission: he had escorted Soviets into the Communications Program Unit. The CIA now believed that the Marines had let the KGB run wild in the embassy and that that had been the source of the security breaches: the Moscow station's secrets had been ransacked, perhaps by a bug implanted somewhere in the Communications Program Unit.

Bracy's ultimate confession was the sole piece of hard evidence to support that theory—and he retracted it almost immediately. But for many at the CIA, the proof was in.

"When I saw the Lonetree-Bracy thing break, I said: Hey! Voilà!," said Milt Bearden, the deputy chief of the Soviet division. "Everything that had been compromised was in a limited but retrievable way shared with the Moscow station. So that was that. Case closed." The CIA's special task force, the small analytical group created to look into the destruction of the Agency's network of Soviet spies, initially agreed with that assessment.

By March 1987, the solution was so self-evident that the Agency began calling in the handful of the newspaper reporters in Washington who specialized in intelligence matters and explaining the case to them in background briefings. The CIA officials confided that there had been a few lapses in security that they had blamed mistakenly on Edward Lee Howard. A couple of cases had gone bad, and a couple of Soviet agents being run by the Moscow station had been lost as a result.

But now the CIA's counterintelligence experts knew what the source of their problems had been: the Marines.

One piece of information they did not share with the reporters was the most crucial one. An impeccable source had confirmed and expanded upon the investigators' conclusions: the KGB.

The Soviets saw the Lonetree and Bracy cases as a perfect way to distract the CIA. Inflating the importance and manipulating the meaning of the affair was a key element of the KGB's deception strategy.

"They made use of the whole Lonetree case—definitely," Ames said. From the moment the KGB learned that Lonetree was under investigation, they took advantage of the fact. They slipped information to the CIA that made the case seem far more significant than it was, amplifying the Agency's worst fears, playing on its predisposition to believe that an electronic bug in the Moscow embassy had killed the CIA's most valuable agents.

The KGB had no problem delivering its message. The rival intelligence services had ways of talking discreetly to one

another. There were always informal contacts in foreign capitals. There was also a secret channel of communications—a
hot line, like the one President John F. Kennedy and General
Secretary Nikita Khrushchev had set up in June 1963. It
linked the CIA's Soviet division with the KGB's First and Second Chief Directorates; the Second Chief Directorate was
primarily responsible for the internal security of the Soviet
Union, and its duties included catching spies.

Through these established channels, the KGB could offer to
explain certain things to the Agency. They used all of them—
and invented some new ones—as part of their scheme.

They told the CIA anything but the truth, blaming Lonetree, Howard, and bad luck for the disasters. Kryuchkov and
his counterintelligence staff instructed a handful of Soviet
intelligence officers and diplomats who had legitimate and
authorized contacts with the CIA to shake their heads and
commiserate with the Americans and to blame the arrests on
sloppy tradecraft. As part of this plan, a senior KGB officer in
East Berlin sent a letter to the CIA discussing five of the disappearances of the CIA's agents. His explanation dovetailed
with the one offered in 1986 by former CIA operations director John Stein: every one of the compromised cases had contained the seeds of its own destruction. Each was the result of
poor work by a CIA case officer, a blunder by a KGB agent
working for Washington, a missed warning, a broken date. In
each case, he offered elaborate explanations that included
indisputably accurate details. This mixture of truth and lies
was diabolically clever, for the task of sorting out what was
wheat and what was chaff could—and did—take years.

Kryuchkov also spread the word inside the KGB that
Howard had after all been the source who had betrayed all
the Soviet agents who had been arrested, imprisoned, and
shot. Their dissemination of disinformation inside the KGB

helped ensure that anyone who might cooperate with the CIA in the future would pass on the falsehood.

All along, the KGB found ways to utilize the men Ames had betrayed. After weeks or months of interrogation in the basement of KGB headquarters, the doomed spies would be offered a false hope. If they cooperated, the death sentence awaiting them might be commuted. They were ordered to make contact with their CIA case officers or their families living abroad, signaling they were alive and well. Each of those messages would contain false implications to baffle the Americans. For example, in late 1986, a few weeks after he was arrested, Sergei Motorin, one of the KGB officers at the Soviet Embassy in Washington who had spied for the FBI, telephoned his wife, who was still living outside Washington and awaiting his return. All's well, he told her. See you soon. The call, monitored by the electronic eavesdropping National Security Agency, befuddled the Bureau and the CIA. Motorin was executed a few months later.

Yet another deception, following the Moscow embassy affair, sought to reinforce the idea that the Agency's communications links had been penetrated. A KGB officer pretended to volunteer his services to the CIA. He sent warnings that there was a security breach of some kind in the Agency's communications center outside Warrenton, Virginia, the switchboard for top secret messages sent to and from the CIA's headquarters and its stations abroad. He hinted that this breach threatened the lives of CIA sources in the Soviet Union—and, in particular, his own life. Then he vanished.

"They ran a very fancy operation on us in the Warrenton deal," Milt Bearden said. "It was very credible, very well run, and it disappeared into smoke. How do I, as a KGB chess master, do this? I create a source of information, a volunteer. The anatomy of this volunteer is such that you, the CIA, may never lay hands on him. The volunteer says, 'I will lead you to something that tells you your weakness has killed me.' And then the volunteer disappears."

The CIA believed in the ghostly source. The Agency's credulity created a hypothesis: the KGB had somehow wormed its way into Warrenton, perhaps with an electronic eavesdropping device that snatched telecommunications from the ether, perhaps by recruiting a source who had implanted a bug that intercepted the center's transmissions. Maybe the KGB recruit had moved into headquarters and had gained access to information about the cases by tapping into messages from the Moscow station.

The possibility became so plausible that the CIA placed at least ninety of its employees under investigation. The investigator on the case was a twenty-eight-year-old neophyte named Dan Payne, who was assigned part time to the special task force. He eventually narrowed the list of suspects down to ten people—and then gave up. Among the ten, he reported, "there are so many problem personalities . . . that no one stands out." The Warrenton communications center was perhaps the most sophisticated of the KGB's ruses. It took five years before the CIA realized it had been duped.

"They were really playing chess now," Bearden said.

The comparison was apt. When it came to deception, the Soviets were grand masters and the Americans amateurs, said Charlie Emmling, then the Soviet division's Western Europe branch chief. Emmling said he learned everything he needed to know on the subject by playing the game with his KGB counterpart while stationed in Burma. "I was no good at it," he said. "After I made a few opening moves, he usually would have me. I remember he beat me once and leaned forward and said, 'Charlie, do you want to know the secret of chess? You look for the weak point and you push everything through it.'"

The weak point of the CIA's investigation was the tiny special task force—two full-time employees and one part-time investigator up against a cadre of world-class fabricators. Even when the task force realized that it had been fooled by one operation or another, that realization brought it no closer to the truth.

Theories rose and fell, formed and evaporated. "Everybody thought the disappearances could be explained by a number of things," Emmling said. "The fact is, it's unusual for an active source to remain active for a long time. Their access to information changes. They get shifted to a job where they are inaccessible to us. They have guilty feelings and quit. They drink too much. They get caught. They die.

"What a rat's nest it all was," he sighed.

"And on top of everything, there was Iran-contra. It was a time of great upheaval. I mean, we always thought we were the shield of American democracy, and people were walking around saying, Is anybody in this place honest? The D.O. has a mandate to lie. Overseas, you are not what you are. The flip side of that is, you need to have great integrity in everything else you do."

13

Bordeaux and Budweiser

On March 3, 1987, a politically wounded President Reagan nominated William Webster, the square-jawed, sixty-two-year-old director of the Federal Bureau of Investigation, to run the Central Intelligence Agency. He praised Webster as "a man of honor and integrity, a man who is committed to the rule of law."

Well, official Washington sighed, that would be refreshing. Reagan was about to go on television and tell the American people, in so many words, that he had lied to them about the Iran-contra affair by saying he had never traded arms for hostages and that he knew that he had lost their trust and confidence as a consequence. So much of the affair had had its roots in Bill Casey's CIA. The appointment of Webster was seen as an attempt to pull up those roots and begin again.

A former federal appeals court judge, Webster had been named to head the FBI by President Jimmy Carter nine years earlier. He had presided over the Bureau's painful recovery from its misconduct in the Watergate scandal and its slow emergence from the nearly fifty-year reign of J. Edgar

Hoover. Surely he could keep the CIA out of trouble and out of the headlines. Judge Webster, as everyone called him, projected the image of an ethical man.

Yet his appointment horrified many of the old-time covert operators. They were appalled at the idea that an FBI man would run the Agency—and Webster, of all people, a teetotaling Christian Scientist, innocent of the CIA and its culture. Their mood was not improved by the fact that thirty-five FBI agents assigned to investigate Iran-contra were crawling all over the CIA, opening safes and pulling out classified records, looking for information that would lead to the indictment of some of the Agency's top officials.

Surely, the old guard grumbled, Webster would bring a whole squad of FBI men to Langley to run things—those clumsy, earnest gumshoes. The corridor chatter at the CIA was filled with gloomy metaphors. Webster's nomination was a raid on the Agency—we know you're in there, come out with your hands up! It was a hostile takeover. No, it was a Frankenstein experiment, grafting the Bureau's head onto the Agency's body. The operators settled on the image of a transplant and knowingly chuckled that the body would reject it.

Webster, of course, had to be replaced at the FBI, and Reagan's attorney general, Edwin Meese III, hastily searched for a candidate. He found William S. Sessions, a federal judge in San Antonio. Sessions was a pleasant man, not particularly brilliant, with a reputation for honesty: a plain-vanilla candidate, a safe if uninspired choice. Rumblings of dissatisfaction began rising at the Bureau's headquarters, the J. Edgar Hoover Building, widely considered to be the ugliest pile of concrete in Washington. The career FBI men who worked directly under Sessions complained that the man had a habit of asking completely irrelevant questions, suddenly bursting into country music songs, and taking a nine-to-five attitude toward a twenty-four-hour job. His mind did not focus; things just didn't stick. No one at the FBI was too thrilled about Sessions.

In Congress, on the other hand, Webster's ascension was greeted by the Senate intelligence committee with a unanimous vote and palpable relief. If nothing else, the members agreed, Webster would keep the Agency on the right side of the law.

And perhaps he could tackle the forty-year-old problem of coordinating the counterintelligence operations of the CIA and the FBI.

The rivalry between the two agencies dated back to the creation of the CIA in 1947, and the war against Soviet espionage had been continually sabotaged by their battles. The cultures of the Bureau and the Agency clashed in almost every respect, and mistrust had tainted their mutual endeavors.

FBI agents said that many CIA officers treated them with polite condescension, were ignorant of the justice system, and were unschooled in the realities of criminal investigation. To their CIA counterparts, FBI agents were blind to the intricacies of intelligence, where people stole secrets and refined them into subtly shaded reports for the nation's leaders. Each saw the other in old stereotypes. The CIA was Bordeaux; the FBI was Budweiser. The Agency was college professors; the FBI was cops. Under Hoover, agents had dressed in starched white shirts and dark suits, and until the late 1960s they had been required to wear hats and forbidden to drink coffee at their desks. CIA officers often affected the faintly shabby, Anglicized air of men who had stepped into the cold war from ivied campuses, bringing along their briar pipes and tweed jackets. The few FBI agents who had left to join the

CIA, especially in the early years, had often been struck by the intellectual vibrancy and freedom from petty rules.

The legacy of J. Edgar Hoover had lived on years after his death in 1972. Hoover's insecurities and idiosyncrasies had hobbled the FBI's institutional growth and left it a tyranny of clerks. His idea of counterintelligence had been a permanent blot on the Bureau's record. He had insisted that Moscow's hidden hand was at work when Americans opposed the war in Vietnam or marched against segregation in the South. That had been made manifest by COINTELPRO—Hoover's domestic counterintelligence programs. FBI men had spied on and sabotaged the antiwar and civil rights movements; undertaken "black-bag jobs," breaking into houses and offices without search warrants; infiltrated legally established political groups; and generally stretched their constitutional powers beyond the breaking point.

In 1970, Hoover had halted all liaison with the Agency, cutting off all cooperation except for written communications. The incident that had provoked this divorce had been petty—the Agency had refused to reveal the identity of an FBI agent who had talked to the CIA without Hoover's permission—but the consequences had been large. Without the FBI to do the fieldwork necessary for counterespionage against the Soviets, the Agency had been hamstrung. Not until well after Hoover's death in May 1972 had the CIA and the FBI resumed talking to each other on counterintelligence matters, but the conversation had often included bitter arguments that had led to long silences. The CIA had routinely refused to share counterintelligence information with the Bureau. And the Bureau's counterintelligence agents, the only people with the power to catch spies inside the borders of the United States, had resented that deeply.

Director after director of both agencies had denied there was a problem, and the problem had therefore continued to fester. But who better than Webster, who had run the FBI for a decade, to solve it? In announcing the nomination, President Reagan pointed out that the Bureau had "dramatically increased its counterintelligence . . . capabilities" under Webster. "I expect Bill to bring the same kind of leadership and achievement to his new position," Reagan said.

Webster's way of harmonizing relations between the Bureau and the Agency was to create a new Counterintelligence Center, where everyone would work together as one big family at the CIA. He put Gus Hathaway, Casey's counterintelligence chief, in charge of the new center. An up-and-coming covert operator named Hugh E. Price, whom everybody called Ted, was Hathaway's number two man. The Counterintelligence Center brought in officers from the Agency's operations, intelligence analysis, technology, and security divisions and opened slots for FBI counterintelligence specialists to come to the Agency and share their insights on how best to do things.

To smooth over the long-standing differences between their agencies, Webster and Sessions signed a "memorandum of understanding" on counterintelligence issues. It said the CIA would notify the FBI immediately whenever it had reason to suspect that someone might be undertaking "activities harmful to the United States."

In theory, the creation of the Counterintelligence Center should have spurred the investigation onward. It did not. It proved to be a huge distraction. The CIA's special task force was simply subsumed into a new investigations unit at the center. Its chief, Jeanne Vertefeuille, was given a dozen new duties. She received no additional help on the most important case of her life. Vertefeuille had one aide and one part-time investigator to help handle the mystery of the disappeared and dead Soviets. She could have asked for more people, more money, more information. She did not. She never took her troubles to the top of the CIA.

William Webster ran the Agency for four years, from 1987 to 1991, but was never more than dimly aware of the special task force and the full scope of its investigation. It appears that no one told him that its origins lay in one of the biggest disasters in the Agency's four decades. Webster says he never knew that ten Soviet agents were dead or that scores of operations had been compromised. As best he can remember, he was told that four or five cases had gone bad in some way a few years back—which is precisely what had appeared in the newspapers after the CIA's background briefings on the Moscow embassy debacle. Had he known more, he later said, he would have paid more attention. But all he knew was that there was a low-level research team trying to figure out a few old unsolved mysteries.

"My knowledge was of a very limited effort that was made to see if they could rationalize some losses," he said. "Was it communications that were being penetrated? Was it human penetration? Was it happening overseas? They were trying to narrow that circle of possibilities. Maybe the losses were related. Maybe they were unrelated. And it was an exercise, nothing more. If they found something, fine. If they didn't find a sinister reason, maybe they'd find another reason or no reason at all. That's all I ever heard about it. I knew almost nothing about this investigation."

So the thread of the investigation was lost. It disappeared in the tumult that surrounded the Iran-contra affair, Casey's death, Webster's succession, Clair George's departure and subsequent indictment, the deep confusion over the Lonetree case and the Soviet deception operations, the endless tensions between the CIA and the FBI, the disruptions caused by the creation of the new Counterintelligence Center—and the withholding of information from the Director of Central Intelligence.

It would be years before the thread was found again.

14

Kolokol

Rick Ames sat at his home computer in his high-ceilinged apartment on the Via Bellini one evening early in September 1987, tapping out a message to the KGB.

The note said that Ames's station chief in Rome, Alan Wolfe, had held a briefing for a few select officers that afternoon—Ames included. Wolfe told the gathering that he had just returned from an annual conference of station chiefs at CIA headquarters, attended by most of the Agency's barons, where he had had a private conversation with Gus Hathaway. Hathaway had reviewed the CIA's Moscow station investigation. He remained deeply worried that a penetration somewhere in the station was the cause of the present crisis.

Ames reported that the CIA's counterintelligence czar still thought that the Moscow station was the root of the evil. He said he was confident the Lonetree affair would divert the CIA's attention for the foreseeable future.

And he said he had dug up another traitor.

The man's CIA code name was MOTORBOAT, and he was an officer of the Czech security service, based in Rome. The man had volunteered his services to the CIA, and in due course Ames had been assigned to be his case officer. The association was fatal to the Czech. MOTORBOAT returned to Prague a few weeks later. He never came back.

But this was not a simple matter of arrest and execution for the KGB. Now Moscow was trying to be more careful about killing the traitors exposed by Ames, in order to keep from endangering him further. The KGB had to alert its Prague residency and its own counterintelligence and internal security directorates about MOTORBOAT without revealing the original source of the information.

"They have to figure out a cover story, sanitize it in such a way that it can be made available and used," Ames observed. "This put a very strong limitation on their ability to exploit the masses of information I was giving them. In a sense, they had a lot more than they could use." Indeed, when Ames received his annual visit from Vlad in September 1987, the KGB case officer told him that his cornucopia of stolen secrets was overwhelming the Soviet intelligence service.

Ames said that the KGB officer told him: " 'You know, there's an awful lot of the information that you give us, even though it is very valuable and very interesting, that we simply can't handle.' The implication to me was very clear: that they have a very small group of people working on my case and that when I would give them, over the course of a year in Rome, a thousand documents dealing with all different kinds of topics and different places, they are not going to ship those documents all over the KGB or break out the information and ship it all around. It had to be managed very carefully." The CIA had always had the same sort of problem, Ames said: "In our own operations, our own Soviet operations, historically, we would wind up with safes full of information that we felt we couldn't do anything with because it would be too dangerous for the source."

While working as hard as he could for the KGB, Ames was angling for a promotion at the CIA. He wanted more money and a better job with more access to deeper secrets. He was overdue, he argued. He had been stalled for five years at the GS-14 salary grade, which paid upward of $60,000 a year. GS-14 is a grade with some significance to government bureaucrats; it is the top of the middle range. Those above it possess status; those below it are ordinary. He fully expected to win that promotion. He failed to do so. His superiors in Washington and Rome considered him for promotion in late September 1987 and turned him down. They cast him as a terminal GS-14, a middleweight, a man on a treadmill going nowhere.

The failure further embittered Ames. He started drinking even more, and more often, and it began to affect what little work he did for the Agency.

The KGB had warned Ames about his drinking. Vlad had seen it firsthand, and he worried out loud that it would ruin Ames's career or lead to a fatal blunder. Ames had made a complete fool of himself a few months earlier at the U.S. Embassy's Fourth of July party, a traditional gathering at which members of the diplomatic community could enjoy hot dogs and hamburgers in the garden of the ambassador's residence. Ames went alone; Rosario was visiting her mother in Bogotá. He started drinking at noon and never stopped. His fellow officers recall that he began a spirited and increasingly stupid argument with a foreign diplomat before he staggered away and disappeared in the general direction of the Borghese Gardens.

"I have no recollection of the latter half of the reception," Ames said. "I walked home, and I passed out on the street beside my apartment building." The police found Ames unconscious in the gutter on the Via Bellini, took him to a local hospital, examined his wallet, saw his phony State Department identification card, and called the embassy. The following Monday, station chief Alan Wolfe ran into him in the hallway at work.

"There was never any discussion of what had happened," Ames said. "He looked at me, and he said, 'You should be more careful,' and I gave him a kind of a hangdog and apologetic look and said, 'I know—I have—I must—that was really something'—something to that effect. And that was that." The matter was dropped. No official report was made. Nor was any record made in October 1987, when he returned from a luncheon with Khrenkov too drunk to type a message Wolfe had ordered him to send to Washington.

The simple fact was that Ames's drinking did not stand out at the CIA. And neither did Ames. Conspiracy theorists might find some sinister aspect in the CIA's inability to see Ames for what he was. But there was no cabal of covert operators shielding him; he had never belonged to the old-boy clique at the CIA. His superiors in Rome and in Washington simply never took notice of him.

Only one of Ames's colleagues in the covert operations section of the Rome station suspected he might be up to no good. She went so far as to search through the station's records for evidence. But she never shared her suspicions with Alan Wolfe or the deputy station chief, Jack Gower, or the station chief who succeeded Wolfe, Jack Devine, or the counterintelligence investigators back at headquarters.

Ames said he never felt that he was under scrutiny or under anyone's safeguard at the CIA: "I never felt protected or

immunized from either problems with alcohol or lack of promotions or my work with the KGB. I never felt that I was
being protected in any way—or persecuted."

Shouldn't someone have seen him for what he was? "How
could they?" he asked rhetorically. "In retrospect, you can
say, well, Alan Wolfe should have done a little more serious
counseling with me on a couple of problems, drinking problems, I had in Rome. But this is not anything above a normal
level of a personnel problem that frequently arises in the
Agency." Ames saw himself as a normal guy. For many years,
so did the CIA.

By this point, Ames was doing almost no work for the
CIA. The station chief, Alan Wolfe, had come to despair of
his Hard Targets officer. In a job evaluation written in October 1987, Wolfe complained that Ames "handles no ongoing
cases; his efforts to initiate new developmental activity of any
consequence have been desultory."

Ames's only source seemed to be Aleksei Khrenkov, the
Soviet Ministry of Foreign Affairs official who was his go-
between with the KGB. Just as he had done with Khrenkov's
predecessor in Washington, Sergei Chuvakhin, Ames told his
bosses in Rome that he was trying to develop the man as a
potential recruit. Just as before, his bosses gave their bless-
ings for the meetings with Khrenkov, giving Ames a perfect
cover to contact his cutout at his convenience. Just as before,
nothing of value to the CIA came of the meetings; Ames was
careful to walk the fine line between making Khrenkov seem
promising, so he could continue to win approval to meet
him, and not making him seem too promising, which might
prompt his superiors to put someone else on the case.

And just as before, Ames inexplicably stopped submitting
the required reports on the meetings with Khrenkov.

His supervisors paid no attention; they chalked it up to his well-known habits of laziness and procrastination. Ames also failed to file the required financial reports on the money he spent while wining and dining his lackluster source, and this did draw notice. Wolfe confronted Ames over his failure to account for the money. Ames simply began paying his expenses out of his own pocket.

That pocket was seemingly bottomless. Everyone in the Rome station noticed that Ames had a lot of money, and everyone talked about it. Once officially criticized for his sloppy clothes and shabby comportment, Ames was all of a sudden wearing thousand-dollar Italian suits and soft leather loafers. He and Rosario would fly off to Switzerland, Germany, or London for the weekend once a month or so. One of his colleagues knew that the Ameses had a $5,000 monthly telephone bill, most of which Rosario ran up talking to her family in Colombia.

No one knew that Ames occasionally flew to Switzerland for the sole purpose of visiting the Crédit Suisse bank in Zurich. He had two accounts there, one in his name and one in trust for Rosario's mother, Cecilia. He deposited an average of more than $25,000 a month in cash into his own Swiss account—in all, at least $950,000 during his stint. The trips to Zurich had been recommended by Vlad, who had warned Ames never to wire large amounts of money from his bank in Rome. The records of those transfers could be traced, and that would be the end of the game. But Ames carelessly negated the value of these precautions. He was required to notify his bosses every time he left Italy. He did not.

Ames was a hopelessly careless spy, spreading his money around, breaking rules, telling artless lies. He told three different stories to explain his sudden wealth. To his colleagues, he dropped broad hints that he had married into a rich Colombian family that had extensive real estate holdings in South America. To his Swiss bankers, he explained that he was liquidating some of his wife's family properties and salting away the proceeds. To his wife, he told a far more elaborate lie.

"I had prepared a cover story for her," Ames said. The story was as follows: "There was an old friend of mine that I had asked for a loan, that I had known back in college days in Chicago. And I had done a big favor for him once. I never described what it was, but I would ask him for a loan to get us out of the financial hole."

That lie, which Ames had concocted back in 1985, had served to explain only the first $50,000 he had received from the KGB. In Rome, "I had to account for more money," Ames said. "And what I told her was that this friend of mine—I only identified him to her as 'Robert'—and his associates were interested in investing money in Europe. And that when I was in Rome, I would look after some of their investments and manage them. And I would get a commission." In the fall of 1987, after their first year in Rome, Ames told his wife that "we were on the way to becoming, if not exactly wealthy, quite well off."

Ames's work for the KGB was, by that time, bringing in more than $300,000 a year, and he encouraged Rosario to spend it freely. But he also warned her to be discreet—"I told Rosario that while I wasn't doing anything illegal, it was not entirely proper"—and told her to avoid discussing his generous friend Robert with his colleagues.

Rosario trusted him. "He tells me he has investments," she said. "Why would I have any reason to doubt the person I loved?"

Back in Washington, the CIA's special task force and the FBI's counterintelligence analysts had been chasing their tails for more than a year. The FBI's ANLACE team had given up the chase. They had spent month after month trying to understand what could have killed their agents from the Soviet Embassy in Washington, Martinov and Motorin. They had no idea. Edward Lee Howard might have known about Martinov; Motorin was a free spirit, a flamboyant man, and might have brought his doom down upon himself. That was as far as they could take it.

They had been crippled by the failure of the CIA to share information about the case. That was the traditional situation, said the leader of the ANLACE team, Tim Caruso—the FBI had received little or no help from the Agency in 1986 and 1987. The situation improved slightly in 1988. After the failure of ANLACE, FBI counterintelligence analysts arranged to meet with members of the CIA's special task force every few months at an FBI conference room in Quantico, Virginia, to discuss the case. But the conversations remained one-sided. One Agency officer at the meetings wrote a memo to Soviet division chief Burton Gerber warning that "a conscious decision has to be made here concerning the degree to which we are going to cooperate with, and open ourselves up to, the FBI." The decision was made: the Agency never shared its files with the FBI during these meetings. That was the standard procedure in a counterintelligence investigation when there was no reason to believe that there was a "human penetration"—a mole. Instead, the FBI got flat, stale summaries of what the CIA knew.

"I call it the Cliff's Notes," Caruso said. "It's a big difference between reading the Cliff's Notes and reading what Dostoyevski wrote."

People were still dying, and nothing was being done about it. The minutes of a typically inconclusive meeting of the two sides, on July 20, 1988, reflect the CIA's conclusion that sixteen Soviet and Eastern European agents had disappeared from the face of the earth since 1985. As best the Agency could tell, Edward Lee Howard had known about only three of these sixteen people. Among the dead, the Agency had very recently learned, was Top Hat: the legendary Dmitri Polyakov, the Soviet military intelligence officer who had been recruited by the FBI in 1961 and had devoted his life to spying for the United States.

The meeting ended on the unremarkable note that "something had happened, either of a human or a technical nature, which caused the KGB to take action" by arresting and executing nearly every secret agent the United States had inside the Soviet Union. The investigation had advanced no farther than that: something had happened.

Jeanne Vertefeuille, the head of the CIA's special task force, remained focused on the idea that the problem was a technical penetration of some sort—a bug, an eavesdropping device, a broken code. But there was no hard evidence to support that theory. The investigation into the Warrenton communications center had gone nowhere, serving only to waste the time of the CIA team's lone field investigator, young Dan Payne. And Vertefeuille had come to believe that the Lonetree case was, in her words, a "dry hole" insofar as explaining the deaths and the disappearances. The evidence available to the CIA now strongly suggested it was extremely unlikely that Lonetree had let the KGB run wild through the Moscow station. First of all, after Marine Corporal Arnold Bracy recanted his confession, saying he had never let the Soviets into the secret communications unit at the Moscow embassy, the charges against him were dismissed. Bracy went free. The confession had almost undoubtedly been false, the invention of a scared young man. The CIA was not quite sure, but it now looked as if the whole Lonetree matter had, for some reason, been blown far out of proportion.

The only CIA employee who was thoroughly investigated in these years was an officer in the Soviet division whose profile was, in retrospect, strangely similar to that of Aldrich Hazen Ames. The man had had trouble passing a polygraph examination a few years earlier. A fellow officer had reported that the man was spending money far beyond his means. The man was removed from sensitive cases and placed under formal investigation. Dan Payne, in between his CIA classes and his trips to Warrenton, looked into the man's finances. It took him most of 1988 to determine that the money had come from his wife's inheritance. He was no spy.

The investigation, Vertefeuille conceded, was "back to square one" by the fall of 1988. So the task force began thinking about getting around to making a list of all the CIA officials who knew about the compromised cases. But the list was impossibly long; roughly two hundred CIA officers had some knowledge of the existence of the men who died. The task force never finished putting it together. The partial list of potential moles included Bob Gates, who had been the acting director of Central Intelligence after Casey's cancer was discovered; Burton Gerber, the chief of the Soviet division; two dozen different officers in the division, including Gerber's former deputy, Milt Bearden; most of the men and women who had served in the Moscow station in the mid-1980s, and an obscure case officer in Rome named Rick Ames.

Vertefeuille reluctantly came to the awkward and agonizing conclusion that some of the people on the still-incomplete list were "more or less likely to be possible suspects." But the CIA task force did not get around to studying their pasts, reviewing their work, or interviewing their colleagues.

The task force was on the verge of failure. But no one at the top of the chain of command did anything to save it. "Webster never touched it," Milt Bearden said. "And Gerber could not. Because he was a suspect. Just like me."

In October 1988, stymied by Soviet deception and the CIA's inertia and self-deception, the investigation collapsed. It would not be revived for nearly three years.

For the moment, Vladimir Kryuchkov had won. That same month, Mikhail Gorbachev made him the chairman of the KGB. And in his first speech as chairman, he tempered some rare criticism of his service with an old-fashioned attack on the CIA, denouncing its "wide-ranging campaign of spy mania and brutal provocation employed against Soviet institutions." Kryuchkov was one of the few who knew just how brutal the spy wars had become.

A few weeks later in Moscow, Britt Snider, the counsel to the Senate intelligence committee, visited the CIA's station with a colleague. They sat down in the bubble and heard some startling news from the station chief.

"We picked up that there had been, in the past, several CIA assets rolled up," Snider said. It was the first time that anyone on Capitol Hill had heard firsthand information about the case. "We were not told they had been executed or imprisoned," Snider remembered. "We were not told that they had lost everything. All we were told was that, several years earlier, several assets were rolled up and that the station never understood why. We went back to the Agency and asked what had happened. We were told that it was all very sensitive, and we were asked to back off." As a member of the committee, Senator Dennis DeConcini of Arizona, later put it, the staffers had been "stonewalled." The law requires the CIA to notify the congressional intelligence committees of "significant intelligence failures." The committees were not notified of what had really happened to the network of Soviet agents—one of the biggest failures in the history of the CIA—for more than five years after Snider's visit to Moscow.

In the spring of 1989, Rick Ames began preparing to return to CIA headquarters, where he was angling for a top job in the Soviet division. Despite troubles in their marriage, partly due to his drinking, Rosario had conceived a son, Paul, born in November 1988. She had become pregnant a year before that but had miscarried.

After their first and only child was born, Rosario withdrew from her husband, who was infinitely less interesting than the baby. "After Paul was born," she said, "I could have cared less if Rick was there. I had my life, and in a way Rick had his own." She had no idea how true that was.

In June 1989, Ames received a nine-page memorandum from Vlad and the KGB. Not only did he incautiously stash the document in his luggage as he flew back to Washington, he kept and treasured it for the rest of his days as a spy.

Ames now had a code name: Kolokol, Russian for "bell"—specifically, the warning bell that had traditionally hung in the town square of peasant villages to warn of an attack by foreign invaders.

The message from the KGB laid out priorities for Ames. First and foremost, he should keep trying to steal "information about the Soviet agents of CIA." Tips on Soviets secretly working for the FBI or the Pentagon's military intelligence agencies were also welcome, of course. He should look out for information on double-agent operations designed to deceive the Soviets and search for possible recruits for the KGB within the CIA. The memo cautioned Ames to beware when back at headquarters and in particular to avoid using his office computer to seek out and copy secret files, because the machines could record the electronic footprints of intruders. It instructed him how to communicate with his new handlers—not in person but through dead drops and signal sites in and around Washington.

The letter included warm personal regards for Ames and his family.

The Russians thoughtfully had included a balance sheet in the form of a letter from Vlad, dated May 1, 1989. "Dear Friend," it began, "All in all you have been appropriated $2,705,000," nearly $900,000 of which had been set aside in Moscow. "Since December 1986 your salary is $300,000. All in all we have delivered to you $1,881,811.51."

Ames also received five Polaroid photographs. They showed a lush forest, with sun-dappled pines reaching nearly to the edge of a grassy bank, overlooking a shimmering mirror of water. If Ames ever had to run for his life, defect from the United States, and retire in Russia, this would be his dacha, his country home.

A postscript read: "We believe these pictures would give you some idea about the beautiful piece of land on the riverbank which, from now, belongs to you forever. . . . Good luck."

15

Pure Negligence

Nobody back at CIA headquarters had any enthusiasm about giving Rick Ames a new job.

The question of what to do with him hung in the air when a CIA personnel placement board convened in July 1989 to decide the fate of Ames and a hundred of his fellow officers. The Soviet division chief, Burton Gerber, told the board that he had sent Ames to Rome for the sole purpose of being rid of him and he would surely never take him back.

But Gerber was replaced in August 1989 by Milt Bearden, who had spent the past three years ten thousand miles from the confines of headquarters, happily helping to kill Russians in the mountains and deserts of Afghanistan. Bearden, based in Pakistan, had been in charge of a three-billion-dollar CIA paramilitary operation that smuggled Stinger missiles, rocket-propelled grenades, and automatic rifles westward over the rugged mountain passes into the hands of the courageous and half-crazy Afghan rebels, the *mujaheddin,* who had fought off a Soviet invading force for nearly ten years.

At the end of a war that had killed more than a million people, the last Russian soldier in Afghanistan, General Boris Gromov, had left in February. Bearden was convinced that the defeat of the Soviet army was the beginning of the end of the "evil empire." Fresh from battle, newly promoted, focused on finding more chinks in Moscow's armor, Bearden was oblivious to the dismal career of Aldrich Hazen Ames.

Somehow—and to this day no one has admitted knowing how it happened—Ames wound up as the chief of the Western Europe branch of the Soviet division in September 1989.

That was the last place he should have been. Now he had access to secret information on every operation aimed at the Soviets who worked among the United States' European allies. But Bearden, his eyes on the big picture, signed off on Ames's appointment. He had met the man exactly once. All he knew was that Ames had been subjectively judged by the old guard to be a third-rate operations man. Bearden said he "didn't want him out in the world." Better to give him a nice meaningless title at headquarters. The old Soviet division was in for an overhaul, and Bearden figured Ames could not do much damage. Western Europe was a backwater now. The real action was behind the iron curtain, where cracks were beginning to show in the Communist monolith.

Ames lasted three months as Western Europe branch chief before Bearden eliminated his job.

"I reorganized the division when the Berlin Wall fell apart" in November 1989, Bearden said. "I wanted a lot of people moved out. I had a charter to remake the Soviet division, and I was trying to bring it into the mainstream, to break out of the spy-versus-spy thing. Ames ended up on the Czech desk, and we had almost no activities in Czechoslovakia." The Velvet Revolution was under way in Czechoslovakia, and the last thing the CIA wanted to do was run operations against the revolution's leader, the playwright Vaclav Havel, and the poets and artists who surrounded him.

"There was a split in the old Soviet division about that," Bearden said. "There were those who said, 'Hey, what is this? We're supposed to be servicing dead drops in Prague!' They were still servicing them while I was going out to the opera with Vaclav Havel."

Czechoslovakia freed itself from the Soviet orbit days after Ames took over the Czech operations desk in December 1989. The CIA watched in astonishment as Gorbachev decided to let the Czechs go free, declining to send the Red Army into Prague as his predecessor had done in 1968. Ames regarded this remarkable event from afar "with utter amazement that it was actually happening. And my own feeling was—and there were plenty of deniers in the Agency, but I was not alone in seeing this—that the minute Gorbachev said, 'No troops,' that was all she wrote. It was all over" for the Soviet Union's domination of its satellites in Eastern Europe.

Bearden deployed a team of CIA officers to Czechoslovakia but pointedly did not send Ames. By the second week of January 1990, the team was sweeping Havel's office for audio devices and training his security staff. "That was Milt Bearden's style," Ames said. "We just went piling in."

Once the Velvet Revolution was secured, Ames had little to do. Supporting a triumphant new regime was a lot less work than undermining an old repressive one. He spent most of 1990 trying to wriggle out of the confines of the Czech desk. He begged his bosses for a new job, seeking an exalted position befitting his high self-regard and his low motives. Ames desperately wanted access to more information to steal for the Soviets.

First he proposed setting up and taking charge of a special analytical group that would pore over all the CIA's Soviet operations from a counterintelligence perspective. Then he asked to be appointed deputy chief of station in Moscow— "a fitting finale" to his career, he told his flabbergasted superiors in a written request. These brazen requests were rejected out of hand, given Ames's dismal record in Rome.

Without much to do at work, Ames turned his attention to making an elegant nest for himself, Rosario, and their infant son, Paul. He had settled on a house at 2512 North Randolph Street in North Arlington, Virginia, immediately upon their return from Rome. It was an extremely pleasant ten-room split-level with landscaped grounds on a curving street in one of the best sections of the sprawling suburb across the Potomac River from Washington.

And at $540,000, it was quite affordable.

Ames plunked down the money in cash. He told anyone who asked, including the title lawyer who worked on the sale, that the money had come from an inheritance from Rosario's family. He sometimes embroidered the story by saying that Rosario's uncle in Colombia had bought them the house as a present to celebrate Paul's birth. Rosario went along with this deception, on her husband's instructions, to protect his secret—his lucrative and faintly illicit dealings with Robert from Chicago, his invisible old friend.

Ames hired contractors and set them to work redecorating the house, renovating the kitchen, improving the landscaping, and installing a hot tub, running up $99,000 in bills in the process. He bought himself a white Jaguar and a more practical Honda for Rosario. He filled Paul's bedroom with toys and lined the living room with faux antiques. He made arrangements to hire a servant through an agency and then flew the woman in from the Philippines.

A CIA officer named Diana Worthen first stumbled onto this stage set of suburban splendor in November 1989. She knew Rick and Rosario from Mexico City, where she had worked side by side with Rick as a reports officer focused on the KGB residency. She had returned to Washington for a desk job with the Soviet division, had kept in contact with the Ameses when they went to Rome, and considered them fairly good friends.

Worthen was a good CIA officer, trained to notice details and discrepancies, and she noticed immediately that something was wrong in the house on North Randolph Street. The place was ostentatious, to be sure. More striking to her was how the Ameses had changed. They were standoffish and tense. In the past, Rosario had offered her companionship and conversation, but now she was remote, and she proffered expensive gifts in the place of warmth. Rick had aged badly since going to Rome. He looked terrible, despite the fact that he'd had his rotten upper teeth capped and now had half of a perfect smile, pearly on top but dark and gnarled on the bottom.

The most striking thing was the money that must have been spent on the house. Worthen knew Rosario Ames well enough to know that her family was not rich. They were upper-class Colombians, but of the shabby-genteel sort. They were no millionaires. When the Ameses had left for Rome back in 1986, they had been living in a utilitarian one-bedroom apartment in Falls Church. Now they were living in luxury, driving a $50,000 car, being attended to by a maid. It was all a little bizarre.

Worthen left the house deeply troubled. After thinking the matter over for a night, she went to the Counterintelligence Center and reported what she had seen of Rick Ames and his lavish spending. For there was something else on her mind, and it filled her with dread. She knew about the disaster that had struck the Soviet division four years earlier. She knew about some of the cases, and some of the agents, that had been destroyed. And she knew that Rick knew too.

She told all this to the luckless and harried Dan Payne, the young sleuth from the CIA's Office of Security. Payne was now working out of the new Counterintelligence Center. Like his boss, Jeanne Vertefeuille, he had been set to a variety of new tasks at the center, and he had lost his focus on the search for the cause of the Soviet division's distastrous losses. In fairness to Payne, the man had had no real training as an investigator and had received little from the Agency. He was being schooled by the Directorate of Operations in various espionage techniques as he went about his business, but he had to teach himself the basics of being a gumshoe.

On the basis of Diana Worthen's hunch, Payne opened a routine investigation into Rick Ames's finances in December 1989.

He ran up against three roadblocks placed in his path by the culture of the CIA. The first had to do with money. The CIA was not the Department of Commerce. It had always been run by a moneyed intellectual elite. Many of its top managers had come from the upper crust, had gone to Ivy League schools, and hoped to send their children to their alma maters. There were many, many people at the Agency who could have laid down the cash for that house. There were a lot of people who had trust funds and country homes. And there was more than one Jaguar in the parking lot. In this and other respects, the culture of the CIA provided cover for Rick Ames. His sudden wealth looked less strange in this light. And Payne had just spent the better part of 1988 investigating another Soviet division officer who appeared to be living in inexplicable luxury, only to discover the man had been telling the truth when he said that his wife had inherited the money. For all Payne knew, Ames had gone off and married the heiress to a fortune in Colombian coffee or emeralds or cocaine.

Then there was the long-standing inability of the CIA to discipline employees for anything less than clear-cut crimes. For people who had a charter to lie, cheat, and steal when abroad, the lines sometimes got a little blurry. The CIA very rarely fired anyone. People who filched money from operational accounts or went a little crazy at an overseas station or were drinking themselves to death were handled gently. They were reassigned for a while, and, if that didn't work out, they were quietly let go, often with a golden parachute to see them through. From 1988 to 1991, seven station chiefs were recalled for infractions ranging from stealing an icon from a church to waving a gun at a case officer, according to the director of covert operations in those years, Richard Stolz. None of these cases ever went to trial or stirred up a scandal. Prosecuting them in open court would have created far more trouble than it was worth.

There remained, above all, the unswerving and still nearly universal belief at the CIA that there was no mole.

Payne started his investigation by going to the Arlington County courthouse to see if he could find a mortgage on the house at 2512 North Randolph Street. There was none. Then he asked the U.S. Customs Service and the Treasury Department to see if they could find records of Ames having any currency transactions of $10,000 or more; transfers of that size are routinely recorded by the federal government in an effort to track money launderers and drug smugglers. The Treasury Department searched its computerized records for the name Aldrich H. Ames. It came up with three hits. On August 1, 1989, Ames had changed some 28 million Italian lire into $22,107 in cash, which he had then banked. On

February 18, 1986, he had deposited $15,660 into his checking account in Vienna, Virginia. On October 18, 1985, he had made a $13,500 deposit.

Payne had—but did not use—the statutory authority to gain access to all of Ames's banking records. There was, however, a far simpler tack for him to take.

If Payne had picked up the telephone and called the counterintelligence squad at the FBI's Washington Metropolitan Field Office, he could have learned that on or about October 18, 1985, and February 18, 1986, Rick Ames and a Soviet Ministry of Foreign Affairs official named Sergei Chuvakhin had met each other at a restaurant near the Soviet Embassy. The FBI had records of those meetings from Ames's work for the COURTSHIP unit. Matching the bank deposits with the meetings would have been ample evidence for opening a full-fledged criminal investigation, complete with search warrants, wiretaps, and surveillance.

Payne did not check with the FBI. Instead, he dropped the case.

He had a two-month training course at the Directorate of Operations to attend, beginning in January 1990, and that left no time for poking around in courthouses or thumbing through old records. No one at the Counterintelligence Center took over the case for him.

On March 1, 1990, a changing of the guard took place at the Counterintelligence Center. After forty-one years of stalwart service to the CIA, Gardner Rugg Hathaway stepped down. At a private retirement ceremony, the director of Central Intelligence, William Webster, praised him for his expertise in "thwarting counterintelligence threats." There was a medal for Hathaway and a nice letter from President Bush. In truth, he had done good work in his career, and he deserved the accolades. Like so many who had spent all their adult lives at the CIA, Gus Hathaway was a bit at loose ends about what to do with himself. Perhaps he would try his hand at writing fiction.

Webster named Ted Price as the new chief of the Counterintelligence Center. Price was an old China hand, a nattily mustachioed Yale man, quite handsome, with reddish hair now turning to gray and a short, compact body. He was the kind of man who could carry off a bow tie as a mark of sartorial distinction. Price saw the job of running the Counterintelligence Center as a short stop on his way to the top. He wanted very badly to be director of covert operations. This goal would soon be fulfilled.

One of his first acts was to set Dan Payne off on a host of new and promising counterintelligence leads. None had anything to do with Rick Ames.

The first was the unsolved mystery of Karl Koecher. It was an old case, one that Ames himself had studied, a typical counterintelligence nightmare in almost every respect, a puzzle with ten possible solutions, none of which felt quite right. Koecher was the Czech spy who had been trained as an infiltrator in Prague, sent to the United States, hired by the Soviet division as a translator and analyst, and unmasked as a mole in 1984. The CIA and the FBI had quarreled over what to do with Koecher after he fell under suspicion. As was often the case, the Agency had wanted to string him along, to use him as a double agent against the Czech security service, and the Bureau had wanted to bust him. The Bureau won. Koecher had gone to trial in 1984 and been convicted of espionage. The CIA had interviewed him in prison, but the Agency had not known what to make of these debriefings: some of his statements sounded as though they had been canned and preserved two decades earlier in Prague. In 1986, in a celebrated diplomatic maneuver, Koecher had been freed in Berlin and swapped for jailed Soviet dissident Anatoly Shcharansky. After his release, Koecher had settled in Bonn. And in March 1990, he had sent word to the CIA that he was willing to talk about his case and perhaps tie up some loose ends.

Armed with questions supplied by the Counterintelligence Center, Payne traveled to Germany. The CIA wanted most of all to know whether Koecher had been a pawn sacrificed to protect a knight, a far more potent mole inside the Soviet division. But Koecher only served to confuse the case. His story was that he had a "twin"—another deep-penetration agent—who had infiltrated the CIA. Payne debriefed Koecher three times, in March, April, and May 1990. He worked the case with the CIA's Bonn station, trying with increasing desperation to grasp its slippery details. He never resolved the case. No one did.

Then, in June 1990, Payne was assigned to assess the newly available archives of the now-defunct East German intelligence service, the Stasi, to see what counterintelligence clues they might hold. He spent much of the summer looking at translations of documents depicting the cruelty of life on the other side of the Berlin Wall. The Stasi files were mostly internal security dossiers on hundreds of thousands of Germans deemed potential enemies of the state; the Stasi had coerced the citizens of East Germany to become informants on their friends, neighbors, and families. But the Stasi had had very close links to the KGB, and the CIA was eager to learn what the East German spy service had known about U.S. intelligence operations in Germany. Had the East Germans ever recruited a CIA officer? If so, had that recruit had any way of knowing about the cases and the agents compromised in 1985 and 1986? The Stasi files were a rich lode of information, filled with promising counterintelligence leads. But they held not a nugget of proof about a penetration of the Soviet division.

. . .

In late June, as Payne puzzled over the files in Bonn, Ames flew to Vienna to meet with his KGB handler, Vlad. He reported on the changes that were taking place at the CIA, the new personnel and new programs, particularly Milt Bearden's shake-up of the Soviet division. Ames cannot now remember much of this meeting; his memory was dissolved by vodka. He got so drunk, in fact, that he forgot the arrangements for the next assignation. Vlad told him to return to Vienna in October. Ames went to Zurich instead.

Ames considered this blackout part of a larger pattern of behavior that had nothing to do with drinking. Alcohol, he said, "was not a central issue" in his professional and private life. He insisted that his absentmindedness was a kind of voluntary amnesia. "I would forget things," he said. "I would screw up meetings, and this is partly just pure negligence, but partly some mechanism operating that not only allowed me to do that, but motivated me to do that in the first place."

At this stage of his relationship with the KGB, temporarily cut off from fresh information to steal, he was becoming just as laggardly and careless as he was in his professional duties for the CIA.

In September 1990, Milt Bearden sat at his desk in his fifth-floor office at CIA headquarters and focused for the first and last time on Rick Ames. Before him was a written evaluation of Ames's work, and it contained the nearly unanimous opinion that the man had become all but useless. Ames's performance in the year since his return from Rome had been appraised, as was the work of all CIA officers, in an annual review. He was rated third from the bottom among two hundred officers in his cohort at the CIA. His bosses called him a weak, unfocused man who tackled only the tasks that personally interested him, and the list of those tasks appeared to be shrinking. His underlings said he provided no direction.

Bearden read the evaluation and factored in the vague but troubling stories he had heard that Ames might be a security risk. He thought about the matter for several seconds and then threw Ames out of the Soviet division, replacing him on the Czech desk with a younger, smarter officer.

The Agency's managers once again faced the problem of what to do with this mediocre man Ames. Their solution was appalling.

First they placed him on a promotion panel. The panel rated everyone at the rank of GS-12 in the CIA's Directorate of Operations and selected the best ones for advancement. Ames was thus required to review in detail the personnel records of several hundred people, focusing on the really talented, up-and-coming operators who would be sent overseas to spy for the United States. He kept good notes.

Then they assigned Ames to the Counterintelligence Center, the repository of all information about what the CIA was doing to the KGB.

Ted Price, the chief of the Counterintelligence Center, knew enough about Ames to be wary of him. But not wary enough. Scraps of information—Ames's unexplained wealth, his drinking, his propensity to sleep off his lunch, his unfiled reports on his meetings with Soviets, his attempts to winkle classified information out of fellow workers—were in the possession of a dozen different CIA officers. No one put these pieces of the puzzle together.

THE AMESES OF RIVER FALLS

J. H. Ames, Rick's grandfather and president of the River Falls State Teachers College from 1917 to 1946.

Rick Ames was born in River Falls, Wisconsin, a small, tightly knit midwestern community. Jesse "J.H." Ames, the family patriarch and Rick Ames's grandfather, was the president of River Falls State Teachers College. Rick's father, Carleton Ames, taught at the school and was recruited there by the CIA. His first (and last) foreign posting was in Burma.

Carleton Ames, 1950, shortly before joining the CIA.

FATHER AND SON

The CIA sent Carleton Ames, Rick's father, to Rangoon, Burma, to be a spy in 1953. Here he lectures to Burmese students, posing as a scholar. In Burma, he shared the secret of his espionage with his son.

While still in high school, Rick Ames took summer jobs at the CIA. In 1957, he was voted "wittiest" in his senior class.

Rick Ames at a party in Bogotá, Colombia, in August 1990. The KGB had by this time paid him close to $2 million for five years of work as a spy.

A NEW FAMILY

Rick Ames with his wife, Rosario, in happier times—Bogotá, 1990.

Rick Ames dancing with Rosario's mother, Cecilia—Bogotá, 1990. A false account in her name provided cover for his payments from the KGB.

A HANDLER AND TWO VICTIMS

Sergei Chuvakhin, a Soviet diplomat, was secretly photographed by FBI agents outside
the Soviet embassy in Washington. The Russians assigned
Chuvakhin to act as go-between
for Aldrich Ames in his first year
as a spy for Moscow.

Valery F. Martinov (*left*), Sergei M. Motorin (*right*). The two KGB officers were stationed in Washington when they were recruited to spy on the Soviet Union by COURTSHIP, a joint CIA-FBI operation. But after Ames told the KGB about their secret life, each was recalled to the Soviet Union and executed.

A SPY'S W-2 FORM

Dear Friend,
this is Your balance sheet as on the May I, 1989.

- All in all You have been apprpriated ---- 2,705,000 $
- From the time of oppening of Your
  account in our Bank (December 26,
  1986) Your profit is ------------------- 385,077$ 28c
{including I4,468$ 94c as profit on bonds, which we
bought for You on the sum of 250,000$)
- Since December 1986 Your salary is ------ 300,000$
- All in all we have delivered to You ----- I,88I,8II$ 5Ic
- On the above date You have on Your
  account (including 250,000$ in bonds) --- I,535,077$ 28c

P.S. We believe that these pictures would give You some
idea about the beautiful piece of land on the river bank,
waich from now belongs to You forever. We decided not to take
pictures of housing in this area with the understanding that
You have much better idea of how Your country house (dacha)
should look like.

Good luck.

A MESSAGE FROM THE KGB

A SCHEDULE FOR 1992

- MARCH - 3D WEEK "BRIDGE' WITH "SMILE"
TO PASS INFO FROM YOU TO US. AND TO
GIVE AN ASSESMENT ABOUT NEW DD
"GROUND". TO INDICATE WHAT DD WILL
BE USED A NEXT TIME. TO GIVE YOUR
OPINION ABOUT CARACAS MTG IN OCTOBER

- AUGUST - 3D WEEK "GROUND" [OR "BRIDGE]
TO PASS INFO FROM YOU TO US. TO CONFIRM
YOUR FINAL AGREEMENT ABOUT CARACAS
MTG.

- OCTOBER, 5TH AT 18.00 PERSONAL MTG
IN CARACAS. ALTERNATES MTG = 6TH, 12TH
OR 13TH OF OCTOBER 1992

PLACE OF CONTACT FOR CARACAS
A LITLE PARK "PLAZA MIRANDA"
[ALTAMIRA AREA] ON THE JUNCTION
OF AVENIDA SAN JUAN BOSCO AND
AVENIDA ENRIQUE BENAIN PINTO.
A THIRD SIDE OF THIS TRIANGLE IS
A SMALL STREET PLAZA MIRANDA

POINT OF CONTACT.
ON THE LEFT SIDE OF A BUST OF
GENERALISSIMO MIRANDA, WHICH IS
LOCATED IN THIS PARK
INSCRIPTION UNDER THE BUST
"GENERALISSIMO FRANCISCO DE
MIRANDA"

TIME OF CONTACT — 18.00

TO GET A PARK IS BETTER ON TAXI.
AREA ALTAMIRA SOCIAL SAN JUAN BOCCO.
THER ARE CHURCH, THEATER, TENNIS CLUB.

IMPOSSIBILITY FOR YOU TO COME TO
CARACAS MTG IN OCTOBER, SHALL
WAIT FOR YOU HERE AT "THE IRON SITE"
ON THE 1ST MONDAY OF DECEMBER 1992
[IT'LL BE ON THE 7TH OF DECEMBER '92]
ALT. DAYS ARE — THE 14TH OF DECEMBER
PLACE — BOWLING IN UNICENTRO
TIME — 18.00

IN CASE OF LOOSING CONTACT IN 1992
THIS SCHEDULE WILL WORK FOR 1993 AND
SO ON. UNTIL CONTACT REESTABLISHED

A meeting plan sent to Ames by the KGB.

:My dear friends,

.All is well with me and I have recovered somewhat from
my earlier period of pessimism and anxiety. My security situation
is unchanged -- that is to say, I have no indications of any problems.
My family is well and my wife has accomodated herself to understanding
what I am doing, in a very supportive way. I will come to Caracas
for the meeting as planned...

A search of Ames's trash in October 1993 produced a computer ribbon with a 1992 message from Ames to the Russians that prosecutors used to implicate Ames's wife, Rosario, in his spying.

"SMILE"

A mailbox at Thirty-seventh and R streets in Northwest Washington. Ames left a chalk mark (a horizontal line above the postal service logo) on October 13, 1993. It signaled the Russians that Ames was ready to meet them in Bogotá, Colombia.

The Ames house outside Washington, D.C., bought with $540,000 in cash from the KGB.

I AM READY TO MEET AT B ON 1 OCT.

I CANNOT READ NORTH 13 - 19 SEPT.

IF YOU WILL MEET AT B ON 1 OCT. PLS SIGNAL NORTH OF 20 SEPT TO CONFI. NO MESSAGE AT PIPE.

IF YOU CANNOT MEE. 1 OCT, SIGNAL NORTH AFTER 27 SEPT WITH MESSAGE AT PIPE.

Against orders, FBI agents stole Ames's trash in September 1993. In it, they found a torn-up draft of a note from Ames to the Russians. "B" referred to Bogotá, the city where Ames had planned a clandestine meeting with his KGB contacts. "North" was a secret signal site and "Pipe" was a hiding place in a suburban Maryland park. The note convinced the FBI that Ames was a spy, and more, that he was still actively spying for the Kremlin.

THE DIRECTORS

William J. Casey

Ames flourished as a mole for Moscow under four directors of central intelligence: William J. Casey, William Webster, Robert M. Gates, and R. James Woolsey. After realizing that the C.I.A.'s network of Soviet agents had been destroyed, Casey ordered a series of internal investigations that went nowhere. Webster and Gates remained unaware of the molehunt or the damage done by the traitor within. And after Ames was arrested, Woolsey was scarred by criticism of his mild disciplining of C.I.A. officers who oversaw the mole.

William Webster

Robert M. Gates

R. James Woolsey

BOGOTÁ MEET

An FBI agent surreptitiously photographed Aldrich Ames in October 1993 at a shopping mall in downtown Bogotá. Ames was scheduled to meet his Russian contact, but Rick arrived nearly an hour late. The Russians had already left.

THE ARREST

On February 21, 1994, a team of FBI agents arrested Ames as he left his house in his Jaguar. To the arresting agents, Ames sputtered, "You must have the wrong man!"

Calendar page found in Ames's house after his arrest.

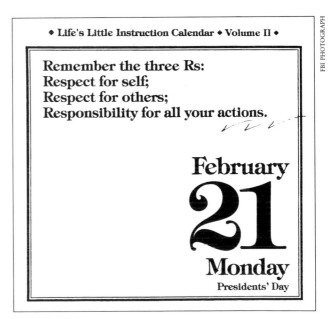

◆ Life's Little Instruction Calendar ◆ Volume II ◆

Remember the three Rs:
Respect for self;
Respect for others;
Responsibility for all your actions.

February
21
Monday
Presidents' Day

THE END OF THE GAME

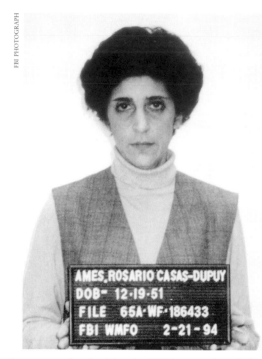

Rick and Rosario Ames were booked by the FBI hours after their arrest on February 21, 1994. That same day, Rosario began to confess that her husband was a spy.

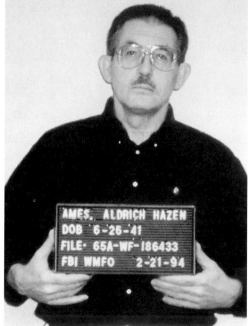

The CIA gave Rick Ames his new assignment because of a simple bureaucratic imperative. The analysis group at the Counterintelligence Center, the team that read and interpreted reports on what the KGB was up to and what the CIA was doing in response, needed to fill a slot with a case officer from the Directorate of Operations. Ames fit the bill. And besides, the man knew a lot about the KGB.

Ames was back inside the heart of the Agency, working with the real secrets. He had access to the identities of Soviet agents and the CIA officers who worked with them, the details of every double-agent operation the United States was running against Moscow, the people and places involved in those operations. He rolled up his sleeves and went to work.

Charlie Emmling, Ames's career-training classmate and longtime acquaintance, had just been placed in charge of training new officers at the Counterintelligence Center when he ran into Ames in the hallway of the CIA. Emmling heard about his new assignment and invited him to come give a lecture to the trainees.

"I was always impressed by his encyclopedic knowledge of the KGB," Emmling said. "He'd picked all this up back when he was the counterintelligence branch chief, back in '84, '85. He'd run you through all the sixteen directorates, all the secondary levels, how they worked and how they fit together. He knew his knowledge was encyclopedic, and he had a certain air of smugness about it, knowing he could snow you on the subject of the KGB. Anyway, I thought he might come give a talk on the KGB, because he knew so much about them. He said sure. But it never came off."

After that encounter, Emmling sometimes saw Ames when he looked through the glass wall of the CIA's first-floor corridors. The wall looked in on the central courtyard of the

Agency's main building, an open-air alcove that was the only place at the smoke-free headquarters where cigarette smokers were allowed to light up. Ames spent close to an hour out there each day, puffing away and chatting with his fellow tobacco addicts, swapping stories and sharing gossip.

"He was always out in that alcove smoking," Emmling said. "I was always struck by how bad he looked. He looked haggard. He looked gray. He looked tired. He looked awful."

16

A Logical Explanation

It had taken the Central Intelligence Agency the better part of twenty years to assemble the stable of spies Ames had destroyed.

Now Milt Bearden was building a new network of Soviet agents with remarkable speed. An astonishing number of Soviet traitors volunteered their services to the CIA between the summer of 1990 and the fall of 1991. A new one would appear every month or two—most of them high-ranking intelligence officers. The KGB, by virtue of its elite status and its access to secret information, had been picking up signals ever since the early 1980s that the Soviet economy was crumbling. Now the rot in the Soviet system was starting to undermine the central pillars of society, the KGB included.

Some of these new recruits had pieces of the jigsaw puzzle that the CIA's counterintelligence officers had been trying to assemble for the last five years. None of them had ever seen the picture on the jigsaw puzzle box. But the simple fact of their existence was pure and unalloyed joy for Milt Bearden.

In October 1990, not long after Saddam Hussein's invasion of Kuwait, Milt Bearden met with some senior KGB officials on neutral territory. These liaisons in European capitals were now becoming commonplace as the tensions of the cold war began to subside. The agenda for the meeting included planning joint operations against drug smugglers and terrorists as well as assessing the war clouds gathering over Iraq.

Eventually the subject of the defections came up. A general in the KGB's First Chief Directorate asked plaintively: "What is going on with all these people? The finest majors and lieutenant colonels, the ones with red diplomas with gold lettering?" Bearden said he told his Soviet counterpart a barbed joke: The chairman of the board of a dog food factory is haranguing his subordinates about the plummeting sales of their product. Our dog food is the best in the world! The most nutritious, most efficiently produced, best-packaged dog food in the world! So why are we going broke? A terrified silence is broken by a junior account executive at the far end of the table. Sir? he says. Dogs don't like it.

The dogs were now turning tail and running into the arms of their old enemy. But not all of them proved faithful to their new masters.

A new Soviet defector offered his services to the CIA in Germany in the fall of 1990. This man had the answer to the case that had consumed the CIA's Soviet division. He said the KGB had recruited an officer from the Soviet division sometime around 1975. This traitor had served in the Moscow station at some point. He had a reputation for living high and wild, spending a lot of money, eating and drinking in nice restaurants.

The defector's detailed information dovetailed with bits and pieces of inconclusive information, hearsay, rumor, and innuendo left over from a dozen cases the Agency and the FBI had pursued off and on for the past fifteen years. It galvanized the CIA's Counterintelligence Center, which plunged into investigations of several current and former CIA officers. But by the end of 1990, the investigators found themselves wandering into blind alleys. One trouble was that the description matched quite a few people. Another was that the defector had disappeared. It took another year for the CIA to reach a devastating conclusion.

They'd been had. The defector was a fraud. He was Vladimir Kryuchkov's last deception.

The case was one of many that caught Rick Ames's attention in his new capacity as the Counterintelligence Center's resident expert on the KGB. He quickly alerted his contacts in Washington to the case and to the many other classified assignments he had in his new position. An officer in the KGB's Washington residency responded to the good news by instructing Ames to go to Bogotá over Christmas for consultations with his controller.

Ames and the KGB communicated with each other in Washington through a network of dead drops and signal sites laid out in the nine-page memorandum he had received in Rome. It was extremely dangerous for Ames to be seen meeting Russians without the cover his official assignments had given him in the past. So the KGB arranged a system whereby information and money could change hands without any personal contact. When Ames had something to tell the KGB, he would signal them by placing a chalk mark on a mailbox near the Soviet residential and diplomatic compound in Washington. These signal sites corresponded with a dead drop in one of the parks in and around the city. For example, Ames would place a mark on a mailbox at the corner of Thirty-seventh and R streets in Washington, a five-minute walk from the Soviet residential compound on Wisconsin Avenue. Upon seeing the chalk mark, a KGB officer would know that Ames had left a package of documents at a dead drop under a stone bridge off the Little Falls Parkway, just outside Washington, a convenient drive from the house on North Randolph Street. Then Ames would go by the mailbox at Thirty-seventh and R. If the chalk mark was gone, that meant the dead drop had been cleared by the KGB. Similarly, the KGB would signal Ames when it had money or instructions to convey. Only when safely overseas would Ames meet face to face with the KGB.

Down the hall from Ames's office at the Counterintelligence Center, Dan Payne kept plugging away, only slightly the wiser for his labors. In November 1990, he dug his files on the 1985 and 1986 compromises out of his safe and realized that he had never done much with the information on Rick Ames that Diana Worthen had conveyed to him a year earlier. He decided it was time to act. After consulting with his superiors, he began to compose a memorandum to Ray Riordan, an investigator at the CIA's Office of Security.

This letter was a milestone in the annals of the CIA: the first official request for a serious look at Rick Ames. It had been nearly five years since the late Bill Casey had ordered that something be done about the case.

Dated December 5, 1990, the memo began: "In connection with our investigation into the compromise of a number of Soviet division operations during the mid-1980's, we request that the Office of Security open a reinvestigation of Aldrich H. Ames." A reinvestigation, in this context, did not mean that Ames had ever been investigated in connection with the compromises. It merely meant reopening the file on the initial background check on Ames that the Office of Security had done when he was hired in 1967.

The memo recounted Worthen's report that the Ameses seemed to be spending huge amounts of money, and it laid out the three cash transactions of more than $10,000 that Ames had had with banks in 1985, 1986, and 1989.

"While we are certainly concerned with the above information, there may be a logical explanation for Ames's spending habits," the memo continued. "Between 1985 and 1990, Ames's mother died. We do not know if Ames received any money or property via insurance or inheritance. A review of public records in the county where his mother lived could answer the question of inheritance. Unfortunately, we do not know the location of his mother's last residence. . . . We have been informed that Ames's mother's obituary appeared in *The Washington Post*."

The obituary said that Rachel Aldrich Ames had died in May 1986 at her son's home, and it noted her hometown of Hickory, North Carolina, her date of birth, the names and addresses of Ames's sisters, and other basic information. A trip to the Catawba County courthouse in North Carolina would have produced the will, as well as the fact that Mrs. Ames had left no fortune to her son.

The memo wandered on through fields of speculation. "The money could have also come from his in-laws," it said—though Diana Worthen had assured Payne that this was surely not the case. "The deposits into Ames's checking account could be explained by loans he may have received from Northwest Federal Credit Union." That question could be answered by the kind of credit check millions of Americans undergo each year.

"There is a degree of urgency involved in our request," the memo concluded. Ames had been assigned to the Counterintelligence Center, it explained, and "we are quickly running out of things for him to do without granting him greater access" to classified files and secrets. "It is our hope to at least get Ames through polygraph before we are forced to take such action."

Noting the degree of urgency in Payne's memo, Riordan immediately opened a formal investigation of Rick Ames.

That same week in December 1990, Ames betrayed another Soviet agent working for the CIA—a KGB officer code-named PROLOGUE. Ames never knew the man's real name. But he was given a file about the case in early December and told to write an analysis about it. From these classified papers, Ames learned that the man worked for the Second Chief Directorate (SCD) of the Soviet intelligence service—the counterintelligence division. Ames immediately passed on this information through a note placed in a dead drop. Back at his office, Ames asked for more files on the man so he could complete his research.

He finished his analysis of the case for the CIA on December 14. Two or three days later, he composed a follow-up note to the KGB on his home computer. "I did learn that GTPROLOGUE is the cryptonym for the SCD officer I provided you information about earlier," it said. GT was the two-letter prefix denoting the geographical or functional area—in this case, Soviet counterintelligence—corresponding to the real person, place, or thing behind a cryptonym, or code name. The CIA had its own cryptonym: PNINFINITE.

The next week, Ames and his family flew to Bogotá. For Rosario, it was her annual family reunion. For Rick, it was his regular Christmas rendezvous with the KGB.

Once again, Ames drank his way through the assignation. "In Bogotá, I left that meeting at maybe two A.M., having had the better part of a bottle of vodka," he recalled. Once again, he forgot the plan for the next meeting, which was to have taken place in Vienna. He recalls only going over the case of

PROLOGUE and discussing details of double-agent operations that the CIA and the Pentagon were planning against the KGB—operations in which an American would pretend that he had been recruited by Soviet intelligence, in order to pick the pockets of the KGB.

Ames returned to CIA headquarters in January 1991 to find a set of routine forms from the Office of Security on his desk. The forms were a standard series of questions, much like the ones asked during a polygraph test, asking Ames if he had done anything untoward. They were in keeping with a new policy, of which all CIA employees were aware, to try to enforce the requirement that everyone at the Agency submit to a security reinvestigation, complete with lie-detector test, every five years.

Ray Riordan and his security officers waited for two months, until March 4, 1991, for Ames to return the routine forms. Then they began to talk to about twenty people who knew Ames and had worked with him in Mexico City, in Rome, and at headquarters.

The interviews were striking. One of Ames's colleagues said he wouldn't be surprised if Ames were a spy. It was an instinctive feeling, he said; he did not trust the man. He told the investigators how Ames had disobeyed his bosses in Rome by giving a laptop computer to Aleksei Khrenkov, his purported agent, after he had been ordered not to do so. Another said that Ames had repeatedly left his office safe open when he left the Rome station for the day, although no one had ever disciplined him for it. A third said Ames had received an unusual number of phone calls from Khrenkov at work in the Rome station, violating basic security practices. A fourth said Ames's newfound wealth was common knowledge; the man flaunted it. A fifth recounted Ames's heavy drinking and lackadaisical work habits. And a sixth said that the Soviet division did not trust Ames—nor any of the agents he had handled over the past decade.

The CIA's Office of Security read these interviews and the rest of the record on Rick Ames. It decided that there was nothing unusual about any of it and there was no need to look deeper into Rick Ames's life. The security office submitted a report to Dan Payne, who agreed there was no point in following up on Ames.

All that remained to complete the reinvestigation was for Rick Ames to submit to a lie-detector test.

"I was extremely worried" about facing the machine again, Ames said. But he did not need to be concerned. Neither the Office of Security nor the Counterintelligence Center shared any of the information they had developed with the polygraphers. Neither the examiner nor his supervisor knew anything about Ames that made him any different from any other longtime CIA employee undergoing a routine reexamination. There was nothing special about the man. They did not even know that the background investigation that had started eighteen months ago had ever existed. That made the test a great deal easier to pass than it might have been.

Still, Ames said, the polygraph was a crapshoot; there were plenty of honest people who could not pass one. And he had become dimly aware, through gossiping with his fellow smokers, that there was some kind of low-level analytical effort within the Counterintelligence Center that was aimed at solving the mystery in the Soviet division. He thought it could not be aimed directly at him, and he was right. Still, just to be safe, he had gone to the trouble of creating false documents, complete with a notary's stamp from the U.S. Embassy in Bogotá, stating that his mother-in-law had given him the money for the house on North Randolph Street.

In keeping with the normal practice, the polygraph examiner interviewed Ames before strapping him into the machine. Ames decided that "it seemed like a good time to volunteer" some information about his finances. "I mentioned that my wife got an allowance of sorts from her mother in Colombia," and that this was his nest egg. The examiner nodded and made a note of this freely proffered disclosure before beginning the formal test.

He attached cuffs to Ames's biceps to measure his blood pressure and other receptors to record his heart rate, breathing, and other indicators of stress. He began rattling off the standard list of questions. Was Ames concealing any financial difficulties from the Agency? No. Was he working for a foreign intelligence service? No. Was he concealing any unauthorized contacts with foreigners? No.

The needle on the machine jumped. The examiner asked the last question again and again. The machine kept saying Ames's answers were deceptive. The examiner turned to Ames and, following normal procedures, told him that they had a little problem. " 'Come back, and we'll resolve it,' " Ames said the man told him. " 'This is not unusual.' "

Four days later, on April 16, 1991, Ames returned. This time there was a different examiner handling the test. Like his predecessor, the tester had no idea that there was anything unusual about his subject. They went through all the same inquiries, including the matter of unreported contacts with foreigners, with one exception. There were no questions that had anything to do with money.

Ames passed with flying colors. The only blot on his record came from a written note from the first polygraph examiner who had handled him four days earlier. "I don't think he is a spy," the note said, "but I am not 100 percent convinced because of the money situation."

The CIA investigators made one last attempt to clarify the situation. The Office of Security sent a poorly briefed and untrained investigator down to Bogotá. The man was unable to find Rosario's father's last will and testament. He did manage to dig up cursory, secondhand information that the Casas clan had donated some land for a public soccer field and sports center a few years back, and he learned that the family had some real estate and import-export business holdings. A week's worth of work convinced him that Ames was telling the truth when he said the money had come from Rosario's family.

Ray Riordan at the Office of Security and Dan Payne at the Counterintelligence Center reviewed the record one last time and officially put the inquiry on hold. The Office of Security said it now had no concerns whatsoever about Ames. Payne sent the file on Ames—the report from Bogotá, the superficial background investigation, the results of the lie-detector tests—over to the CIA's special task force.

The task force reviewed the file and gave Rick Ames a clean bill of health.

. . .

Six years had passed since Ames had first become a spy, and five and a half years had gone by since the Soviet agents who had trusted the CIA with their lives had started dying. The case had gone nowhere. The Agency was no closer to solving it than it had been in 1985. But there was one man at the CIA who had never stopped thinking about it: Paul J. Redmond.

Redmond was the man who had taken over the Soviet counterintelligence branch from Ames. He was now fifty years old, and time had not improved his dyspeptic view of the world. But his reputation was rising at the CIA, and he was about to be promoted to deputy chief of the Counterintelligence Center. He and Ames had crossed paths—and occasionally swords—over the course of the past decade.

"Paul's an intelligent guy with an abrasive manner that he cultivates," Ames said. "He has developed ideas that are sort of neo-Angletonian"—by which he meant the elaborately nurtured, exotic strain of hothouse paranoia that had flourished in the counterintelligence staff under James J. Angleton. Others at the CIA saw a healthy strain of suspiciousness in Redmond—whose job, after all, was to ensure that nothing and no one penetrated the Agency.

In late April 1991, a few days after Ames passed his polygraph test, Redmond had a long talk with Jeanne Vertefeuille, the long-suffering chief of the special task force.

Redmond had been trying to move the immense machinery of the CIA toward a serious investigation into one of the great disasters in the Agency's history. He had failed. The Counterintelligence Center had been in existence for three years, and no one had even the beginnings of a solution. Of course, everyone had theories. Ted Price, the center's director, was starting to develop an idea that someone somewhere in the CIA had sold the Soviets secrets in the mid-1980s and then retired. Some continued to think a bug in the Moscow station was to blame. Still others subscribed to the opinion that each of the agents had self-destructed.

Redmond rejected all of it. Every test of the CIA's communications links had found them intact. The idea that the deaths were a terrible coincidence was a canard. The assumption that the problem was solved because the Soviet agents had stopped dying was absurd. By 1988, there were almost none left to kill.

There was one theory of the case that the CIA was institutionally incapable of contemplating. And that was Redmond's theory.

It might be a mole.

Redmond decided it was time to take a radical course of action. It was time to call in the FBI.

"The Agency came over here and said, 'We have a continuing problem, and we need the FBI's help to solve this problem,' and other peppy, dramatic phrases that they used," said the FBI's Tim Caruso, then the chief of the Bureau's Soviet counterintelligence group. The FBI's top officials had never known how bad things were, for the CIA had never confided the fact that almost its entire network of Soviet agents had been destroyed in the mid-1980s. Now, for the first time, "they were talking to each other," said Bear Bryant, who was about to become chief of the FBI's Washington Metropolitan Field Office.

It was high time that "we looked at just about everything, went back and retraced just about every case that had gone bad," Bryant said. "Just put it all together, once and for all. Because we'd been living with a lot of misinformation. Wrong information."

The CIA would take a hard look at the facts locked away in its files. It would share the facts—selectively—with the FBI. Together, they would conduct a serious investigation. Two teams took shape over the summer of 1991. The FBI's was code-named PLAYACTOR. The CIA's was SKYLIGHT.

One idea held sway from the start, and its influence on the investigation was subtle and powerful. The thinking about the case would flow from the precept that a machine was not to blame. Chance was not the culprit. A man was. In time, the SKYLIGHT investigators would focus on a suspect and create what the CIA calls a "deep chrono," an extensive chronology, on every aspect of his life.

They began with a simple question: Who is this man? The answer would be far richer and stranger than they had ever imagined.

17

The Ames Files

Aldrich Hazen Ames was born on May 26, 1941, in River Falls, Wisconsin, the son of Carleton Cecil Ames, an undistinguished history professor, and Rachel Aldrich Ames, a high school English teacher. He spent the first ten years of his life in the town, which had the midwestern innocence of the mythical Bedford Falls, the outwardly perfect yet secretly troubled town in the Frank Capra film *It's a Wonderful Life.*

Then as now the town was surrounded by farms and small houses that dotted the prairie. The briskly flowing Kinnickinnic River, a first-rate trout stream that attracted people with the patience the sport demands, ran through it. Its main industry was education; it was the site of River Falls State Teachers College, an obscure institution later incorporated into the University of Wisconsin. Most of the students were sons and daughters of dairy farmers, and many anticipated nothing grander than going on to inherit the family farm. Others saw teaching as a way of bettering themselves, of setting off on a life whose central concern wasn't the making of cheese.

The patriarch of River Falls was Rick Ames's grandfather Jesse Ames, known to all as "J.H." He was a lumberjack's son who served as the autocratic president of the college from 1917 to 1944 and transformed it from a "normal school," which accepted eighth-grade students, into a full-fledged four-year college.

Throughout the 1940s, President Ames's son Carleton taught European and Asian history at River Falls. He was an outwardly easygoing man whose hardest work was aimed at concealing his inner demons. His wife, Rachel Aldrich, had been one of his students. She was thirteen years younger than her husband and much admired by their friends and family. She came from nearby New Richmond, a community that held bad memories for Carleton. He had been a high school English teacher there and had been asked to leave under murky circumstances having something to do with liquor. After Carleton's difficulties, J.H. stepped in and saw to it that his son came to teach at River Falls, first at the elementary school, then at the college. The college faculty resented J.H. for using his influence to employ his son, whom they saw as unqualified. "We all thought it was nepotism," said Walker D. Wyman, a former agronomy professor at the college and local historian.

J.H. was a tall, taciturn man whose bearing suggested he was wearing a stiff collar and a boiled shirt even when he wasn't. Photographs show his unmistakable air of hauteur, qualities people later found in his grandson Rick. In fact, Rick Ames—Carleton's and Rachel's first child and only son—grew up to look quite like him, down to the small moustache and the long face framed by prominent ears.

J.H. was a hard man to please, and three of his four children plainly failed him. They became notorious alcoholics. Only his daughter Avery seemed to have no taste for the stuff.

His daughter Ruth and son Ken were well known in River Falls as binge drinkers, according to Walker Wyman. Ruth died of drink in the local hospital.

On one occasion, J.H. was walking out of the Gladstone Hotel with his wife and two other couples when he saw his son Ken, obviously drunk, stagger out of a bar and cross his path. The others were embarrassed for J.H., recalled Benny Kettelkamp, the biology department chairman who was there, and wondered how the college president would deal with this awkward moment. J.H. simply pretended not to see his son. But Carleton hid his drinking. He developed a practice of asking friends to go into bars and package stores to buy his liquor while he waited in the car, remembered Maruca Jurgens, a family acquaintance.

In 1951, a stranger from Washington, D.C., came to River Falls to talk to Carleton Ames about his earlier work on a doctorate in Asian studies. Shortly thereafter, Carleton let it be known that he wouldn't be staying on for the fall semester. He was vague and mysterious about it, but he confided to a few flabbergasted colleagues that he was taking a one-year leave from the college and joining the State Department. He never returned.

Carleton Ames had been recruited by the Central Intelligence Agency. In 1951, the CIA was only four years old, and it was just beginning to get its bearings in Asia. The Agency cast its net very wide for people who thought they knew the Asiatic mind, and Carleton Ames turned up in the haul.

"My father joined the Agency in a high spirit of adventure and as a fervent member of the anti-Stalin liberal left of the 1940s," Rick Ames said more than forty years later. "A lot of that certainly rubbed off on me."

Carleton Ames began a six-week training and indoctrination course with the CIA's Directorate of Operations, then euphemistically called the Directorate of Plans. He was one of several thousand new recruits in the early 1950s, all of whom reported for their first days of work at the Agency's patchwork of a headquarters, a collection of wooden buildings and Quonset huts near the reflecting pool at the base of the Lincoln Memorial.

In early 1953, the Agency dispatched Carleton Ames to Rangoon, Burma, under the cover of a scholar with a grant from the Ford Foundation. After almost three days on airplanes that leapfrogged from Los Angeles to Honolulu to Tokyo to Bangkok, the whole family—Carleton, Rachel, Rick, and his sisters, Nancy and Alison—landed in Rangoon.

In the 1950s, few more remote or exotic places existed on earth than Burma. Some of the world's most beautiful gilded temples and Buddhist shrines graced the country. Children astride water buffaloes worked the rice paddies outside the capital, and red-robed monks carrying lacquered begging bowls dodged bicycle rickshaws in the city streets. The nation had suffered immensely under a Japanese onslaught during World War II. Then the cold war had come. After China had turned Communist in 1949, thousands of Chinese Nationalist troops had taken refuge in northern Burma. The CIA had sent a team of officers to lead the stateless soldiers in cross-border attacks on China. By 1953, thousands had died, and not much good had come of it.

Into this stew of intrigue came the Ameses of River Falls. The family lived north of the capital, near the University of Rangoon, attended by a security guard, a house servant, a cook, and a gardener. They became part of a self-contained society created by American expatriates in Rangoon—bridge games and cocktail parties at the American Club, the annual Monsoon Madness tennis tournament on the club's clay courts, and the Lower Kenmendine Bible and Roulette Society, where U.S. officials and English-speaking Burmese could congregate, drink, and socialize.

Carleton Ames's assignment was clear-cut: recruit Burmese agents as sources of information; gather intelligence on Burmese political leaders and tribes; keep an eye on the Russian and Chinese missions. In all these tasks he was a failure. For Carleton Ames was a feckless spy. He was forty-eight years old when he first went to Burma, but he looked far older. His hair was pure white, his face baggy as a rumpled suit, his gait a slow shuffle.

"He was obviously a drinker," said James Cassedy, an academic serving as a U.S. Information Agency officer in Rangoon. "He had a very florid complexion, and sometimes when I would see him coming into the center he had a thickened voice. He wasn't a sociable person. He was dour. Kept to himself. Rather a loner. He didn't have close acquaintances among any of the other Americans. I remember him as plodding, trotting around with an old man's look. I can see him in my mind's eye—Rachel too. I always thought: 'How did she get mixed up with him?'"

Toward the end of his two-year tour, Carleton Ames took his son on a steamboat up the Irrawaddy River toward Mandalay and told him a secret: Your dad works for the CIA. Don't tell anybody. The trip up the Irrawaddy became a seminal part of family lore, a legend of bonding between the once and future spies. It was told and retold like a classic story out of Rudyard Kipling.

Carleton's life of foreign intrigue ended when the CIA brought him home from Burma after the minimum stint of two years. He never worked abroad again, not after the disastrous evaluation he received in 1955. He was forced to undergo a humiliating six-month probationary term before being accepted back on staff, and for the rest of his career he served without distinction in the Directorate of Operations, with a brief and unremarkable tour on Jim Angleton's counterintelligence staff.

The family returned from the strange smells and sounds of Rangoon to the familiar Ozzie-and-Harriet suburb of McLean, Virginia. Rick developed a reputation in high school as the class clown, the wittiest boy in the room. Some of his classmates had fathers who worked for the Agency. All knew what to say if ever they were asked about it: "My dad works for the government." What part? someone might ask. "The government" was the only reply. Those in the know could share a silent but thrilling understanding.

In the summer of 1957, Rick Ames, then sixteen years old, took a summer job as a handyman and clerk at the CIA with the help and encouragement of his father. He found the place intriguing.

After graduating from high school, he enrolled as a freshman at the University of Chicago in 1959. He studied drama and theater and had vague ideas of being an actor. But he also planned to take courses in history and foreign cultures and languages, and to master one or another in pursuit of his idea of serving his country overseas. He did not make it past his sophomore year. He was flunking out, in part because he was enjoying the company of his theatrical friends too much to study, in part because of his growing fondness for alcohol. He hung around Chicago for almost a year, however, working as a director's assistant at a small theater, until his money and his will to persevere gave out.

In February 1962, he went home and applied for a full-time job at the Agency. Though he could not become a full-fledged spy until he had earned a college degree, he had the advantage of being the son of a CIA man, and that counted heavily in his favor. Carleton could now help his son Rick, just as J. H. Ames had used his sway to help Carleton. He went through three months of testing and evaluation before the Agency hired him as a records clerk.

In June 1962, three weeks after his twenty-first birthday, Rick Ames became an officer of the Central Intelligence Agency. For the next five years, he worked as a clerk, trudging up and down the hallways with secret papers to file. At the same slow pace, he pursued a college diploma. Finally, in September 1967, after eight on-and-off years of college and much procrastination and delay, Rick Ames, age twenty-six, was awarded an undergraduate degree in history at George Washington University. He had racked up a B-minus average, partly as a consequence of the self-destructive sloth that was becoming part of a pattern in his life.

Without thinking too much about it, he signed up for training to become an officer in the clandestine service. "By the time '67 rolled around, and when I got my degree, I had sort of insensibly committed myself to going into the career-training program. Not unconsciously. Insensibly," Ames said. His decision coincided with his father's retirement. Carleton, now sixty-two years old, had had enough after fifteen years. One Ames replaced another in the Company, like a factory hand following in his father's footsteps on the assembly line.

Ames believed he had been tapped for an exclusive fraternity. "I felt proud and selected," he remembered. "They made a great effort, as do some units in the military, the Foreign Service, to cultivate a sense of being in the elite. Kids respond to that. Young men and women respond to that. And certainly I did. The ethics of espionage, of telling lies, cover stories, this didn't bother too many people. It didn't bother me."

He began the career-training program in October 1967. After lectures on the history and structure of the CIA, he was shipped down south to Camp Peary, a 480-acre site in the piney woods outside the restored colonial settlement of Williamsburg, Virginia. An old Seabees camp from World War II thinly disguised as a Pentagon research and development center, Camp Peary was replete with weapons ranges, obstacle courses, and a mock-up of a border checkpoint in a hostile nation. Ames was taught how to be a case officer, how to get out and meet people and recruit them. He learned tricks of the trade: coding and decoding secret messages, evading surveillance, surreptitiously opening and resealing mail, exchanging documents with a source without being detected, and handling a "dead drop"—a secret hiding place, such as a hollowed-out brick, used for delivering messages.

Charlie Emmling met Ames in career training, as did Frederick Hitz, who later became the CIA's inspector general. Ames and Emmling struck up a casual friendship as trainees, and their career paths intertwined over the next twenty-five years.

"The training was very, very intense—as much an endurance contest as anything else," Emmling said. "An ordinary day ran from seven A.M. to eleven P.M., though on Fridays they'd let you off at five. There was four months of operations training, four months of paramilitary training after that. If you got through the training, you were told that you were pretty good.

"At the end there was a field exercise to put together what you had learned. They broke us into groups of four or five and dropped us in New York City. We would get an anonymous phone call, saying 'Meet me at such and such a corner.' You'd meet somebody, debrief him, and if you asked the right questions you'd get the right answers, which would lead to the next person. Push the right button, get to the next level."

Ames was a team leader. "He worked hard and did a good job," Emmling remembered. "I do remember, though, that he was under a lot of stress and that he spent two or three nights that week barfing his brains out. Mostly I remember a witty guy who liked to tell jokes and play with words."

Early in his training, Ames underwent a routine psychological test. His evaluators reported that he lacked the right stuff to make it as a spy. He was a thinker, not a doer; an introvert without the social skills necessary to recruit foreigners. But by the end of the program, his supervisors thought Ames had shaped up: he appeared smart, enthusiastic, and ready to go out and spy for his country. He was a different man. During his CIA training, at age twenty-seven, Ames fell in love. The bonding that naturally takes place between people undergoing a rigorous common experience had happened between Ames and Nancy Jane Segebarth. They were married in May 1969 and spent the summer preparing to set off on a great adventure. They were going overseas, to Ankara, the capital of Turkey.

With borders on the Soviet Union, Bulgaria, Syria, Iraq, and Iran, Turkey was a cultural crossroads and a paradise for spies. The CIA station was hidden inside the U.S. Embassy, on a hill overlooking the city. A good CIA man could bump into a lot of interesting people in Ankara. "Everyone's there," said V. J. Maury, who was a CIA officer stationed in Ankara a few years after Rick Ames. "It's Europe to the Europeans and Middle Eastern to Middle Easterners and a little Russian for the Russians. The Turks had a close relationship with the Soviets. But there were people in the station who never interacted with Turks. They went from their home to the embassy to the PX at the Air Force base to their home."

That was Rick Ames—much to the consternation of his station chief in Ankara, Dewey Clarridge. Not yet forty years old, Clarridge was already something of a legend inside the Directorate of Operations. He would go on to serve as station chief in Rome and as chief of operations for the Near East, for Latin America, and for Europe. Clarridge liked to surround himself with good people. He did not regard Rick Ames as good. He wrote a devastatingly critical evaluation of Ames in 1971, which called him lazy, unfocused, unfit for the life of an operations officer overseas, and best suited for a slot far behind the front lines of the cold war. The criticism stung Ames so sharply that he seriously considered quitting the CIA.

"Now, what do you do with a guy like that?" said Charlie Emmling, who himself had a successful career as a case officer and a manager of clandestine operations. "Here's Ames. He's been through this rigorous selection, he passed all the tests, you've spent thousands and thousands of dollars training him. Then he gets out there in the field and you find he doesn't fit in. Do you flush him down the toilet? No. You let him evolve. Ames had a talent as a thinker, a writer, and an analyzer. Guys like that are very, very valuable. But it was clear that he was not going to progress past a certain level. People who do well as case officers become glamour boys. People who don't become second-class citizens."

Ames did not quit. In 1972, he returned to headquarters and fastened on to a new course, one that he would cleave to for the better part of twenty years. He joined the Soviet/East European division of the Directorate of Operations. He went to language school to learn Russian and became fairly proficient. Over the next two years, he did a creditable job handling paperwork and planning field operations against Soviet officials in the United States. He secured himself a small and anonymous billet on the home front in the cold war.

Ames's arrival in the Soviet division coincided with the outbreak of détente. In May 1972, President Richard Nixon was toasting Soviet General Secretary Leonid Brezhnev in

Moscow. Their leading diplomats, national security adviser Henry Kissinger and Ambassador Anatoly Dobrynin, had opened secret lines of communication that had led to a summit meeting, diplomatic agreements, and a treaty limiting nuclear weapons. But no new understanding limited the game of espionage. As the cold war thawed a bit, the KGB was rapidly expanding its presence at its three U.S. residencies: the United Nations in New York and the Soviet embassies in Washington and San Francisco. The number of Soviet intelligence officers in the United States nearly doubled, from about 120 in 1970 to 220 in 1975. Those known to be spies were kept under surveillance, but the flood of new talent made it difficult to keep track of them. Ames was supposed to try to help figure out who was who among the Soviets, to read and write dossiers and to coordinate assignments for other, more talented field officers.

Ames's personnel and security files from those years contained commendations, but also noted his inability to concentrate, his procrastination, and his inattention to detail. And the distinct aroma of alcohol wafted up from the classified dossier. Twice, the in-house cops from the CIA's Office of Security had cited Ames for drunken and untoward behavior. In both cases, the incidents took place at Christmas parties. At a holiday gathering on December 20, 1973, Ames had become so drunk that a couple of security officers had to take him home. The next Christmas, Ames had gotten drunk again, and the report in this case drily noted that he had been found "in a compromising position with a female CIA employee." The reports went into his security file, but nothing suggested that his bosses were notified of his behavior. There were plenty of people at headquarters who had bigger battles with the bottle. Getting drunk at a Christmas party? Who didn't? Good old Rick. What a character.

As they read his files, the SKYLIGHT investigators wondered at Rick Ames's rise through the ranks of the CIA. Then they arrived at the story of Sergei Federenko and began to understand. The Federenko case had made Ames's career, though in retrospect it should have been his undoing. It had showed he was capable of serving as a case officer, and it had helped him win promotions in the 1980s. But the Federenko case had turned out to be another counterintelligence conundrum.

. . .

Sergei Federenko was a member of the Soviet elite by birth, marriage, social standing, and professional accomplishment. An engineer by training, he worked on arms control issues at the disarmament division of the U.N. secretariat. Good-looking, hard-drinking, with a beautiful wife and a young girlfriend at a college in the suburbs north of New York City, Federenko was a charmer. Mirroring his double life as husband and lover, he began a relationship with the Central Intelligence Agency in the fall of 1974.

The Agency took a gamble and assigned Rick Ames the task of serving as Federenko's case officer. At first, Federenko provided Ames with what appeared to be solid information. Ames would go up to New York for monthly meetings with Federenko that usually took place at a CIA safe house not far from the Soviet residential compound in Riverdale, on the northern edge of New York City. Federenko provided a who's who of the Soviet delegation—including, in some cases, the personal foibles and character flaws of the KGB officers.

Everybody was happy with the case except Paul Redmond, then an up-and-coming Soviet counterintelligence officer. Redmond thought there was something suspicious about the way Federenko conducted himself—the fact that he lived such a carefree life, apparently unconcerned about surveillance by the KGB. Something was not quite right, Redmond argued. He did not trust Federenko—or Rick Ames.

The Federenko case went swimmingly for about a year, until Rick Ames did something so stupid that it almost ended his career. He bungled things so badly that the memory would pain him for the rest of his life.

Ames's normal practice was to carry a page or two of his agenda for the meeting with Federenko in a briefcase that had a concealed compartment. He would take the Metroliner up to New York, then catch a subway to the safe house. Ames was sleepy that morning; he had arisen at four o'clock to catch the first train out of Washington. It was approaching eleven as the IRT subway rumbled into the north Bronx. Ames became drowsy with the rocking of the train. With a jolt, he realized that he had arrived at his station, and he ran off the train just as the doors closed behind him.

"And then I realized—I left my briefcase." He began a frantic search in every station to the end of the line, clawing through trash cans. "After about an hour, I had done what I felt I could myself, and so I went to the safe house, which was nearby, and I called the chief of base"—the senior CIA officer assigned to the United Nations. "I have to come down and meet you immediately. We've got a real problem," Ames told the chief.

"We were worried to death," Ames said. The Soviets rode the same subway line from their residential complex to Manhattan. And there were pictures of Federenko in the briefcase—"some snapshots he had given me at an earlier meeting with pictures of him and some of his friends, Soviet friends. And that was a great concern." Hours later, the CIA men decided to go ahead and meet Federenko. Without telling him about the lost briefcase, they gave him a new set of emer-

gency telephone numbers and safe houses. Then Ames went
to the base chief's apartment, where several CIA and FBI men
were at work, "drafting a little ad to go down in the bottom
of the front page of *The New York Times*." The telephone
rang. It was the FBI's New York office. A schoolteacher—a
Polish émigré—had found the briefcase, examined the contents, and called the FBI. Perversely, Ames's idiocy had saved
the day: he had left his papers, including one that mentioned
the FBI, in the open pockets of his briefcase, not in the secret
compartment. The schoolteacher had seen them and called
the Bureau.

"So it was a tremendous relief," Ames concluded. "I was
going through agonies. I was thinking: I am just going to
have to quit, retire, or something."

But a few months after his snafu on the subway, Rick Ames
won a promotion.

In June 1976, shortly after his thirty-fifth birthday, he
began work at the CIA's station in New York City. It was the
best posting the Agency had to offer inside the United States.
Rick and his wife, Nan, had a fine apartment on the East Side
near the United Nations, subsidized by the CIA, and he enter-
tained potential recruits on a generous expense account. He
also made a new friend within the ranks of the Soviet press
corps.

Tomas Kolesnichenko was a *Pravda* correspondent who
filed virulently ideological dispatches about U.S. foreign policy. Kolesnichenko had also written the book for a ludicrous
musical called *Rock and Roll at Dawn*. The plot was something about hip American kids struggling against the military-
industrial complex who were betrayed by a scheming, Maoist,
dope-dealing Chinese nightclub owner who was in cahoots
with the Pentagon. The *Pravda* correspondent became one of
Ames's favorite partners for drink and conversation. Ames

and Kolesnichenko met at least once a month for three years at restaurants ranging from East Side coffee shops to the elegant Tavern on the Green in Central Park. Kolesnichenko knew his companion as a political scientist named Frank Madison, and he found him a fine conversationalist. They talked about everything from Watergate to the Warsaw Pact, and all of it went into Ames's reports, some of which he was now filing promptly for the first time in his life. There was a profoundly conspiratorial bent to the Soviet mind when it regarded the United States, and the same held true for the American perception of the Soviet Union, the two men agreed. The Soviet view grew out of a lack of understanding of American ways and the experience of life under Stalin. The Americans caricatured Russians as robots and slaves.

Ames did not come close to recruiting the Russian; he never recruited anyone in his life. But he remembered absorbing a great deal from those long discussions, which he felt gave him great insight into the way the Soviets really worked. Kolesnichenko remembers things differently. He says he filled his companion's head with ideas he thought would find a receptive ear: the promise of détente, the problems of U.S. foreign policy, the prospects for peace.

Deeper thoughts—and genuine intelligence—came to Ames from his meetings with Arkady Shevchenko. In 1978, to his astonishment and pleasure, Ames was given the task of debriefing Shevchenko, the highest-ranking Soviet diplomat to serve as an agent in place in the history of the cold war. Shevchenko was under secretary general of the United Nations. Disgusted with the Soviet Union, he had sought to defect in 1975. But a CIA officer had persuaded him to remain at his post for a year or two, in order to serve as the Agency's eyes and ears inside the high councils of the Soviet Union, and he had been spying for the United States for two and a half years when he publicly defected in 1978. Now, instead of rushed, nervous meetings at the Agency's safe house on East Sixty-fourth Street, Ames and Shevchenko could meet in more relaxed circumstances in Washington and New York. Most of the defectors of the 1970s had portrayed the Soviet leaders, from a distance, as a monstrous, murderous rabble. Shevchenko knew these leaders personally, and he had a more detailed story to tell. While there were people in the Kremlin who genuinely believed that the United States was run by a secret cabal of Wall Street capitalists and warmongering generals, some of the members of the Soviet leadership were reasonable, he told Ames.

The conversations with Shevchenko provided a boost to Ames's career, one that would compensate for the loss of Federenko. In 1978, Federenko's five-year tour of duty at the United Nations ended, and he returned to Moscow. Great plans were afoot for Federenko to become a source from within the Ministry of Foreign Affairs in Moscow. But Federenko fell strangely silent upon his return to the Soviet Union, a fact that some inside the CIA found greatly troubling. Federenko would not resurface for a decade, and when he did, his reputation and reliability would be the cause of deep contention.

"That case smelled to high heaven," Milt Bearden said. "Nobody liked Federenko but Ames." Federenko's bona fides were the subject of long arguments between Ames, who trusted Federenko, and counterintelligence officer Paul Redmond; the outcome was Redmond's growing disbelief in Ames's judgment and trustworthiness.

But in 1979, Ames was at the high point of his professional life. He had won three promotions in four years, as well as a bonus for handling Shevchenko, and had collected the best appraisals of his career, including one that called him "superior." His drinking was also under control.

He was offered several assignments overseas. But his wife, Nan, preferred to stay in New York, and the issue became one of many strains between them. As his career reached its apex, his personal life began a long slow slide. At the beginning of the summer of 1981, after long and sometimes desultory discussions about their relationship and the future of their childless twelve-year marriage, they decided to separate. She would stay in New York; he would take the post he'd been offered in Mexico City.

Rick Ames, now forty years old, went off to spy in a strange country. Down in Mexico, his life began to run off the rails.

The Mexico City station was a mess. The station chief, Stewart Burton, was under enormous pressure from Bill Casey, the new director of Central Intelligence, to discover evidence of the Communist plan to disrupt the Western Hemisphere.

"Casey had a feeling that there was a lot going on in Mexico that the station didn't know about," said John Horton, a former Mexico City station chief who was the CIA's senior analyst on Latin America in the early 1980s. "Casey's thesis was that Mexico was another Iran—so badly covered that we didn't know what was going on and the next thing we knew the Communists would be in Missouri. He placed a great reliance on rumors about arms smuggling and Cuban infiltration. It was fiction, but appealing fiction. So that was a strain, to be told to look for something that isn't there and then prove that it isn't there."

Casey was right on one point. The station did not produce a great deal of useful information on Mexico, in part because most of its officers could not speak Spanish, in part because they were busy chasing Soviet, East German, and Czech intelligence officers. The KGB maintained one of its largest overseas residencies in the Mexican capital, and Communist intelligence officers from around the world used the Soviet Embassy as a business center, social club, currency exchange, and guildhall.

In his two years in Mexico City, Ames worked on one, and only one, important counterintelligence case. It eventually led to the arrest and espionage conviction of Alfred Zehe, an East German physicist who lived in Mexico and frequently traveled to the United States seeking military secrets. At one point, Ames was even considered—briefly—for the post of deputy chief of station in Bogotá. But he withdrew from the hard business of recruiting spies and running agents. He closeted himself in his office. He began drinking as never before, and the few friends he made in the CIA's station were the office drunks. He began a pattern that he would hold to for the rest of his career: arriving at the office sometime between nine and ten in the morning, staring into space or into the muddle of an old, unresolved case for most of the morning, going out for long lunches with a few like-minded souls from the station, drinking himself into semi-oblivion, and sleeping it off for the rest of the afternoon.

The downward spiral of his life and work was rapid. In 1982, at a diplomatic reception in the U.S. Embassy, Ames started drinking heavily. He began a discussion with a Cuban who was, like most of his countrymen in diplomatic circles, a member of Fidel Castro's foreign intelligence service. The conversation grew in intensity and stupidity until it became a loud, embarrassing argument that verged on becoming a small international incident. A few months later, Ames got behind the wheel of his automobile so drunk that he could not see straight or speak coherently. He quickly got himself into an accident and proved to be incapable of thought or speech: he could not answer the questions put to him by the police, nor could he recognize the U.S. Embassy officer sent out to extricate him from the embarrassing altercation.

These chapters in Rick Ames's career were the subject of a message, sent via a private channel reserved for the most sensitive cables, from the station chief in Mexico City to the CIA's office of medical services back at headquarters. He recommended that Ames receive professional treatment for alcoholism. Nothing came of it.

Ames also flouted regulations by indulging in at least three adulterous relationships. One of these affairs proved to be lasting. It had an unusual genesis.

One of Ames's drinking buddies in the Mexico City station was Dave Samson, a longtime clandestine services officer with a reputation for charming the pants off potential recruits. In February 1982, Samson met a woman at a diplomatic cocktail party. She mentioned that she had a check on a Colombian bank that she couldn't seem to get cashed in Mexico City. No problem, said her newfound friend, I'll take care of it. This casual encounter developed into a complicated relationship.

The woman was the new cultural attaché at the Colombian Embassy in Mexico City, María del Rosario Casas Dupuy.

Rosario Casas was thirty years old, and until she moved to Mexico City she had never lived anywhere but under her parents' roof. She was a member in good standing of Colombia's traditional elite, a group of a few hundred families who all knew one another in some fashion and accepted the notion that they had been chosen to run the country. Her father, Pablo Casas Santofimio, was a mathematician who had long since given up numbers for political power. He had held various government jobs, once serving as secretary of the interior, and he was the secretary general of the Liberal Party, one of the country's two dominant political groups. Her mother, Cecilia Dupuy de Casas, was a professor of literature, a position to which Rosario aspired. Rosario had attended an American secondary school and spoke unaccented English. Her baccalaureate thesis at the Universidad de Los Andes had been a comparative study of the urban sensibilities in the poetry of Baudelaire, T. S. Eliot, and Federico García Lorca. By the time she had finished college, she spoke Greek and fluent French.

Rosario had anticipated a life in the shelter of the university. "I was dedicated to academia," she said. "It was my world and I loved it." But she was fascinated by the larger world, too, and she had traveled to New York, Paris, and Rome while in her twenties, usually chaperoned by relatives. As her thirtieth birthday had approached, her father had died, and she had "decided it was time for a change." She had set her sights on Mexico City.

She had used her connections to secure a diplomatic posting. For someone in her social circle, it was easy. The president of Colombia, Julio Cesar Turbay Ayala, and the Colombian ambassador in Mexico City, Ignacio Umana, were family friends. They had simply arranged for her to be named cultural attaché at the embassy.

Her job consisted of overseeing scholarships and art exhibits and even dealing with journalists. The embassy staff was so small, she was also obliged to serve as press secretary. She also served as a member of the board of a diplomatic association known as AMCOSAD, an acronym of its full Spanish name, which served as a gathering place for attachés, consuls, junior diplomats, and spies. A KGB officer named Sergei Shurygin, known to the CIA as an aggressive recruiter of foreign agents, also served on the board of AMCOSAD. So did the CIA's Dave Samson; he was the treasurer. Samson urged Rosario to run for secretary of the diplomatic association. She did, and she won.

After she and Samson became friendly, he told her he was not really a diplomat but an officer of the CIA. She was taken aback, but she quickly got over it. Eventually, she agreed to help Samson out on a few matters, such as letting him use her apartment as a safe house when she was away. He paid her for her help, a few hundred dollars here and there.

She never got over the fact that she had allowed Samson to recruit her. "Let's not kid ourselves," she said. "I mean, the image of the CIA in Latin America is not a good one."

In her new capacity at the association, she attended most of the events it sponsored. On one of these occasions, an evening lecture on ancient Aztec culture at the Museum of Anthropology in October 1982, she talked at length with Rick Ames. Dave Samson had introduced them once before. They met again at a party in January 1983, and soon they were going out to dinner regularly. Unlike Samson, Rick Ames did not tell her that he worked for the CIA.

The relationship grew quickly. Rosario had most of the social graces but very little experience with men. As she put it, she was "very sophisticated intellectually, but in this field totally naïve." She said she had found Rick worldly, cultured, and well read—but "clearly an unhappy person." The unhappiness showed in his drinking.

"I saw Rick get drunk a lot of times," she said. "I attributed it to the fact that he was not happy with his marriage." The Colombian Embassy was near the U.S. Embassy, she said, and she had often looked out her window in the afternoon to see Ames and Samson coming back from lunch, having had a lot to drink. "There were some embarrassing times in Mexico, there were times when I'd have to drive him home, and I didn't enjoy that at all." But she had thought "a little tender loving care" would heal him: "Once I thought I was totally in love with him, I said, 'I'm going to change this. He just needs to be happy.' "

Ames was scheduled to return to the United States in September 1983. Mexico City may have been a professional disaster, but as his assignment neared its end, he reached a personal milestone. He would divorce Nan and marry this cultured, intelligent woman who thought she loved him. Shortly before his departure, Rick sat down with Rosario and told her two secrets: One, he wanted to marry her. Two, he worked for the CIA.

Her head aswirl, she said yes to his proposal. They decided she would remain in Mexico City and keep her job until he could extricate himself from his marriage to Nan.

But Rick found he did not possess as much patience as he had thought. In November 1983, he called Rosario and told her to quit her job and come to Washington and move in with him.

At one time the Agency had tried to prohibit marriages between officers and agents, but in the late 1970s it had capitulated in the face of their frequency. A growing number of officers were falling in love with the foreigners they recruited, and it became a burden having to fire them or ordering the romance ended. The CIA's regulations still required an employee to report any romance with a foreigner and formally request permission to marry one. Ames did not reveal his relationship with Rosario until Thanksgiving 1983 and kept his intent to marry her secret for another six months. Finally he filled out the written request for permission to marry. Attached to it, as required, was an unsigned letter of resignation.

The CIA's personnel and security offices recommended that Ames should be kept out of extremely sensitive positions at CIA headquarters if he married a foreigner. The recommendation was ignored. So were all the disastrous elements of his stint in Mexico—the drinking, the sloth, the aberrant conduct, the traffic accident, the incident with the Cuban intelligence officer, the flouting of Agency rules. So was his station chief's request that Ames receive treatment for alcoholism. Nor did the chief of the Latin American division— Dewey Clarridge, Ames's station chief in Ankara, who knew him as a ne'er-do-well—alert his colleagues that they were inheriting a personnel problem. None of this entered the picture when the CIA's Soviet division hired Rick Ames for one of the most sensitive jobs in the entire Agency.

And so it was that Rick Ames became the Soviet division's counterintelligence chief in the fall of 1983 and began calling for the files on every important CIA operation involving Soviet spies in every corner of the world.

18

PLAYACTOR

Six miles above the north Atlantic on a July afternoon in 1991, two middle-aged men in business suits sat huddled in deep conversation in the coach section of a commercial airliner.

One was Tom DuHadway, the outgoing special agent in charge at the FBI's Washington Metropolitan Field Office. The other was Robert M. Bryant, who was about to take DuHadway's place. They were headed for Lockerbie, Scotland, the site of the downing of Pan Am flight 103, the airliner blown from the sky by a terrorist's bomb in December 1988, killing 259 people on the plane and another 11 on the ground. Washington Field had a counterterrorism squad on that case, and it was nearing an indictment of two Libyan suspects.

But DuHadway had another disaster on his mind. Sipping a Grand Marnier, he quietly related the facts. Bryant swore into his beer as he learned that there might be a mole inside the CIA.

The Agency had come to the FBI three months earlier with its glimmer of a suspicion that it had been penetrated by one of its own employees. Not everyone at the CIA agreed with that supposition, but the general feeling was that a serious effort would have to be made to revitalize an investigation that had gone nowhere for more than five years. This was an open wound that needed professional attention. The FBI, in turn, had suggested that the rival agencies join forces, and the Agency had immediately agreed. It was quite a proposal—to renew long-broken vows of togetherness and cooperation after years of estrangement, in which the two warring tribes had stood on opposite banks of the Potomac, throwing rocks and shaking their spears at each other.

Catching spies was DuHadway's line of work, not Bryant's. DuHadway was steeped in the world of espionage; he was even married to a counterintelligence supervisor in the Washington field office. Bryant had little experience in the arcana of spy versus spy. He had investigated racketeers in Las Vegas, run a field office in Salt Lake City, and, during his most recent tour at headquarters, had handled organized crime and drug cases.

Now an enormously complicated spy investigation was landing on his head. At least, he figured, he could count on help from DuHadway, who was transferring back to headquarters as the Bureau's top counterespionage official. But a few weeks after their return from Lockerbie, DuHadway dropped dead of a heart attack on a golf course in suburban Maryland. He was forty-nine years old. Bryant would be on his own.

Bryant was a sandy-haired lawyer from Little Rock, Arkansas, known throughout the Bureau as "Bear," like the legendarily tough University of Alabama football coach. His stints in Nevada and Utah had given him an affinity for the old West, and he kept books on the subject on his office coffee table, along with a pair of brass cowboy boots and a framed print of buffalo standing in the driving snow of a prairie blizzard. He had an irreverent, blunt manner that sometimes bothered his more orthodox colleagues at FBI headquarters, the bureaucrats and yes-men who often told him no. But his troops in the Washington field office instantly liked his battering-ram style.

Bryant won the promotion to run the Washington field office at a time when headquarters was increasingly preoccupied with cocaine, guns, and street gangs—threats that were actually on the periphery of the traditional jurisdiction of the FBI but that were terrorizing urban America, including whole sections of the District of Columbia. He had been under the impression that his biggest assignment would be making a transition from the cold war priorities of the FBI, redirecting its firepower back to the streets of the city and away from ivory-tower issues like counterintelligence.

Bryant had a practical approach to the festering case. He was a criminal investigator. If a crime had been committed, somebody had to have committed it. And if the Central Intelligence Agency had a problem with a mope—that was what they called criminal subjects at the FBI—Bryant would find him. Then he would hand him over to a prosecutor with enough evidence to send him to prison for a very long time. His allies at FBI headquarters quickly discovered that he was totally committed to the investigation now known as PLAY-ACTOR. They saw him working it exactly like any other criminal case. They saw him clashing with the counterintelligence types at the CIA, the thumb-twiddling theorists who were content to leaf through old files until they reached retirement. And they knew he was prepared to lay waste to the entire intelligence community in order to find the mope.

When Bryant took over the Washington field office, PLAY-ACTOR, along with the CIA's parallel SKYLIGHT investigation, was just getting under way. PLAYACTOR/SKYLIGHT was a reunion of sorts, pulling together some of the same investigators who had tried without success to analyze the CIA's losses during the 1980s. Jeanne Vertefeuille, the head of the old CIA special task force, and her colleague Sandy Grimes, who had spent years digging dry wells in the Lonetree case, were on the case. The Bureau sent Jim Holt and Jim Milburn, two agents who specialized in counterintelligence investigations, over to the CIA.

Holt and Milburn—"Jim Squared" to their FBI colleagues—were two of the Bureau's best Soviet analysts. Holt had a personal interest in the case, having handled KGB Lieutenant Colonel Valery Martinov and having watched helplessly as he had disappeared in 1985. Holt and Martinov had daughters about the same age. The two men had spent many days and nights together in the early 1980s. Milburn knew all about the disappearance; his colleagues said he knew the KGB better than anyone else in the Bureau did.

When PLAYACTOR began, Holt had not been terribly optimistic. There had been so much time wasted and so many dead ends. "But maybe," Holt said, "if we pooled our resources and took one more crack at it, we could make some headway."

They started from square one, throwing out the old logic, stripping away the layers of assumptions that had accumulated through years of following false leads and falling for Soviet disinformation. The way the CIA, and even some at the FBI, had seen the case "just didn't make sense when you started looking at it," Bryant said. The analysts had been "looking for a needle in a haystack" of old cases instead of compiling a list of suspects—which was what any criminal investigator would do.

The four investigators worked to assemble a roster of all the CIA employees who could possibly have revealed the Soviet agents who had been betrayed. This was known as a BIGOT list, the names of people authorized to know a certain secret. It was a term the CIA had appropriated from British intelligence during World War II; legend had it that it was simply a backward reading of a list of people authorized to go "to Gib"—that is, to Gibraltar.

The investigators concentrated on compiling the most comprehensive list possible. Tim Caruso, who had run the FBI's futile ANLACE investigation in 1986, compared the process to drawing a series of concentric circles. In the first circle, the smallest, were the people who had actually recruited and run and analyzed the work of the Soviet spies who had been burned. In the second ring were the technical and clerical employees who had helped the first group. Last came the outer circle of people plugged into the loop through corridor gossip. "You've got people who'll say, 'I hear you got something really great,' " said Caruso, "and the guy or gal puffs out their little chest and leaves a hint. And the circle just gets wider and wider and more ambiguous."

The compilation of the BIGOT list took three months because the list was so long, a fact that astonished the FBI. The cases that had been compromised were supposed to be the holiest of holy secrets at the CIA. And yet there were 198 people on the list. Arranged by rank, the list went from a lowly analyst in the Soviet division to the newly nominated director of Central Intelligence, Robert M. Gates.

It was impossible to investigate 198 people; that would take until the turn of the century. So while Holt and Milburn focused on the smallest circle of people, the ones who had direct access to the blown cases, Vertefeuille and Grimes went to work subjectively plucking the names of people from the BIGOT list, singling them out for closer scrutiny. In many cases, they knew the people personally, knew their problems and their pasts. The investigators relied on instinct, or what old-time CIA officers called *fingerspitzengefühl,* an untranslatable German word that literally means "fingertip feeling." This was art, not science.

At the end of August 1991, the investigators sat down and compared notes. Twenty-nine people stood out as potential suspects. Rick Ames was on everyone's list.

19

Hopeless Romantics

As the investigators first began to focus their attention on the possibility that Rick Ames was a mole for Moscow, he received a new and fascinating assignment. He was ordered to help finish off the KGB.

The Soviet intelligence service had been gravely wounded by its own hand. On the afternoon of August 18, 1991, its chairman, Vladimir Kryuchkov, had tried to take over the Soviet Union. His coup had lasted less than a hundred hours. When it was done with, Kryuchkov had been placed under arrest and the people of Moscow were storming KGB headquarters and painting swastikas on its walls.

This was the spymaster to whom Rick Ames had pledged his allegiance and who had worked so hard to protect him by brilliantly deceiving the CIA.

Kryuchkov had planned the coup for months, gathering support among the old regime's hard-line Communists. He had stirred up old fears, warning the Soviet legislature that the CIA was plotting "the pacification and even the occupation" of the Soviet Union—and as proof pulling out an old report he had written in 1977 entitled *C.I.A. Plans to Recruit Agents Among Soviet Citizens,* which detailed the Agency's master plan to destroy the motherland.

Kryuchkov had been convinced that the reformist Soviet leader Mikhail Gorbachev was a deluded rabble-rouser who was hell-bent on destroying the system that the KGB had served for so long and that had served the KGB so well. Gorbachev had been set to sign a treaty granting autonomy to the republics of the Soviet Union. Kryuchkov had secretly organized a junta of reactionaries, fools, drunks, and generals to protect the old order.

The politicians who opposed the coup had taken refuge in the Russian parliament. Tens of thousands of people had gathered at the building, known locally as the White House. Kryuchkov had ordered the KGB's Alpha Group, which had a deserved reputation as the world's most brutal and efficient SWAT team, to storm the parliament. The Alpha Group's attack was to have been backed by close air support, tanks, and troops with rocket-propelled grenades.

The Alpha Group hadn't shown up.

A revolt within the KGB had been building in counterpoint to Kryuchkov's coup plans. It was open and unmistakeable. Donald Jameson, a retired CIA Soviet division branch chief, had traveled throughout Russia in the weeks before the coup, and he said he had heard "a lot of internal dissent" from KGB officers "who had a realistic assessment of how rotten Soviet society was." When the crisis had come, the up-and-coming majors and lieutenant colonels in the Alpha Group, as well as officers throughout the KGB in Moscow, had opposed the junta and refused to assault the parliament. The refusal of the younger generation to go along with the old guard had broken the back of the coup.

Kryuchkov had been arrested, and that week his loyalists

had worked around the clock burning files. Muscovites had gathered at the spy service's headquarters, shaking their fists and shouting "Gestapo! Gestapo!" That night, with the help of a crane sent by the city fathers, they had toppled the statue of Feliks Dzerzhinsky, the founder of Soviet intelligence.

The Soviet Union began to dissolve, and with it the old KGB. The spy service started losing its powers as a brutally effective tool of internal repression. Its foreign intelligence component lived on, though its new chief, Vadim Bakatin, complained shortly thereafter to the U.S. ambassador, Robert S. Strauss: "I don't know what my future is. I don't know who pays my salary. My government doesn't pay it anymore."

Milt Bearden, the CIA's Soviet division chief, had witnessed the August 1991 coup. He had returned to headquarters convinced that he could finish off what was left of the KGB. "I got the idea that we could kill this virus once and for all," he said. "We could get under the KGB's skin. We'd make contact with the Russian parliament and inject it with ideas, like the concept of oversight of intelligence agencies." In September 1991, two weeks after the coup, Bearden created the KGB Working Group, a committee of covert operators, analysts, and Russia hands at the CIA, and he ordered them to come up with creative ideas to subvert and destroy the KGB. He told one of his deputies to create a staff.

Rick Ames was named chief of the KGB Working Group.

"Milt Bearden's charge to me was to put a stake through the KGB's heart," Ames said. "That's his dramatic expression. The point being that the coming dissolution of the union and the shocks to the KGB after the coup were such that the KGB was extremely vulnerable, or was at least potentially vulnerable, to what we may be able to do to discredit it politically, bureaucratically, with the new Russian leadership."

Bearden said that "Ames never did anything" with the assignment. On the contrary, Ames said, the CIA itself was unable to do anything with Bearden's ambitious ideas and his own plans to execute them. "By the time I had my next meeting with my KGB handler" at the end of 1991, he said, "I told him that I thought it was unlikely that anyone was going to carry on with it."

In the fall of 1991, the CIA was in trouble, too; like the KGB, it was imperiled by the end of the cold war.

In September and October, the Senate intelligence committee held confirmation hearings on the nomination of Robert M. Gates to be Director of Central Intelligence. They turned into a public bloodletting. Gates started out sounding like a real reformer. "The old verities that have guided this country's national security policies for forty-five years, and thus its intelligence service, have disappeared in an historical instant," he said. "The CIA and U.S. intelligence must change, and must be seen to change, or confront irrelevance and growing sentiment for their dismantlement." It was a politically adept statement that had the added advantage of being true.

But Gates, as head of the CIA's intelligence analysis division and deputy director of the CIA, had been one of the great cold war ideologues of the 1980s, and some of the most preeminent CIA analysts who had worked under him testified that he had forcibly altered their work to conform with the late Bill Casey's biases, cutting the cloth of the facts to fit the fashion of the day. Hal Ford, a highly respected thirty-year CIA veteran, told the committee that Gates had been "dead wrong on the central analytic target of the past few years, the outlook for change in the fortunes of the USSR and the Soviet–Eastern European bloc." Mel Goodman, who had been the CIA's chief analyst on the Soviets' role in the Third

World, testified that the effect of Gates's leadership had been to "corrupt the process and the ethics of intelligence." Gates survived the hearings; his reputation did not.

That autumn, the victory over the KGB turned bittersweet. The collapse of the Soviet Union left many at the CIA bereft of their life's work. "We were chock full of hopeless romantics who never thought we would win like this, that all of a sudden it would all fall down," Milt Bearden said. "What we also didn't know was that the collapse of our enemy ensured our own demise."

In October 1991, the depths to which the Agency was falling were measured when Bearden received a startling report from one of his case officers in Bonn. The case officer reported that he had recruited a KGB source who knew all about a mole inside the CIA.

According to the report, the new recruit said that the Agency had been penetrated in the mid- to late 1970s by one of its own officers, an ethnic Russian born in the United States. The mole had handed over to the KGB information about all CIA operations in Moscow, including the identities of at least two of the Soviet agents arrested and killed in 1986. The two dead agents had worked out of Germany, as had the new KGB source.

The mole was reported to be alive and well and still working for Moscow from somewhere inside the Agency.

Several aspects of the CIA officer's report on his KGB recruit matched the tip from another mysterious Soviet source that had launched the misguided five-year-old investigation into the imaginary penetration of the Warrenton communications center. No one yet understood that the whole Warrenton story had been a KGB deception.

The PLAYACTOR and SKYLIGHT teams immediately dropped what they were doing to focus on the report from

Bonn. Milt Bearden said he had flown to Germany to interview the case officer.

"At a certain point I just stopped talking, and I listened and I watched his eyes and hands," Bearden said. "And I came back and I said, 'The guy's lying. It's a fraud. This is a guy who's gone wacko and he's making stuff up. He invented the recruitment.' And there was a great sadness over that."

The CIA case officer in Bonn was recalled to headquarters for questioning in October 1991. After a week of interrogation, the CIA concluded that he had fabricated the recruit and invented the report to enhance his career and win a raise. The case officer resigned from the CIA, and in 1992 the case was referred to the Justice Department for possible prosecution. Nothing ever came of it.

The bogus report cost PLAYACTOR and SKYLIGHT nearly a month. They got back on track by scheduling interviews with the top twenty-nine suspects on the BIGOT list. These included Milt Bearden, Ames's boss; Colin Thompson, Ames's colleague in the counterintelligence group back in 1985; and Ames himself. But the interviews almost never came off.

The FBI has a standard procedure for interviewing that includes creating a transcript listing the names of all participants—the interviewers as well as the subjects. The CIA refused to go along with that. The Agency felt it would be a breach of security to record the true name of a CIA officer on a piece of paper that might end up as a public record in a criminal trial. The Agency demanded that the transcripts omit the names of Jeanne Vertefeuille and Sandy Grimes.

Bryant angrily refused. Leaving out the names would create a false document, and that could taint a prosecution against a mole, he argued. The CIA reluctantly backed down, but the episode, a petty dispute over procedure, brought the deep animosity between the Bureau and the Agency boiling back to the surface.

Finally, the interviews got under way. Vertefeuille and Grimes from the CIA usually did most of the questioning; either Holt or Milburn usually accompanied them.

They went to see Milt Bearden. "I knew I had to be on the list," he said. "We were down to about twenty people, and I was one of them." A few weeks after the interview, the new Director of Central Intelligence, Bob Gates, ended Bearden's tenure as chief of the Soviet division and made him station chief in Bonn, effective in February. It would be Bearden's final assignment at the CIA.

Next, the investigators went to see Colin Thompson, who had retired from the CIA in 1988. He also was expecting them. "I knew there was an investigation going on, and I knew I was one of the suspects," he said. "I had been in the counterintelligence group since 1978. I had handled Boris Yuzhin"—the KGB man code-named TWINE who had been betrayed by Ames, convicted of espionage in Moscow, and, in 1987, sentenced to fifteen years at hard labor.

"The gist of the questions was: If you were a spy, how would you work it?" Thompson recalled. "They were interested in how I handled Yuzhin, how requirements were passed on, did I carry documents out of the building." Bearden and Thompson remained on the list of suspects after the interviews, despite the fact that the investigators had learned nothing new of consequence from them.

On November 12, 1991, they got around to interviewing Rick Ames at CIA headquarters. "He was calm, cool, and collected," said Holt. "We broached the subject with him just like we did with everybody else, and we told him that we were working to determine the reason for the compromises that began occurring in 1985, and we would like the benefit of his thoughts on that."

The interviewers asked Ames to explain where he had been assigned, how he had handled his assignments at the Agency, the extent of his access to the blown operations, the names of the people he had worked with, and whether he had any theories on what had gone wrong.

"It was somewhat generic," said Holt. In a half hour, the interview was complete.

"I thought it was routine," Ames said. During the interview, Ames twice volunteered that he had received a letter admonishing him for leaving his safe open back in July 1985, the only written reprimand of his entire career at the CIA. He told the investigators that the safe had contained case histories of some of the Soviet agents who had been betrayed, along with combinations to other safes that held more secrets about the dead and disappeared spies.

Ames left the interview relieved. "I didn't see it as a probe aimed at me specifically," he said.

In fact, he had aroused the investigators' curiosity. Shortly after the interview, they ordered a full computer scan of records in the Directorate of Operations regarding Ames; he was the only employee singled out for such scrutiny. The printouts provided a new and provocative piece of the puzzle.

It was a copy of a cable the FBI's Washington field office had sent to the CIA back in July 1986—a second request for reports from Ames on his meetings with the diplomat Sergei Chuvakhin. These were the contacts that Ames had never reported but that had been witnessed by the FBI counterintelligence officers who were keeping watch on the Soviet Embassy. The records showed that the CIA had promised the Bureau that it would respond to the requests but never had.

Bear Bryant grew impatient. He had a crime, but no suspect and no evidence. So he organized another investigative squad at the field office that would report to him. The man he tapped to run it was Tim Caruso, the ANLACE veteran with thinning hair and a droll sense of humor, the Bureau's chief of Soviet counterintelligence analysis.

On a cold, threatening day in November, Caruso was ushered into the carpeted inner sanctum of Division Five, the main intelligence arm of the FBI, on the fourth floor of the J. Edgar Hoover Building. "There were a lot of blue suits around," Caruso said. Bryant was there, as was Pat Watson, the deputy assistant director of operations in the intelligence division. Watson served as an FBI goodwill ambassador to the CIA, trying to salve bruised egos and ease tensions when there was a row.

"We're back to the penetration issue, Tim," Caruso was told as he settled in a chair. The discussion was matter-of-fact, like doctors discussing a cancer patient whose disease had been in remission but now had returned in a highly virulent form. Bryant and Watson told Caruso of the interrogations that were under way and ordered him to put together a group of agents to investigate what came in from the ongoing analysis and match it with old counterintelligence leads that had never been resolved. Caruso thought back to the fruitless work of the ANLACE team, the long months inside the tiny vault. He was returning to the bureau of missing persons, the rag-and-bone shop of the cold war. He moved from his headquarters office to Bryant's shop at Buzzard Point to run the new squad. They began poring over a long list of blown cases, recruitments gone bad, ambiguous anomalies.

They tried looking at the cases from new angles. For months, they stepped through the looking glass of intelligence to try to identify the mole's Russian controller. If there were a mole, he would have to have had a handler—almost certainly a KGB officer assigned to Washington in the mid-1980s. The information the mole handed over would have been sent straight to Moscow by diplomatic pouch. But if the Russians had stuck by their standard tradecraft, they would have set up a system for secret communications, probably by way of prearranged dead drops and signal sites. And someone would have to have served as the man who placed the signals and picked up the stolen information.

"We identified about thirty or so intelligence personnel in the Russian colony of Washington, D.C., that we believed would be involved in the running of an American agent in Washington," Caruso said. And then they set about tracing the surveillance records they had compiled on those officers, which often included minutely detailed accounts of their comings and goings in Washington. The average tour for a KGB officer in Washington was four or five years. The squad had to examine every day in the lives of the thirty KGB men—a total of 150 years. The task sent agents rummaging through the files for daily reports on long-forgotten surveillances, searching for something slightly askew, maybe even something missing that should have been there—a gap of fifteen minutes when a KGB officer might have slipped his tail to empty a drop site. The inquiry was a long shot. But if they found that a KGB officer had dropped from view at the same time as a suspect from the BIGOT list had gone on vacation or taken a leave of absence, that could lead them straight to the mole. "You look at those times that we found were unaccounted for," said Caruso, "and then start to narrow things down."

By the time they were done, Caruso's investigators had prepared minutely detailed chronologies on both the Soviets and some of their CIA suspects, keeping logs of their daily activities by drawing time lines on long rolls of butcher paper, somberly unfurling them at briefings like religious scrolls. They hoped the lines would converge at some point and reveal the mole meeting his handler. The butcher-paper charts grew longer and longer, stretching from wall to wall in the office at Buzzard Point. But they never reached a conclusion.

In December 1991, Caruso's team sought to push its investigation overseas. It wanted access to the files of the Stasi, the newly dismantled East German intelligence service, once probably the most lethally efficient spying operation outside of Moscow. With the crumbling of communism, the files were available to the CIA. Could the Stasi have run a U.S. intelligence officer as a mole on behalf of their Soviet patrons? If not, had the Russians been giving the East Germans a look at any of the mole's information? After all, two of the blown Soviet agents had spied for the United States from Germany. Perhaps the files would yield a clue.

But the CIA's station chief in Bonn blocked the FBI's access to the Stasi files and the Agency's translations of them. He bluntly told the Bureau that they could not fish in his waters.

Bryant was furious. This was a criminal case. His agents needed information. This station chief was stonewalling him. Bryant screamed his rage into his secure telephone, his profanity booming down the halls of the field office. He accused FBI headquarters of gutlessly refusing to stand up for the investigation. He threatened to indict the station chief for obstruction of justice and warned that he had already gone to federal prosecutors about the case.

In the end, Pat Watson paid a courtesy call on the Agency. Two months later, Milt Bearden became the new station chief in Bonn. He smoothed the waters, the FBI got access to the files, and the idea of prosecution was quietly shelved. But the bad blood remained.

At Christmastime, Rick Ames and his family made their pilgrimage to Bogotá. Ames parked his wife and son at the house of Rosario's relatives and set off for his annual face-to-face meeting at the Russian Embassy.

Ames had both good and bad news for the Russians. They worked out their plans for the coming year, and Ames shared his progress reports on the KGB Working Group. He also provided details on double-agent operations that he had gleaned from his work at the Counterintelligence Center. But, unhappily, he reported that he was being transferred out of the Soviet division yet again.

Ames was being assigned to the Agency's Counternarcotics Center. It was a kind of Siberia, one of the least desirable posts at the CIA. The idea of centers—Counterintelligence, Counternarcotics, Counterterrorism—had come into vogue under William Webster's tenure. They had been intended to be think tanks where people could share ideas within the intelligence community. But they had never worked that way, especially not the Counternarcotics Center, which had been set up largely as a way to get money from Congress for the never-ending war on drugs.

The CIA and the nation's principal counternarcotics agency, the Drug Enforcement Administration, were mortal enemies. "The DEA hated and feared us, and we had contempt for DEA," Ames said. The relationship had been poisoned by cases such as the kidnapping, torture, and murder of Enrique Camarena, a DEA official in Mexico who had disappeared in 1985. The DEA had linked a high-ranking Mexican law enforcement official—a long-standing CIA agent—to the killing. Then, in 1990, the CIA, which was supposed to be coordinating its work on a drug-smuggling operation—one involving a Venezuelan general—with the

DEA, had managed to ship a ton of nearly pure cocaine to the United States. The drugs had wound up on the streets of south Florida. "A most regrettable incident," the CIA said when reporters found out about it.

The relationship between the CIA and U.S. law enforcement agencies was a perfect mismatch. As Gates delicately stated the problem during his confirmation hearings, "there has been friction over time between the CIA and law enforcement agencies in terms of the intelligence that the CIA collected. The law enforcement agencies want to use that information in court. They want to use it to prosecute people. And there is a concern in CIA, naturally, for the protection of sources and methods, and to be able to prosecute, that would require revealing the sources and methods."

So the CIA's role in the war on drugs was, to put it politely, circumscribed. And the Counternarcotics Center, appropriately located in the Agency's basement, was a demoralized and demoralizing place to be.

But to Rick Ames's complete surprise, he liked the job. To his colleagues' surprise, he was fairly good at it. He even came up with a splendid idea: the Black Sea Initiative.

The idea was to work with the intelligence services of Russia, Turkey, and the Eastern European nations to focus on heroin flowing west from Afghanistan through the former Soviet republics. The CIA had run guns into Afghanistan for a decade to help the Afghan rebels fend off the Soviet invaders during the 1980s but had no idea about the flow of heroin base—hundreds of tons a year—that was coming out of Afghanistan now that the invaders had been vanquished.

What Ames loved most about the project was the prospect of liaison—going abroad on a regular basis to meet with foreign intelligence officers. "I had never been in liaison before," he said. "I had never sat down as a CIA officer talk-

ing to any other service, never in my career. And all of a sudden, I'd be sitting down, wheeling and dealing with the Russians, the Bulgarians, the Turks, and putting them all together and having a grand time. It was really exhilarating."
Upon his return to headquarters, Ames spent January and February 1992 laying the groundwork for the first of his liaison trips.

He'd be going to Moscow soon.

20

"Don't Worry, Rosario"

Rick Ames might never have told his wife the truth were it not for an accidental discovery that Rosario made in the early summer of 1992.

She was hunting for a dark red leather wallet of Rick's in a second-floor closet in the house on North Randolph Street. It was a small wallet that Rick rarely used, and she needed it that afternoon to fit inside a small purse.

"And so it's sitting on a shelf in this part of the closet and I go and pick it up and I see there's a piece of paper in it," she recalled. It was a note with some cryptic typewritten sentences. She couldn't figure out what it all meant. But one sentence stood out and alarmed Rosario. It referred to "the city where your mother-in-law lives." Another sentence referred to an embassy in that city. Rosario knew that Rick's work had nothing to do with Latin America.

That evening, she confronted her husband. "I saw a mention of my mother in there," she said to him. "What in hell does my mother have to do with your job? You know I don't want her or my family involved in your affairs, the CIA stuff."

At first, he lied. "It's nothing," he told her. "Don't worry." But she did worry. And she continued asking about the meaning of the paper and its oblique reference to Bogotá. He wouldn't be shaken. "When he doesn't want to say anything, he just closes up," Rosario said. But about two weeks later they drove into the District of Columbia on a Saturday night for dinner at Germaine's, a popular restaurant in Northwest Washington that serves a range of Asian cuisines.

The dimly lit restaurant is a favorite of Washington political celebrities and reporters. Germaine Swanson, the hostess and co-owner, is a former Vietnamese journalist working to restore relations between her native country and the United States. On any crowded Saturday night, Germaine's might be feeding both the guests and the hosts of the next morning's public affairs talk shows. The restaurant, on the second floor, is also two blocks down Wisconsin Avenue from the Russian residential compound on Mount Alto.

After the meal started, Rosario asked her questions again. This time, to her surprise, Rick responded. He looked up from one of Germaine's satays and said, "Oh, I'm working for the Soviets."

Though the disclosure would eventually turn Rosario's world upside down, Rick offered it in the most casual of tones. "He said it in the same way a person would say, 'Oh, by the way, I'm selling vacuum cleaners,' " she remembered. He was vague about what exactly it was that he did for Moscow. "He never told me something like 'I am stealing and giving them top secret or highly classified documents,' no, he never said anything like that," she said. He did tell her he was meeting with the Russians and that they were giving him some money in return. She asked him if he was doing it as part of some CIA operation. No, not at all, he replied.

"I thought it was the most absurd thing I had heard in my life," she said. "I mean, what does one do when one's husband announces that he's a spy? Run immediately to the nearest FBI headquarters and turn him in? That's ridiculous."

Rosario Ames knew that the household money at her disposal came from somewhere other than Rick's salary at the Agency. But her husband had already given her a cover story about the source of the income: Robert, his Chicago friend who paid him a handsome fee for helping with his investments. Rosario said she had never been inclined to question Rick in too much detail. She had, after all, married him as a middle-aged man when his financial habits were set. And, she said, a woman with her Latin American heritage did not question her provider.

Even now that he had told her he was receiving money from the Russians, she said, she continued to believe the household funds she was spending extravagantly came from Robert. Rick didn't say that the story about Robert was false, and Rosario said she had never made the connection herself.

More importantly, she had to confront a larger issue: What should she do now that her husband had confessed that he was a traitor? The significance of what he had told her took time to sink in. Rosario said she lived in a state of panic for the next several weeks. "I never made a rational choice from the start," she said. "I guess you could say I chose family over country," she said.

But if Rosario was fearful over Rick's secret life, he brushed her qualms aside. In his notes to his Russian handlers, he reassured them that she was dutifully standing by him. Several weeks after the dinner at Germaine's, he wrote to them, in a misspelled note he stored on his home computer: "My wife has accomodated [*sic*] herself to what I am doing in a very supportive way."

Ames's notes to the Russians from 1992 reflect how badly he was addicted to their money. Though he had been paid close to $2 million over the past seven years, he pleaded for more.

"My most immediate need, as I pointed out in March, is money," he wrote on June 8. "As I have mentioned several times, I do my best to invest a good part of the cash I received, but keep part of it out for ordinary expenses. Now I am faced with the need to cash in investments in order to meet current needs—a very tight and unpleasant situation! I have had to sell a certificate of deposit in Zurich and some stock here to help make up the gap. Therefore, I will need as much cash delivered in Pipe as you think can be accomodated [*sic*]—it seems to me that it could acomodate [*sic*] up to $100,000." "Pipe" was a dead drop—a galvanized steel drainage pipe under a horse trail in Wheaton Regional Park in suburban Maryland.

That summer, the PLAYACTOR and SKYLIGHT teams, on instructions from Paul Redmond, the deputy chief of the CIA's Counterintelligence Center, began digging into Rick Ames's finances. Redmond specifically ordered Dan Payne, the luckless investigator who had started but never finished a cursory look at Ames's financial background back in 1989, to complete the task.

The Agency had had the power all along to seek Ames's financial records from banks and credit card companies but had never used it. The CIA's squeamishness at the prospect of peering into Ames's private affairs was a matter of club rules and manners. Intelligence officers who would not flinch from thumbing the check stubs of a Middle Eastern sheik grew indignant at the thought of scrubbing a colleague's accounts. But the time for traditional courtesies had ended.

Once the requests went out, the results were quick and alarming. The Ameses were charging up to $30,000 a month on their credit cards. The charge records produced other unpleasant surprises, including the first evidence that Ames was traveling overseas without telling the Agency. Ames's bank records produced an even more astonishing find: statements from 1985 onward showed that Ames had deposited $1.5 million into his bank accounts—including hundreds of thousands of dollars in wire transfers from the Crédit Suisse bank in Zurich.

And then two strands of the investigation crossed like high-voltage wires to produce a blinding flash.

The FBI's PLAYACTOR team had always been puzzled about Ames's failure to file the required reports on his meetings with Sergei Chuvakhin back in 1985 and 1986. After seeing the computer records that revealed the FBI's futile request to the CIA for the reports, the investigators started searching to see if the FBI had its own records of Ames's visits to the Soviet Embassy in Washington. The Bureau had always thought it was a little strange for Ames to be courting a potential recruit at the embassy itself. Why meet there, when the target would be forced to explain the meeting to the KGB?

It took months to find the records. But the crucial evidence was sitting in a locked file cabinet in the Washington field office at Buzzard Point. It had been sitting there for years. The FBI's counterintelligence surveillance had indeed recorded each and every one of a dozen unreported visits to the Soviet Embassy.

The PLAYACTOR team turned the files over to the CIA. The CIA's SKYLIGHT team matched them up with Ames's bank deposits. They fit together like two halves of a torn dollar bill. Beginning in October 1985, Ames's checking account had bulged shortly after his undisclosed meetings with Chuvakhin. The implication was staggeringly obvious: he had been taking money sent from Moscow straight to the bank. And the proof had been available to the Agency and the Bureau all along.

By September 1992, the principal SKYLIGHT investigators had reached the inescapable conclusion that Ames was probably a spy. But they did not officially alert the FBI. Vertefeuille reported the findings to Ted Price, the chief of the Counterintelligence Center. Her memo said: "We have not briefed the FBI in any formal manner and do not plan to do so at this time." They would not do so for another three months.

Ames was a happy man when Charlie Emmling, his career-training classmate, bumped into him in the corridors of the CIA that month. He had a ticket to Moscow in his desk.

"I said, 'So, what are you up to?' " Emmling remembered. "He said, 'Oh, I'm working in the Counternarcotics Center now.' I said to myself, 'What the fuck is going on here? Here's the guy who was the counterintelligence chief of the Soviet division on the counternarcotics desk.' He must have seen my expression, because he said, 'No, no, no, it's great. I'm going off to liaise with the Russians and the former republics, get shitfaced with all these guys and have a great time.' "

This was a highly accurate depiction of what Ames did when he took his first overseas trip for a conference he had arranged on his Black Sea Initiative that September. On the trip to Moscow, Ames was accompanied by several colleagues from the counternarcotics team. He had no plans to make contact with the Russian intelligence service in Moscow. Under any circumstances, such a meeting would have been foolhardy. But afterwards no one back at headquarters was happy to hear that Ames had arrived at an informal evening meeting with his Russian counternarcotics counterparts halfway drunk and had then gotten so enthusiastic during the toasts to fraternal cooperation between former enemies that he had made a series of highly inappropriate remarks about the CIA, its operations, and its covert operators, then passed out at the table. No one who witnessed this thought to make a note for the record or to recommend counseling or some form of discipline.

On October 4, 1992, shortly after returning from Moscow, Ames flew to Caracas, Venezuela, to meet his Russian handlers. But he provided little information for his friends. In a note he left in a dead drop prior to the meeting, he complained that his new job at the Counternarcotics Center made it harder for him to find fresh facts about the CIA's covert operations. "My lack of access frustrates me, since I would need to work harder to get what I can to you," Ames wrote. "It was easier to simply hand over cables!"

Still, Ames had new ways to pass his information to the Russians—on computer diskettes that could be used only by entering his password: Kolokol. Ames had started using his WordPerfect software to write his notes to the Soviets back in Rome, printing them out and passing on the paper. In Washington, he had started slipping them the disks themselves. Unfortunately, his Russian associates had only rudimentary computer skills. They were pleased at being able to punch up his messages on a personal computer, but they never communicated electronically.

Not long after his return from Caracas, he signed on to his computer at work and discovered to his great surprise that he had been granted access to a restricted message delivery system that originated in the Directorate of Operations. People within the D.O. could not download information from the message system, which contained extremely sensitive information about ongoing covert operations. But Ames could. His access to secrets, combined with the compactness of the computer disks, put him back into the game in the best way possible. He could tap into some of the CIA's most highly classified circuits, and no one would ever know.

The new year arrived, and the PLAYACTOR and SKY-LIGHT investigators were bogged down trying to write a final report. Then, in late January 1993, the CIA received an intriguing report from a highly placed intelligence source in Moscow. The source, who is still in place and working for the CIA, did not identify a mole by name or provide the Agency with a smoking gun. But what he had to say closely matched the conclusions the investigators were drafting. Still they waited. It had been seven years since the CIA had started looking into the case. Surely another few months would not make a difference.

The ghost of James Jesus Angleton still haunted the CIA. The Agency's counterintelligence officers had been scarred so badly by the memory of his hunt for an imaginary mole that they hung back, reluctant to confront a real one when it stared them in the face.

In February, the mole hunters briefed the new director of Central Intelligence, R. James Woolsey, a Washington lawyer and skilled arms control negotiator who was a newcomer to the Agency. It was a terrible way to start the job. Woolsey was enraged, but he kept the secret to himself.

Finally, on March 15, 1993, the investigators issued their final report.

"We are virtually certain there was a KGB penetration of the CIA who followed closely on the heels of the CIA defector Edward Lee Howard," it said. "This subject probably began to disclose CIA/FBI operations to the KGB by July

1985 if not sooner. The KGB then proceeded to roll up our agents throughout 1985–86."

The subject of the investigation, the report continued, had been assigned to CIA headquarters in 1985 and had been in a position to expose nearly every operation the Agency was running against the Soviet Union—which, in all likelihood, he had in fact done. The subject had worked in the Soviet division or in one of a very few slots on the counterintelligence staff.

Only five people fit that description. Only one fit it perfectly.

21

Nightmover

On May 24, 1993, Les Wiser walked through Bear Bryant's open door up on the eleventh floor of the Bureau's Washington Metropolitan Field Office. He sat down in a red leather chair in front of Bryant's spacious desk. Helicopters shuttling military brass in and out of the city thudded past the window, banking over the bilious waters of the Anacostia River below.

"How would you like to run one of the biggest cases in the Bureau?" Bryant asked.

"Are you kidding?" Wiser said.

Bryant quickly briefed the counterintelligence squad supervisor. Most of the Soviets working for the Agency and the Bureau had been murdered in the mid-1980s. Wiser was to focus on a single target: Aldrich Ames. The target had been spending hundreds of thousands of dollars and was depositing more in the bank. The investigators had checked his story about the money coming from his wife's family in Colombia. It was false. Maybe he was selling intelligence stolen from the Counternarcotics Center to the Colombian cocaine cartels.

Maybe he was smuggling emeralds. Maybe he was the Kremlin's mole inside the CIA.

"It was clear to me he was guilty of something," Wiser said, recalling Bryant's briefing. "But let's see if he's guilty of espionage."

Wiser had been waiting all his life for a case like this. He gave it a sexy code name—"Nightmover"—and began making plans. The FBI had opened a formal criminal investigation of Ames on May 12, almost eight years to the day since he had taken his first $50,000 from the KGB. That meant Wiser could use the government's most intrusive and powerful investigative weapons against Ames: wiretaps on his home, office, and car telephones; concealed microphones in his house; a video monitor trained on his driveway; a full financial analysis of his bank accounts; and around-the-clock surveillance.

"My philosophy was to build an intelligence base about Ames, and learn about him, and learn as much as I could, to begin to understand," Wiser said. "What I know about him is that he is a CIA officer who has been trained in counterintelligence techniques. He has worked overseas. I presume that he is going to be looking for surveillance. And I don't know how good this guy is. Let's look at him for a little bit and see how good he is. And then we'll ratchet it up."

Wiser, the son of a Pittsburgh truck driver, had spent seven years working East German and other foreign counterintelligence cases. Even so, the FBI veterans of the cold war regarded Wiser as a newcomer. That, of course, was one reason Bryant had picked Wiser for the job. Wiser was young, aggressive, and willing to take risks to crack a case. Nevertheless, in the stratified, paramilitary culture of the FBI, he ranked a step below the criminal investigators who hunted down serial killers, corrupt politicians, and crooked financiers. In the FBI, big cases meant big careers. But counterintelligence agents worked in secret and rarely made an arrest. When they scored a direct hit, like recruiting a Russian intelligence officer, they couldn't brag about it, not even to their fellow agents. The work demanded unusual people with peculiar talents.

Wiser began selecting agents for his team and set them to work in a shabby room near Bryant's office, a squad bay that had been used for the investigation of the bombing of Pan Am flight 103. From his intelligence squad, Wiser chose two young agents, Mike Degnan and Julie Johnson. Their main chore was the tedious business of monitoring the wiretaps and bugs in the Ameses' house. To complete the financial profile on Ames, he selected Mike Mitchell, an accountant by training and an expert on legal seizures of ill-gotten gains. Mitchell was in charge of analyzing Ames's finances, searching his house, and cataloguing its contents. John Hozinski had the job of managing the evidence the squad collected. Dell Spry and Mike Anderson were already up to speed on the case from the PLAYACTOR investigation, as was Jim Milburn, the KGB expert. Mike Donner, the SWAT team agent built like a football linebacker, was in charge of the surveillance and would play the role of the tough cop if and when Ames was arrested and interrogated.

Rudy Guerin would play the role of the soft cop, the understanding one who offered cigarettes and conversation. Guerin had almost fifteen years of counterintelligence work under his belt but retained a criminal investigator's outlook on the human condition. He was a professional interrogator, a pale, wiry man skilled at getting inside other people's heads. He had to be prepared to grill Ames on short notice. If Ames caught on to the fact that he was under investigation or if any of a thousand other little things went wrong, the case would close down in a hurry. In that situation, a face-to-face interview would be the best hope, maybe the only hope, of obtaining enough incriminating information to convict him. Guerin needed to learn everything that everybody else knew about the case if he was to be ready when the time came to deal with Ames.

Guerin started with the two-hundred-page chronology of Ames's career, the one assembled by the CIA. It was a bare-bones record of the man's life: the precise times Ames had clocked in and out of the Agency's headquarters every day he had ever worked there, the dates and places and amounts of his credit card charges and bank deposits, the dates and destinations of his personal travel, the sketchy records of his authorized meetings with Russians in the mid-1980s, and a list of his official comings and goings in Ankara, Mexico City, and Rome. A hundred different questions arose in Guerin's mind. He had to put some meat on those bones.

"I've got to try to figure out who this clown is," Guerin said. "I never liked this idea that, hey, he's a lazy, drunken bum. Say what you want, it still takes a certain amount of chutzpah to commit espionage—in a sick way." Ames was a risk taker, that was sure, Guerin said. But once you knew that, you knew nothing. "We don't know what he's giving. We don't know how much he's giving. Are people in danger? What access does Rick have? Who's he talking to? What old buddies of his are telling him about other cases that he shouldn't know about?

"Espionage cases are probably the hardest cases in the Bureau to solve, because a lot of the time, there's no evidence," Guerin said. "The other side has the evidence—that is, documents, verbal information. You might have a cold body, but you don't have anything else. Another problem that you have to overcome in espionage cases is, a lot of times, only one guy knows about it—Rick."

Guerin said the Bureau was terrified of the possibility that they might arrest Ames and then lose the case in court for lack of proof. "We have to develop certain evidence and prove beyond a reasonable doubt that Rick Ames is a spy. Prove it to a jury," he said. And prove it without Ames ever knowing that his every move was being watched.

The electronic monitoring of Ames's telephones started on June 11, approved by a special panel of federal judges who met in secret to review (and invariably grant) requests for wiretaps, electronic eavesdropping, and search warrants in national security cases. The Nightmover squad took turns on the wiretaps, sitting in a tiny cubbyhole hour after hour listening to the drone of the Ameses' everyday existence.

"Oh, the calls were just ludicrous," Guerin said. "Fake lovey-dovey stuff all the time. It's like they're newlyweds, but it's just not real." Working the wiretaps was mind-numbing, but it had to be done. It was a good way to build a feel for the rhythms of Ames's life. And there was always the hope that a snatch of conversation could be used as evidence.

The FBI agents moved cautiously at first, digging into Ames's life like archeologists, using artist's brushes rather than shovels to strip away the layers of his past. They combed CIA and FBI files for additional tidbits of information, piecing together an increasingly intricate mosaic of his work habits, his finances, his friends.

The team took an especially hard look at Ames's two years in Mexico City, thinking maybe that was where it had all begun. They uncovered the fact that Rosario, Rick's drinking buddy Dave Samson, and KGB officer Sergei Shurygin had all served on the board of the diplomatic association in Mexico City. Had Shurygin recruited any of them? Had he been one of Ames's handlers? Ames was still friends with Samson, one of the few real buddies he had ever had at the Agency. Were they in cahoots? Samson had left the Agency under something less than the best of terms and had landed at the University of

California at Berkeley, across the bay from San Francisco. What was his story? The FBI asked him for an interview, but he insisted, as was his right, on immunity from prosecution. Another blind alley. But it had to be followed to the end.

In June, Bryant and Wiser slowly turned up the pressure. First they assembled drivers, pilots, and agents for a concentrated stakeout, believing they had figured out Ames's schedule for filling his dead drops. Then, at the last minute, they pulled back. Instead, they began to deploy the FBI's Special Surveillance Group. The "Super Gs" consisted of dozens of FBI employees, men and women of all ages, races, shapes, and sizes. They were not special agents or criminal investigators. They were the watchers, their eyes and ears attuned to the sophisticated techniques of covert surveillance. They were too valuable for work on routine criminal cases and were used only for high-priority counterintelligence and counterterrorism cases. They were trained in surveillance, long-range photography, and following a subject undetected by car and on foot. In class and on the street, they studied the habits, personnel, and countersurveillance techniques of foreign intelligence services.

"They can follow a fly through an ice storm," Bryant said. "They're slick. And I love 'em."

They gradually wrapped Ames in an invisible web. When Ames left his house in his purring Jaguar, the Super Gs, in eight cars, drove behind him and ahead of him. When he went to the supermarket, the movies, the bank, the shopping mall, or the airport, they were there. It was a tricky job, seeing without being seen. It wasn't like in the movies, where a pair of wisecracking detectives in a car can follow a subject for hours without being spotted.

But Ames was never aware of them, not for a moment. He remained oblivious to the tightening noose.

On the night of June 25, a search team surreptitiously entered Ames's basement office, Room GV06, in the glass-enclosed New Headquarters Building of the CIA. The Counternarcotics Center occupied a large room divided into workstations; Ames had his own private corner office, painted beige with gray trim, with his name on the door.

The search team found stacks of files and papers strewn around the room. In all, there were 144 documents marked "Secret" and 10 stamped "Top Secret" or "Top Secret—Code Word," which designated documents deemed to be extremely sensitive. Some of them had nothing to do with narcotics. There were "Top Secret" papers that revealed how much the CIA knew about key aspects of the Russian military and the Kremlin's spying operations. Interesting, Wiser thought, but not surprising. Ames was a Russia expert, and intelligence officers often kept classified documents on issues unrelated to their current assignments. But spies also sometimes kept copies of documents they had provided to their controllers.

One nugget turned up in the search. It was a copy of a cable Ames had sent to the CIA's Bogotá station, notifying them, as a requisite professional courtesy, that he would be in Bogotá during the first week of October 1992 to visit his mother-in-law, Cecilia, and attend to family business. The investigators already knew from their analysis of Ames's credit card records that he had gone to Caracas that week. So the cable was a lie. After the search, the Bureau checked the records of international airlines and learned that Ames's mother-in-law had been in Virginia that same week in October, on a visit to Rosario and Paul. Then a review of Ames's financial records showed that he had made a dozen trips to the bank in the space of two weeks after his return, depositing a total of $86,700 in all. He had broken the deposits down to sums of less than $10,000 each time to avoid triggering a report to the Treasury Department. Something illegal had happened in Caracas.

As the July Fourth weekend approached, Nightmover was beginning to take shape as a full-fledged criminal investigation. But at FBI headquarters, things were unusually chaotic.

Morale at the agency was in free fall. The FBI's director, William S. Sessions, was struggling to keep his job after a damning Justice Department report on his misuse of FBI aircraft and other official perks. He had lost command in the face of a simmering rebellion by his senior staff, who were torn between their loyalty to the institution and a galloping disdain for Sessions. Sessions was particularly weak on matters concerning espionage. After six years of counterintelligence briefings, Sessions still confused the GRU, the Russian military intelligence agency, with the KGB and its successor, the political espionage service. Nevertheless, Sessions was always eager to help out, and his offers to meet with foreign officials alarmed some of his subordinates, who feared he might inadvertently blurt out a state secret. He had to be treated like a mushroom: kept in the dark. Sessions was briefed on the Ames case, but the information was kept very basic.

The Sessions situation was hardly the only distraction. The intelligence division, which had overall responsibility for espionage and terrorism cases, was still working on the February bombing of the World Trade Center by a group of Islamic militants. And the Bureau was still dealing with the aftermath of its siege of the Branch Davidian religious cult near Waco, Texas. The confrontation had ended horribly in April, with a catastrophic fire and the deaths of more than seventy people after the FBI had launched a tear gas assault on the compound on the authority of Attorney General Janet Reno. The fallout from that fiasco had preoccupied the Bureau and damaged its standing with the public.

Finally, on July 19, after months of tension at the FBI, President Bill Clinton sacked Sessions. He replaced him with a federal judge from New York City named Louis J. Freeh. Only forty-three years old, Freeh had been a choirboy, an Eagle Scout, an FBI agent, and a federal prosecutor who handled major organized crime and drug-smuggling cases, rising from a working-class New Jersey family to the federal bench. His appointment breathed life into the demoralized, depleted Bureau. But he would not take over until September, and the FBI bided its time until the new chief arrived.

In July, Nightmover moved into a phase of laying traps.

On July 20, FBI officials invited Ames to a mid-morning meeting—a contrived counternarcotics briefing—at the Hoover building. As anticipated, he arrived in his red Jaguar, parking it in the driveway that cuts through the building at street level. When he headed upstairs, a team of technical services agents, who had made themselves a set of duplicate keys, dashed to the car, installing a tiny but powerful homing beacon that beeped out the location of the vehicle. It proved invaluable.

Over the next four weeks, the agents stepped up their physical surveillance of Ames. They carefully watched his mail, writing down the names and return addresses of the senders, and they dug up more financial information from his banks and his credit card companies. They sifted, analyzed, and collated more details of his life in Mexico City and at CIA headquarters.

In late August, Ames, Rosario, and their son took a vacation to Miami Beach. The FBI went with them, thinking that Ames might hop a plane for Bogotá or Caracas for a quick meeting with the Russians. The Ameses stayed in the Doral Hotel, the agents at the nearby Fontainebleau. The agents eavesdropped on the Ameses' conversations in their room, rolling their eyes as Rosario complained about the service. They followed their target at a distance. They watched the family on the beach. They waited at the pool. Nothing happened.

The FBI had the beginnings of a solid circumstantial case. But it still had no proof that Rick Ames was a spy. Had he broken off contact with his handlers? Was he acting alone or in concert with someone else? What was Rosario's role in the whole affair? What Wiser wanted most of all was to watch Ames meeting with a Russian or unloading a dead drop stuffed with cash. "We wanted to understand how he was operating in his totality," Wiser said, "and we thought the best way to do that was to catch him in operational activity."

Thursday, September 9, 1993, was the perfect day to catch him. And the FBI missed him—twice.

The agents had a feeling from cryptic comments they had picked up on the wiretaps that Ames was getting ready to deliver a package of documents to the Russians before taking Paul to his first day of kindergarten that morning. But by the time the surveillance teams assembled on the side streets and cul-de-sacs surrounding the house on North Randolph Street at 6:30 A.M., Ames had already left his house and returned.

They could reconstruct the precise times because they had a videotape from a concealed closed-circuit television camera that was keeping watch on the Ames residence from a telephone pole across the street. It showed that Ames had pulled out of his driveway at 6:03 A.M. and returned at 6:23 A.M. "That was really unusual, because Ames was not really a particularly industrious guy," Bear Bryant said. "He's lazy as hell. And for him to move out at 6:03 in the morning meant something was up."

Unseen by his pursuers, Ames had taken the Jaguar into Washington, driving to Garfield Terrace in a residential neighborhood in upper Northwest. There he had left a chalk mark on a mailbox, signifying to the Russians that they would find a package that evening at a dead drop two miles away, on a ledge under a pedestrian bridge off Beach Drive in Rock Creek Park. But the FBI had no idea what Ames had been doing, where the signal site and the dead drop were, or how the man communicated with his contacts. They needed to catch him in the act.

"That afternoon, we set up out at the Agency," Bryant said. No matter how good the Super Gs might be, spying on a CIA officer at the Agency's headquarters was a headache. They could not loiter around the lobby of the CIA or hang out in the parking lot. Access to the Agency was tightly controlled in normal times, and these times were not normal. Nine months earlier, a man named Mir Amal Kansi had walked calmly alongside the morning rush-hour traffic stuck at the Agency's entrance, firing bursts from a semiautomatic rifle and killing two CIA men, a middle-aged doctor and a young officer. Kansi had fled to his native Pakistan and disappeared into Afghanistan. Jittery CIA security guards now patrolled the public roadway outside the Agency's main gates. The guards had rousted the Super Gs from the roadside once before, forcing them to pull back the perimeter of their surveillance. Since the security officers could not be trusted with the information that there was an FBI stakeout under way, the whole arrangement put the Bureau's nerves on edge.

Around three P.M., the FBI listened in as Ames telephoned Rosario at home, saying he was leaving work early. For an hour, the Super Gs waited nervously in their command post, an unmarked trailer parked at an Exxon station a quarter mile down Route 123 from the CIA's entrance. They told the curious gas station attendant that they were conducting a security exercise.

The beacon on the bug underneath Ames's Jaguar told them that their man was approaching. As the Jag went by the Super Gs' stakeout, its rear directional signal indicated Ames was turning onto the George Washington Parkway, a four-lane highway paralleling the banks of the Potomac River, headed for the capital. "And the guy gets out on the G. W. Parkway and just takes off like a bat out of hell," Bryant said. "And we lose him."

For the second time that day, Ames had slipped under the radar. The directors of both the CIA and the FBI knew that Ames was under surveillance that day. When they heard that Ames had gotten away, they started "asking a lot of very painful questions," Bryant said.

The surveillance detail responsible for staking out Ames's house was waiting for him when he returned at 5:50 P.M. The listeners picked up the Ameses' plans to attend a parents' night at Paul's private school in Alexandria, Virginia, that evening. The watchers tracked the Jaguar as it pulled into the school's parking lot. They sat and waited. The Ameses and their son left the parents' meeting at about eight P.M. and got into their car. They did not go home. They crossed the Potomac River into the District of Columbia, tracked by a light aircraft flying slow and low, outfitted with a sophisticated video camera trained on the Jaguar.

The Jaguar rolled through the quiet, darkened streets of the upper Northwest, past single-family brick colonial houses, home to the city's lawyers, politicians, and diplomats. Ames neared the intersection of Garfield Street and Garfield Terrace. He slowed dramatically at the intersection and turned into Garfield Terrace. He backed up in a driveway, turned around, and headed back home to North Randolph Street in Arlington.

"We figured, 'There's something at that intersection,' "
Wiser remembered. Agents swarmed over the corner, carefully inspecting trees, curbs, a fire hydrant, telephone poles,
and the mailbox for signs. Wiser guessed correctly that Ames
was looking for a signal confirming that the Russians had
picked up his package. But where was the evidence? What
was Ames doing?

"We're looking all over the place," Wiser said. "We're
looking for something." They found nothing. There was
nothing to find.

The FBI still did not understand the simple tradecraft the
KGB had taught Ames. Had they trailed the early-rising CIA
man that morning, they would have seen him place a chalk
mark on the mailbox at the intersection. They would have
staked out the corner. And they would have seen an officer
from the Russian intelligence service come by in the early
evening and erase the chalk mark, confirming that the package in the dead drop had been picked up.

"We're looking for something, when he looked for nothing," Wiser said months later, when he finally understood.
"We saw nothing and didn't know what it meant. He saw
nothing and knew what it meant."

All in all, a terrible day for the FBI. That night, Wiser experienced the depths of despair. He managed to salvage a hopeful
thought out of the wreckage of the day. Yes, they had blown
the coverage. Yes, there would be hell to pay for it. But he now
was convinced of one thing: Ames was acting like a spy.

22

The Right Guy

The next day, Friday, September 10, 1993, everybody on the Nightmover team was a little tense. Failure was bad for the spirit. Wiser tried to be upbeat. From now on, he told his squad, there would be more agents to work the case, around-the-clock surveillance on Ames, fake CIA employee badges for the Super Gs so they could follow Ames into the Agency's parking lot and tail him after he left. Despite the screwups, they had remained undetected. They had the target in their crosshairs. They would live to fight another day.

This time, Wiser would pick the time and place.

He wanted to search Ames's trash, and sift it for evidence. The idea did not please Bear Bryant, who was smarting from being chewed out by his new boss, Louis Freeh, and thought the risk of detection outweighed the potential return. Bryant was less than enthusiastic when Wiser requested permission to search Rick Ames's garbage as soon as possible.

Trash covers were disgusting. Usually, junior agents were delegated to the task. Wiser had done his share, dumping malodorous bags of dripping refuse onto his desk, pulling out a can of insect spray to kill the bugs as they squirmed to the edge of his desk—but they were often very useful. Streetwise criminals, who would never utter a secret over a telephone, would unthinkingly toss incriminating evidence into the garbage. More important, under the law, Wiser did not have to obtain any court approval to sift a suspect's trash. It was there for the taking. And the Super Gs had it down to a science.

But sending agents in at midnight to steal Ames's trash posed obvious risks, especially in an affluent suburb where strangers were noticed. A lot of risks were already being taken. There was an active Neighborhood Watch program on North Randolph Street, and some of Ames's neighbors had occasionally called the local police to report the presence of strangers. When the Super Gs had used a nearby church as a staging base, the congregants had complained to the local police. A retired naval officer had noticed the frequent presence of the low-flying plane and queried the cops. When the cops had called the FBI, suspecting that someone had stumbled on to a surveillance in progress, Bryant had taken the call and offered a vague cover story to explain the flights. Then there was the problem of Ames's drinking: he often woke up late at night, especially when he'd had a few nightcaps before bed and the drink wore off before dawn.

But the coming week offered Wiser an opportunity that might not be repeated soon. Ames was leaving the country on Monday, going to Ankara for a week-long international conference on drugs. Wiser went to Bryant for permission, but the chief was dead set against it. He said: "Les, I don't think that's a very good idea. If we get burned on this thing, we can't ride too much heat." And he remembers Wiser replying "Okay, boss."

Wiser recalled the conversation a little differently. "He just said, 'No, you'll get caught.' And I said, 'No, no, we won't. You've got to trust me.' " Then yet another problem arose. A just-published book about the FBI had suggested that the Bureau had recently obtained a new Soviet source, a KGB officer who was helping unravel old counterintelligence cases. Ames had become nervous about this and had started pumping a colleague of his for information while they shared a cigarette break out in the alcove at CIA headquarters. The colleague happened to be an FBI agent, detailed to the CIA's Counterintelligence Center, who was well aware that Ames was under investigation. He had reported the conversation back to the Nightmover team. "So there was a lot of concern about that from our headquarters and Bear," Wiser said. "And of course, he already doesn't want to do the trash cover, so he says, 'This guy's antennae are going to be up. . . . Stop the trash cover.' "

On September 13, Ames flew to Ankara for the international conference on drugs. His supervisor at the CIA's Counternarcotics Center was with him. The conference had originally been scheduled for Moscow, but another huge political crisis was brewing in Russia—a few weeks later, President Boris Yeltsin ordered tanks to shell the Russian parliament to quell an uprising—and at the last minute the gathering was moved to the Turkish capital. There was the inevitable confusion over hotel reservations, and the U.S. government delegation had to move to new lodgings on the evening of the fifteenth.

Ames's CIA supervisor was waiting in the lobby, where the luggage belonging to the U.S. delegation was piled up, awaiting transportation to the new hotel. He watched with alarm as a hotel employee casually lifted a laptop computer off the stack of suitcases and started walking away. He confronted the man, took back the laptop, and noted with chagrin that it had Ames's name tag on it. It was another instance of his casual rule breaking, a blatant breach of security practices, bringing his own computer abroad. Ames was nowhere in sight, so his supervisor kept the laptop as the bags were transferred to the new hotel. Later that evening, he rang up Ames in his new room, and Ames sounded irritated at the interruption. There were voices in the background. His boss said he had the computer. Ames's tone changed immediately. Gee, thanks a lot, he said, I'll be by to pick it up in an hour or so. By now deeply suspicious, the supervisor asked if there were any games on the computer that he could play to while away the time. He wanted to see what Ames had with him. Go ahead, help yourself, Ames said. The boss logged on and hit the directory.

"I was overwhelmed at the incredible amount of classified info that Ames brought to the conference," he told the FBI after returning to the United States. File after file of copied classified cables and memos filled the laptop's hard drive. It was an extraordinary violation of the rules—and an incredibly stupid risk. Ames's boss had also seen two files in the computer's directory that he did not pull up. They intrigued the FBI deeply. One was labeled "$." The other was "Vlad."

That same night, six thousand miles from Ankara, a black van with an open side door prowled slowly and silently past the darkened homes on North Randolph Street. Each house had a trash can placed at the end of its driveway.

Wiser had decided to go ahead with the trash cover, despite Bryant's injunction. Now that Ames was in Ankara, the time was ripe to steal his trash. He had an explanation planned for when Bryant asked—as he inevitably would—why he had disobeyed his command to stop the cover. Wiser's shaky defense was that he had interpreted Bryant's instruction less as a cease-and-desist order and more as a temporary suspension, pending developments.

The van slowed to a stop. A team of agents and Super Gs was inside, dressed in blue jeans, sweatshirts, and tennis shoes. They bounced out of the van and switched the Ameses' trash can with an exact replica they had brought along. In seconds they were gone. When they had finished their search, they would return to the house and switch the cans back again.

The squad sorted through the household debris. As they rooted deeper in the rubbish, Dell Spry saw tiny fragments of unlined yellow paper—a Post-it note, torn up and tossed away. It took a while to piece it together, and there were a couple of words missing. But before dawn, the team had it figured out:

> I am ready to meet at B on 1 Oct.
> I cannot read North 13–19 Sept.
> If you will meet at B on 1 Oct. Pls signal North
> w . . . of 20 Sept. to confi . . .
> No message at Pipe
> If you cannot mee . . . 1 Oct.
> signal North after 27 Sept. with message at Pipe.

The team phoned Wiser at home before dawn. It was after six by the time he made it into the office. Mike Anderson of the Nightmover squad was there with a blown-up photograph of the note; the original had been sent out for handwriting analysis. Wiser took a long, satisfied look at the photo.

"If there was a reservoir of doubt that existed before—which there was, this little bit of doubt about what was really going on here—it was gone," Wiser said. "We knew now. We had the right guy, for sure. I'm convinced we've got the right guy. I'm convinced that he's active, he's an agent, and I know we're going to get him."

Bryant came into work at about 6:45 A.M. He saw Wiser, glowing with undisguised glee, standing outside his office. "I thought, holy God, this is unusual," Bryant said. "Wiser looked like the Hallowe'en pumpkin. I mean, he was so happy it was unbelievable. And that's when he came up with that note. In twenty-seven years in the FBI, that's probably my favorite document. . . . We knew we had the guy. It was just a matter of time."

And what of Wiser's decision to disobey him and delve into the garbage?

"That," said Bear Bryant, "is the finest piece of insubordination I've ever seen."

The note was pure gold. Nightmover did not have a very difficult task in assaying it. It was a rejected draft of a message from Ames to his handlers. "North" and "Pipe" were obvious references to signal sites or dead drops. Then, on September 19, the day after Ames returned from Ankara, they listened as he picked up his telephone and made a plane reservation to travel to Bogotá ten days later. "Ready to meet in B on 1 Oct." was self-evident: Ames had a date with his handlers in Colombia.

Wiser immediately spun a bigger, finer net of electronic and human surveillance. The Bureau now had a circumstantial case, but that was nowhere good enough. Now they needed to catch Ames in a face-to-face meeting with the Russians or take a picture or videotape of him placing documents at a dead drop. Wiser decided to lead a team of twelve FBI agents down to South America.

"The good news is, we have a leg up," Guerin said. "The bad news is, he's going to Bogotá, Colombia. So now we got another logistic problem here." Should they notify the U.S.

ambassador in Bogotá? No. The CIA station chief? Yes. The Colombian government? A tough call. After years of trying to work together against cocaine traffickers, mutual distrust between the Colombians and U.S. law enforcement agencies ran deep. The FBI did not want to alert the Colombian government to its presence, but under diplomatic protocols, they had no choice if they wanted to mount an aggressive surveillance operation that might end with an arrest of Ames.

On the other hand, "this was such a special case that we couldn't make the normal notifications," Wiser said. They compromised. They would go down to Bogotá without guns, without diplomatic immunity. They would not mount an aggressive surveillance operation. They would not even tail Ames. They would go to well-trafficked spots near the Russian Embassy—a popular shopping mall and restaurants that the Russians might use as a rendezvous. They would look like tourists with video cameras. They would wait and watch and learn.

On Wednesday, September 29, they staked out the international airport in Bogotá, awaiting Ames's arrival and looking out for any stray Russian intelligence officers who might show up. Then the agents monitoring the wiretaps on the house on North Randolph heard Rosario pick up the telephone. It was her husband. And it was a local call.

"There's news. No travel," he said. He asked her to call her mother in Bogotá to let her know he wasn't coming.

"And does that mean you retrieve something?" Rosario asked.

"Yeah," he said.

Ames was about to go to a dead drop to retrieve a note from Moscow. But where? Tailing Ames directly to the site would require very tight surveillance. That was not the smartest move. "It's not just him that might discover the surveillance," Wiser said. "We had to be concerned about the Russians. They have ways of figuring out what we're doing." It was a delicate balance between wanting the evidence and fearing detection. Sometimes the Nightmover team made the wrong decision. The team returned from Bogotá; the Super Gs dropped their physical surveillance on Saturday, October 2, and waited with their wiretaps for Ames to make the next move.

Ames left the house in his Jaguar at dawn on Sunday, October 3. An hour later, he called home on his cellular phone.

"All is well," he told his wife.

"Financially, too?" she asked.

"Wait till I get there," he snapped.

Wiser could not wait when he heard the listeners' transcripts of the Ames's telephone calls from the weekend. The Ameses were leaving town next Friday for a wedding in Pensacola, Florida. Wiser began planning a surreptitious entry— a black bag job, a search without a judicially approved search warrant—for the coming weekend.

First he ordered another trash cover for Wednesday night, October 6. Again the Super Gs rolled in in their silent black van. They unearthed another find, a printer ribbon from Ames's home computer. But the Nightmover team was too busy to read it; that would have to wait until after the clandestine operation set for Saturday morning, October 9, 1993, at one A.M. The team had been dying for a chance to break into Rick Ames's house. They had been drafting elaborately detailed plans ever since May. The Super Gs canvassed the block, watching the houses to see who might be awake late at night, recording when the neighbors went to bed. They found a real estate brochure with a floor plan of the Ames house. They even found the same kind of house nearby and prevailed on the owner, who turned out to be a retired FBI agent, to allow them to inspect it.

Nothing could be left to chance. If something went wrong, if they were spotted or caught, headquarters would be looking for someone's scalp, most likely Wiser's.

A warrantless search was a highly unusual procedure. Back in the 1960s, when J. Edgar Hoover's FBI had run COINTELPRO operations against the civil rights movement and antiwar protesters, such searches had been far more common and far less controlled. Nowadays, they required the approval of the attorney general of the United States. "That's not given lightly—and thank God it's not given lightly," Rudy Guerin said. "I don't think any of us would want anyone going in our house and putting a damn microphone in."

Three members of the Nightmover squad were assigned to the main search team. Tom Murray was the computer wizard; he would download whatever he could from Ames's files. Mike Mitchell and Rudy Guerin would conduct the search, gathering evidence, photographing it, then carefully replacing it. A technical team would plant tiny bugs throughout the house, and FBI agents from the Bureau's training academy in Quantico, Virginia, would pick the locks to let them all inside.

They assembled at the Washington field office on Friday evening. Wiser stayed behind and waited as the break-in team drove out to Virginia. It took them about forty-five minutes to handle the entry; the locks were tricky. Luckily, there was no security system.

"That's Rick," Guerin said sardonically. "He's got a five-hundred-forty-thousand-dollar house and he's making about three million in cash, but he won't spend two hundred bucks to put an ADT alarm system in."

The Nightmover crew put a big black drop cloth over the picture window in the living room and got to work. The technical surveillance team started placing its electronic bugs throughout the house, including the bedroom, the kitchen, and the living room. Tom Murray calmly attacked the computer in Ames's study, pulling files from the hard drive and copying floppy disks.

Though Guerin had studied the floor plan until he thought he knew the house by heart, he kept bumping into furniture in places where he didn't expect to find it. He tiptoed carefully, scanning the dark rooms with a penlight. The place was full of paintings and picture books and coffee tables with ceramic ashtrays and silver cigarette boxes and little purple glass fish—rich people's knickknacks. He was wary of disturbing anything.

"We don't really know Rick that well," Guerin said. "Some people are very meticulous. They'll come in and say, 'Oh, my God. Someone was here!' But as soon as I opened up his top dresser drawer, I can see Rick is not one of these Type A personalities. It was a mess. I mean, shit was all over the place."

Jammed in with the stale socks and used handkerchiefs was a crumpled note written on a classified advertising form clipped from the *Washington Times*. It said, "Are ready to meet at a city well known to you on 1 Nov. Alt dates are 2, 7, 8 Nov. If it does for you put Smile before the 17th of October. Best Regards." Guerin knew immediately that it was a message from the Russians rescheduling the canceled trip to Bogotá, the one that had been set for October 1. "Smile" sounded like a signal site. The note was devastating evidence.

Guerin and Mitchell photographed the clipping with a document camera—a suitcase with a pop-up lens that had an automatic focus. They set up the camera in a downstairs bathroom, one without windows, so the flash could not be seen outside the house. Guerin replaced the note exactly where he had found it and walked into Rick's closet. The smell of tobacco on the man's clothes nearly knocked him over as he felt through the pockets of the suits. All manner of litter was in them. One piece of paper looked interesting. It was a note from 1991—Rick had saved it for nearly two years, as if it were a ticket stub from the World Series—with a telephone number, the initials A.B., and instructions to call the number, hang up, and call again. The number turned out to be the Russian residential compound in Vienna. A.B. was Aleksandr Belinkov of the KGB.

By 4:30 A.M., it was time to wrap things up. They managed to make their way out of the house with only one hitch: Mitchell overwound the document camera and broke the delicate tool. They left North Randolph Street and sent an all clear to Buzzard Point. Wiser, exhilarated and exhausted, went home to bed.

On Sunday morning, October 10, Murray telephoned Wiser from the field office. "I've got some stuff I think you'll be interested in," he said calmly.

Ames's computer held some of the most incriminating documents ever unearthed in an espionage investigation. They detailed his secret relationship with the Russian intelligence services with remarkable precision. One of the files contained a copy of Ames's note to the Russians dated June 8, 1992, saying that his "most immediate need . . . is money" and asking for $100,000 in cash to be delivered to the dead drop in a Maryland park that was code-named "Pipe." Another logged and dated his payoffs. For example, he had made a record of receiving $150,000 on October 8, 1992—one day after he had returned from the unauthorized trip to Caracas.

He had even installed accounting software that helped the FBI reconstruct his financial relationship with the Russians.

Ames had also recorded the dead drops and signal sites he used. "Smile" was a mail box at Thirty-seventh and R streets in Northwest Washington. A chalk mark on Smile corresponded to a dead drop named "Bridge," a pedestrian bridge off Massachusetts Avenue near Little Falls Parkway, just over the District line in suburban Maryland. The signal site the Russians used to alert Ames was on Military Road, conveniently located along the route he took to CIA headquarters each morning. The signal sites Ames used when he wanted to send a message were all near the Russian compound in the capital, the dead drops closer to Ames's home.

The Nightmover team was amazed at how careless Ames was, keeping this kind of material at his home. It broke every rule of tradecraft. And the huge sums of money confirmed that Ames was not only a spy but an agent of great significance to the Kremlin.

The team was still sifting through the bounty from the search when Wiser and two other Nightmover members got around to looking at the discarded printer ribbon that had turned up in the latest trash cover. Reading it was simpler than might be imagined. They simply rolled it off its cartridge and onto a couple of large take-up reels from an old-fashioned tape recorder. They stuck a pencil into the center of each reel, unspooled the ribbon, and read the letters from a mirror held underneath. Wiser remembered laughing over the scene. "You know," he told his fellow agents, "In the movie"—of course, there would be a movie—"they're going to send this over to the lab and they're going to have this big computer and it will spit it out and give us the answer. It's actually pretty funny that we're sitting here doing this."

It took a few days, but the ribbon revealed two letters that Ames had written fourteen months earlier. Ames must have been drunk when he typed them, there were so many spelling mistakes. The first confirmed that Ames had been on a clandestine mission when he went to Caracas in October 1992. One paragraph in particular stood out:

> Besides getting cash in Carascus (I have mentuoned how little I like this method, though it is acceptable), I still hope that you will have decided on some safer, paper transfer of some sort of a large amount.
> Until we meet in Caracas. . . . K

"K" was a little baffling. The Bureau figured it must have been Rick's code name with the Russians. Still, the first letter was a solid piece of evidence. The second letter, however, was the clincher. It began:

> You have probably heard a bit about me by this time from your (and now my) colleagues in the M.B.R.F. . . .

The MBRF was the Russian Federal Ministry for Security, the successor to the KGB's counterintelligence service. Ames was corresponding with the boys in Dzerzhinsky Square.

The letter discussed CIA operations, CIA officers, and the trip Ames had taken to Moscow for a narcotics conference in 1992. It ended with Ames saying that Rosario had adjusted nicely and was very understanding of his work.

In the month since the first successful trash cover, Nightmover had picked Ames clean. They had everything they needed to make a case—except direct evidence of Ames meeting with the Russians.

The note that Guerin had found in Ames's dresser drawer told Ames to signal the Russians at Smile, the mailbox at Thirty-seventh and R, if he was coming down to Bogotá in November. On Tuesday, October 12, the new bugs in the Ames household recorded Rick telling his wife that he had to leave early for work the next morning in order to "put a signal down . . . confirming that I am coming." Rosario bristled.

"Why didn't you do it today, for God's sake?"

"I should have, except it was raining like crazy."

"Well, honey," she replied, "I hope you didn't screw up."

He did not, for once. The FBI's cameras saw Ames leave his house at 6:22 A.M. the next day and return at 6:44 A.M. Fifteen minutes later, the Super Gs found his freshly scrawled chalk mark on the mailbox at Thirty-seventh and R. The Bogotá trip was on.

Rosario fretted that Rick might lose his luggage—and the cash he would receive from the Russians—while returning from South America. On October 25, five days before his departure, the agents overheard her telling him to use a carry-on and prodding him to be more careful. "You are going to have to be a little more imaginative," she said. "You always have this envelope with this big hunk. I mean, really."

Rudy Guerin went down to Miami to watch Ames changing planes on October 30. "We just needed to cover all the bases and make sure nobody met Rick in the Miami airport," he said. There was a chance that the Russians could meet him in a bar, pick up a suitcase crammed with CIA documents, and send him off to Bogotá, where he would receive some cash and some cosseting—a little eating, drinking, and ego stroking. Guerin was all set to watch Ames operate. "But—typical Rick—he came in, he just went right to the bar and started throwing down some booze. He just smokes nonstop, watching television and drinking." Guerin saw him board the flight for Bogotá and then telephoned the Washington field office to say their man was on his way, carrying a laptop computer case and a bellyful of vodka.

Rick phoned home from a hotel in Bogotá that night. Just as Rosario had feared, his garment bag had been temporarily lost by the airline.

"You didn't have anything that shouldn't have been in that bag?"

"No, honey," he said. He had it with him, in his computer case. He reminded her, elliptically, to lie to his bosses if they called looking for him. "You tell them I went up to Annapolis. You don't have to explain why." He had not told anyone at the CIA where he was going.

Wiser and the contingent from the Nightmover team down in Bogotá had a good idea where Rick was going. After their dry run a month earlier, they had figured, on the basis of an educated guess, that Ames might rendezvous with the Russians at the downtown Unicentro shopping mall. They were right.

It was pouring rain in Bogotá on the evening of November 1 when Yolanda Larson spotted Ames. He was wandering aimlessly through a bowling alley in the shopping mall, dripping wet, with a big bulge under his trench coat. It was the computer case, though the agents did not know what Ames had inside it. Larson checked her watch. Six forty-five. Under the rules of engagement, she could not trail Ames, only watch him from a fixed position. She did manage to take a few pictures as he strolled about the mall. Around seven o'clock, he wandered off. The FBI was a bit mystified. Was Ames dry-cleaning himself, trying to evade a surveillance? Had he handed something off to a Russian contact? Had he gone off to meet his handlers?

Later that evening, the telephone rang at the house on North Randolph Street. Rick was calling from his mother-in-law's. Rosario was confused, then angry. She knew the meetings with the Russians lasted late into the night and suspected something was wrong.

"Did you really meet?" she asked him. He assured her he had. The questions continued. "You swear to me that nothing went wrong? You're sure? You wouldn't lie to me, would you?"

He would. Ames had missed his appointment, arriving at the Unicentro mall forty-five minutes late. Typical Rick. He finally did meet with the Russians, but only after blowing another date and so thoroughly confusing the FBI's surveillance team with his ineptitude that they failed to see him strolling into the Russian Embassy the next afternoon. He swapped a sheaf of CIA documents in his computer carrying bag for $50,000 and a promise of $190,000 to be delivered in dead drops in the coming year.

On the evening of November 3, Wiser sat in Bogotá, planning his next move. Was it time to arrest Ames? "I had to decide," he said. "Had we achieved all our counterintelligence objectives? Should we pick him up on the way in?"

Wiser wanted an airtight case. He had learned a great deal about Ames's relationship with the Russians. But if he moved in to arrest Ames now, he might find only money, and he could probably obtain all the financial information he needed from the Ameses' banks. It was possible that the Russians had given Ames a shopping list in Bogotá. If he was patient, he might be able to catch Ames filling the Russians' orders, stashing stolen secrets in a dead drop.

"So we waited," Wiser said. "Then in January, we waited. And then in February, we waited." In December, they hoped Ames would get a traditional year-end bonus from the Russians. In January, they expected him to make a drop. In February, they thought he would receive a payment. They kept their twenty-four-hour, seven-day surveillance on Ames. Nothing happened.

The Super Gs were getting nervous. They saw a Russian intelligence officer—they knew him by his diplomatic license plate—driving through their surveillance zone four times in six days. Had they been spotted? It turned out the man had moved and was taking a new route to work. Then they saw a Russian electronic eavesdropping expert in the area. Were their encrypted telecommunications with Buzzard Point being intercepted?

The listeners grew weary of the domestic discord at the Ameses, the phony endearments and the pained silences of a bad marriage. Guerin remembered listening to Rosario whining in the upstairs bedroom on Sunday mornings after Rick brought her breakfast in bed, complaining that her eggs were hard and her toast was cold and ordering young Paul from the room when he spilled his food on the carpet.

On the basis of the intercepted telephone conversations in which Rosario worried about the money Ames was being paid and urged him to be more careful with his tradecraft, Wiser and Mark Hulkower, the federal prosecutor in the case, decided she should be charged with aiding Rick's espionage. Louis Freeh strongly endorsed the idea on evidentiary and strategic grounds, arguing that she would provide the government with powerful leverage against her husband. If Ames understood that he could win leniency for her by helping the FBI and CIA compile a detailed history of his spying, he might well discover he had a strong motive to cooperate.

At the CIA, Ames was becoming restless. He needed to travel to Ankara and Moscow to continue his work on the Black Sea Initiative, the counternarcotics program he had set up. The FBI and the CIA worked hard to come up with excuses for delaying the trip. They concocted a series of briefings for Ames to give inside and outside the Agency, calling on him to share his expertise on the flow of heroin across the southern tier of the old Soviet republics with a widening circle of people. But the number of people inside the Bureau and the Agency who knew about the investigation was also widening with the passage of time. How long could the investigation be kept secret? How long until someone slipped up and Ames discovered that his every move was under surveillance? How long before Ames grew suspicious of the superiors who kept postponing his travel requests? He was set to travel to Ankara, then Bucharest, then Moscow, starting on February 22. The trip had been put off twice. The Agency would have to let him go this time.

Let him go to Moscow? Were they kidding?

It was time to move. Wiser set the arrest for February 21—Presidents' Day, a federal holiday. He set the trap in coordination with the CIA by having Ames's boss call him in to work to see some really important snippet of intelligence. He wanted Ames out of the house for two reasons. He wanted to arrest Rick and Rosario separately—divide and conquer. And he didn't want to handcuff Ames in front of his son, Paul.

The arrest went perfectly, a textbook street stop. Donner placed Ames in the backseat of the government car. Guerin slid in next to him.

He'd been rehearsing his speech for nine months.

"Rick," Guerin said, "let me explain the situation to you. You are under arrest for espionage."

"This is unbelievable," Ames said. He was hyperventilating.

"It's believable," Guerin said. "And you better believe it." He explained calmly that they were headed to the FBI's office in Tyson's Corner, Virginia, where they would have a chance to talk. Then he stuck the knife in a little: "Your wife, Rosario, has also been placed under arrest," he said. "What do you think her reaction will be?"

Ames looked blank. "She'll be terrified," he said. He never asked what was to become of his son.

The voice of Mike Mitchell, the head of the search team, came in over the car's squawk box: "We have subject number two in custody, and we have the residence secured." When Ames heard that, he dropped his head nearly to his knees and cursed bitterly.

"And then"—Guerin loved telling this part of the story— "it dawned on me: there must be something good in the residence."

There was. In a box in Ames's closet, the FBI found the nine-page letter from the KGB that he had received in Rome and kept for nearly five years. They found documents that revealed how Ames had burned the Czech spy MOTOR-BOAT in 1989. They found the financial report from the Russians, the one that said "All in all you have been appropriated $2,705,000," described the dacha by the beautiful river in the woods, and ended, "Good luck." It was, in effect, a W-2 form from KGB headquarters. In the computer were electronic copies of classified documents describing double-agent cases and CIA operations, stolen by Ames in the five months since Tom Murray had cleaned out the hard drive. In his red Jaguar, among the cassette tapes of Duke Ellington and Vivaldi, was a piece of white chalk, marred at one end by a bit of blue paint.

And over in Room GV06, Ames's office at the CIA's Counternarcotics Center, amid reams of top secret paper that had nothing to do with drugs, the Bureau found a bit of classified history. It was an in-house essay entitled "What Angleton Thought."

Rick and Rosario were taken separately from the garage up the elevator to the FBI's satellite offices in Tyson's Corner. Yolanda Larson, the pregnant FBI agent, handled Rosario's interview along with John Hozinski. Rosario at first stuck to the story that their money had come from Rick's investments with his wealthy friend, Robert from Chicago. Her interrogators told her she was lying. And within three hours, she began to talk.

Down the hall, Guerin sat down with Ames in a room that was a stage set. Half-drained cups of cold coffee and empty Domino's Pizza boxes littered the office. They were props— no one in Nightmover ever used the office. The FBI's crime lab had concocted charts of Ames's career, with all his assignments in neat rows, under a big, official-looking sign that said AMES: ESPIONAGE. Surveillance photographs from the investigation and a blown-up shot of a chalk mark on the mailbox at Thirty-seventh and R streets were hung on the walls and perched on easels. These trappings "made it look like this is where it happened, this is where we investigated his case," Guerin said. "And made it look like this has been quite an undertaking."

Ames squinted at the pictures and charts papering the room as he heard Guerin saying: "Rick. We know what you've been doing. We know what you've been doing with it. We know about the money. What we really don't know is why." Guerin slid a form advising Ames of his rights across the table and asked him if he wanted to waive them and talk. Ames slid the paper right back at him.

"Go ahead," he said. "You can ask me questions. I just won't answer them." The interview was over. Guerin stared at Ames, watching his reactions. The shock was wearing off. The cockiness, the arrogance, was returning. "He's back into Rick Ames," Guerin remembered thinking.

Months later, Ames thought about the arrest and the questions and the photos on the wall and closed his eyes at the memory of his thoughts that day. "I didn't have any flashbacks," he said. "I had flash-forwards of what it was going to be like from then on."

Survivors

A few hours after Ames was paraded in chains before the television cameras on his way to see the federal magistrate in Alexandria on February 22, 1994, Oleg Gordievsky was walking past the television set in his hotel room in Warsaw. It was late in the evening in Poland, and Gordievsky had the television tuned to CNN.

He half-heard a stunning piece of news—a CIA officer had been arrested as a spy for the Russians. Gordievsky was so taken aback that he sat down on the end of the bed and waited, nearly motionless, for fifteen minutes until the news recycled and he could see the whole story.

Gordievsky was the KGB station chief in London who had been recalled to Moscow in May 1985. For eleven years before that he had been an agent in place for MI6, the British intelligence agency, feeding top-grade intelligence to the Brits and, through them, the Americans. A few weeks after he had been recalled to the Soviet Union, his superiors had confronted him with the accusation that he was a spy. In July

1985, MI6 had saved his life by stealing him away from Moscow in a false-bottomed van.

He had always believed that someone had betrayed him.

In time, the television showed a full story about Ames's arrest. When his face appeared across the airwaves, Gordievsky had another surprise. He knew this man. He had met him while on a visit to the CIA five years ago. He had liked him a great deal. He also remembered that Ames had looked at him in a strange way back then. Now he thought he knew why.

In 1989, Gordievsky had made one of his periodic trips to Washington to consult with CIA officers. Still an asset of British intelligence, he had been taken on tour, so to speak, once a year to meet personnel from the CIA and others in the intelligence community who wanted to pick his brain. The 1989 meeting had been held in a first-floor conference room of a hotel in Tyson's Corner, Virginia. Ames had been there with about six other intelligence officers, and they had questioned Gordievsky from ten in the morning until five P.M., with a short break for lunch.

Gordievsky had not liked any of the other intelligence people at the meeting. He had found them to be arrogant, foolish men. But Ames had been different. "He looked like a very kind, nice person, someone with a heart of gold," Gordievsky remembered. "His eyes were full of goodness and kindness."

He now understood just how false his impression of Ames had been.

"He knew very well he was looking at one of the first men he gave away, and he knew I was supposed to die and yet I was there," Gordievsky said. "Alive and in the heart of Washington."

There was another KGB man betrayed by Ames who had escaped with his life.

Almost two years to the day before Ames was arrested, a handsome, graying prisoner named Boris Yuzhin had answered a knock on his cell door at the forced-labor camp called Perm 35, deep in the Ural Mountains on the western edge of Siberia. His jailer, an obese, pig-eyed colonel named Nikolai Osin, told him that the president of Russia, Boris Yeltsin, had proclaimed an amnesty for all political prisoners and a handful of others condemned to Perm 35, the last remaining island of the gulag archipelago.

Yuzhin had been convicted of spying for the United States by the military collegium of the USSR Supreme Court in December 1986. The verdict under Article 64 of the penal code—treason against the motherland—carried a maximum punishment of death. But Yuzhin had been spared and given fifteen years at hard labor. He had spent most of the past five years alone in his cell.

He and four of his prison mates, all Article 64 prisoners, had traveled to Moscow, one thousand miles to the west, and on February 10, 1992, they had held a press conference at the offices of a Moscow newspaper. Yuzhin had told the story of how he had been sent to San Francisco in 1976, posing as a reporter for the Soviet news agency TASS but assigned by the KGB to gather military and industrial secrets from defense companies. He had instead chosen to work for the United States after his exposure to freedom had led him to reject the Soviet system. He had never asked for money.

"I had a chance to pick up some real knowledge about what was doing in my own country," he had told the assembled reporters in rusty but serviceable English. "For the first time in my life, I had access to all publications which were prohibited here in this country, I had a chance to pick up any book I wanted. I just kept reading and reading, and the more I read, the more I realized that the official ideology which I studied here, which I was educated in here, it was nothing but a big lie.

"All of us here, in one way or another, were collaborators or advocates of the totalitarian regime to which we are now bidding farewell. Some served in penal troops, others for the KGB. But an internal protest was ripening in each of us. Each of us violated the law that existed at the time to some degree.

"If you give a moral assessment to our actions," Yuzhin concluded, "they can be justified. I am proud of what I have done. And if I had the chance, I believe I would do it again. . . . There are some things in life that could justify plenty of years' punishment."

24

A War of Words

Rick Ames awoke to the clamor of the Alexandria city jail on the morning of April 28, 1994, ready to make his appearance on the world's stage. He had spent weeks writing the statement he would be allowed to read in open court after he made his guilty plea. Day after day, alone in his cell, he had tried to fashion a mosaic of the shards of rage that had rattled around in his head for so many years, searching for words that would wound the CIA.

The men with the shackles came for him, chained him hand and foot, and led him through the maze of cinder-block corridors, out of the jailhouse, and onto the ramp where the government van was waiting. Five minutes and they were at the courthouse. Back into another maze that led to the jammed courtroom. Rosario was there, and he met her gaze. He looked down, shuffled his papers, and prepared for the ritual of confession.

The court was like a theater, with each person playing a well-rehearsed role. Rosario went on stage first and spoke her bare part. Yes, she understood the charges. No, she had not been coerced. Yes, what the government said had happened had happened. On count one, conspiracy to commit espionage: guilty. Count two, evasion of taxes on the money Rick had taken: guilty.

There was some business to be attended to by the judge, Claude Hilton; Rick's lawyer, the orotund Plato Cacheris; and the prosecutor, Mark Hulkower. Cacheris arose and advised the judge that his client would not challenge the warrantless searches of his home, his office, and his computers. Had Ames had the slightest desire to fight, this might have provoked a ferocious legal battle. But there would be no argument from Rick Ames.

"His desire to aid his wife dissuades him from that course of action," Cacheris advised the court. "He will tell you, Your Honor, that he is pleading guilty because he is guilty."

Ames clutched the manila folder holding his speech as he walked slowly to the witness stand and was sworn in. It was the first oath he had taken outside of the CIA and his marriage vows. As he sat in the dock, the judge began the recitation again: "Do you understand the charges? . . . Do you make any claim that you are innocent? . . . How do you plead?" Yes, sir. No, sir. Guilty, guilty, guilty.

First Hulkower, the young prosecutor, arose for his moment on stage. Anxious to try cases, he had given up the partnership track at a big Washington law firm in 1985 and moved to the U.S. attorney's office. But a man could labor all his life in that office, trying corporate frauds and income tax evasions and drug cases, and never handle a case like this. Hulkower's speech was the government's only chance—outside the indictment, which had been scrubbed by secrecy-minded CIA lawyers until it was practically bloodless—to put a human face on the men Rick Ames had condemned to death. Still, the orders to Hulkower were clear: no names, no details. Secrecy survived the death of the secret agents.

"The defendant's crimes have to be recognized for what they are, crimes which caused people to die as surely as if the defendant had pulled the trigger," Hulkower told the court. "In all the talk about assets, penetrations, compromises of intelligence information, all the spy lingo which has been bandied about in this case, it is easy to forget that what we are talking about, Your Honor, is people."

Hulkower began talking elliptically about Dmitri Polyakov—code-named "Top Hat"—perhaps the best Soviet agent ever to walk into the open embrace of the CIA and the FBI.

"In the 1970s, a Russian general who was disturbed by the course his country was taking volunteered to help this country by giving information to the CIA. He didn't want money. He did it, he said, because it was right. And for years and years this high-ranking officer provided valuable intelligence about the Soviet military buildup and Soviet intentions to this country. This is information that was disseminated and utilized by every branch of our government from the president on down. And even after years when the CIA urged this official to come over to this country, he stayed, working for this country, feeling he could do more for us there than he could over here.

"This individual was arrested and executed by the KGB," he said. "Like so many others whose identities were known to Rick Ames, this individual died because Rick Ames wasn't making enough money with the CIA and wanted to live in a half-million-dollar house and drive a Jaguar.

"Well, Rick Ames bought the house, he bought the Jaguar, and he acquired the other trappings of wealth that he couldn't acquire on a government salary, but at some point Rick Ames has to pay the price for all these luxuries," the prosecutor said. "And the only appropriate payment, the only appropriate price, and the only appropriate sentence for the damage Rick Ames caused to our national security and to the people who assisted us is life in prison without parole."

The judge turned to the prisoner. "Mr. Ames, is there anything you would like to say at this time?" Ames knew there was nothing the Agency wanted less than for him to be allowed to speak. There was no way to stop it; he had the absolute right to be heard. "Yes, I would, Your Honor," he said. "This is my opportunity to say a number of things of very great importance to me."

He began with Rosario and Paul. "I bitterly regret the catastrophe which my betrayal of trust has brought upon my wife and son and upon any who have loved or cared for me. No punishment by this court can balance or ease the profound shame and guilt which I bear." None of the executions he had set into motion meant anything to him by comparison, though in his next breath he turned and lifted his hat in respect to the men he had killed: "For those persons in the former Soviet Union and elsewhere who may have suffered from my actions, I have the deepest sympathy—even empathy. We made similar choices and suffer similar consequences." In his mind, he had become one with the men he had betrayed. They had all taken the same risks, betrayed the same sorts of oaths. He too would be made to disappear, but not before he had his say.

First to the heart of the matter, to the lies and secrecy that had been the daily diet of his marriage ever since Rosario had found that little scrap of paper with the scribbled note in his wallet. "I successfully concealed my relationship with the KGB from her for seven and a half of the nine years of my criminal activity," Ames said, still in that bland, matter-of-fact tone of voice, as if discussing an automobile accident with a claims adjuster. "When she learned of it through my careless mistake, that knowledge was devastating to her and to our marriage. Frightened nearly to death by the possible consequences to me, to her, and to our son, she pleaded with me to break off the relationship with the Russians. I was able to manipulate her, even to blackmail her, into delaying that action. I argued falsely that we dared not anger the Russians. I also falsely implied that extravagance on her part had been and continued to be a continuing factor in my espionage, an implication which I believe came to undermine her own sense of self and integrity, making her even more vulnerable to my blackmail. She shrank from turning me in, hoping against hope that we would survive detection until my retirement."

There was one last thing Ames could do in the aftermath of the disaster that he had brought down on both their heads: he could try to convince the government that she had known next to nothing about his spying. She was facing ten years in prison. It was tricky. He had to minimize her guilt in the face of the tapes, the starkly incriminating snippets of conversation, while admitting the enormity of what he'd done and the fact that she had been more or less clear on that. He plunged on: "Rosario had no knowledge of what information I furnished the KGB; she had little or no understanding of what any consequences of my actions could be. While she knew that I had received a great deal of money, she had no way to associate such sums with the gravity of the information I was passing. Rosario understood me to be cooperating with Russia, a country which she had heard extolled by Presidents Bush and Clinton as a friend and a potential security partner. She had heard me speak since 1991 of the growing confidence of the CIA and the Russian security services in their evolving relationship."

Ames made it sound as if he had been participating in some sort of foreign exchange program, sharing insights about American culture with his new Russian friends, trading warm toasts extolling brotherhood and the family of nations. In fact he had been spying for Moscow, selling out his country, and that was something his wife had known well. Ames's attempt to protect Rosario was straining his fragile argument. Now he tried to contradict his own words, and hers.

"Rosario recognized and feared my sloppiness," he said, acknowledging his hopelessness as a spy, the incriminating evidence he had absentmindedly stuffed into his pockets, the botched rendezvous with the Russians, the records strewn about his home and office. "She ultimately found herself cautioning and counseling me to be careful and precise in my contacts with the Russians. These statements"—recorded with precision for months by the FBI's bugs and wiretaps— "have been used with brutal effect by the government to imply falsely that she supported my espionage activity." But, of course, it had been one of Ames's notes to the Russians— the one that said Rosario had accommodated herself to his spying—that had hung her the highest.

At the very last, Ames hit upon a hard and unassailable fact: "The main explanation for the government's treatment of my wife is the ferocity of the government's desire to punish me, both in revenge and to set an example. To punish her beyond her deserts punishes me."

Now Ames turned to the statement he had been mulling over for a long, long time—his indictment of the CIA. These were to be the last words he spoke before the judge handed down his life sentence and consigned him to oblivion. He meant to strike a blow against the U.S. intelligence community's barons.

Ames first tried to humanize himself by drawing an analogy between his crimes and those committed by the ordinary run of white-collar felons. "In breaking the law," he began, "I have betrayed a serious trust, much as does a corrupt government official receiving a bribe or a stock speculator acting on inside information. I do regret and feel shame for this betrayal of trust, done for the basest of motives."

He then made what amounted to a full, if abridged, confession. Ames recounted how, in April 1985, he had conceived his confidence game to play on the KGB and had given them "the identities of several Soviet citizens who appeared to be cooperating with the CIA inside the Soviet Union. . . . Then, a few months later, I did something which is still not entirely explicable, even to me: without preconditions or any demand for payment, I volunteered to the KGB information identifying virtually all Soviet agents of the CIA and other American and foreign services known to me. To my enduring surprise, the KGB replied that it had set aside for me two million dollars in gratitude." Nothing like this had ever been said in a U.S. courtroom, and the enormity of it took a while to sink in. Ames had destroyed the network of spies developed by the United States in the Soviet Union. He had done so in a casual, what-the-hell state of mind. And he had run free for nearly nine years afterward.

Although he had no standing to attack the CIA, he forged ahead, couching his assault on the Agency in the form of a credo.

"I had come to believe that the espionage business, as carried out by the CIA and a few other American agencies, was and is a self-serving sham, carried out by careerist bureaucrats who have managed to deceive several generations of American policy makers and the public about both the necessity and the value of their work," he said. "There is and has been no rational need for thousands of case officers and tens of thousands of agents working around the world, primarily in and against friendly countries. The information our vast espionage network acquires at considerable human and ethical costs is generally insignificant or irrelevant to our policy makers' needs. Our espionage establishment differs hardly at all from many other federal bureaucracies, having transformed itself into a self-serving interest group, immeasurably aided by secrecy. Now that the cold war is over and the Communist tyrannies largely done for, our country still awaits a real national debate on the means and ends—and costs—of our national security policies. To the extent that public discussions of my case can move from government-inspired hypocrisy and hysteria to help even indirectly to fuel such a debate, I welcome and support it."

The CIA's director, Jim Woolsey, had been dreading this moment. As a lawyer, he knew Ames must have his say, but as the nation's intelligence chief, he knew that no one could stand up in court and shout: "This man is a murdering traitor! Don't listen to him, don't trust a single thing he says!" From the CIA's perspective, the speech Ames delivered was nothing but another act of treason. And the worst thing was that the press and the Congress would take him seriously, as if he were some savant on the Sunday-morning talk shows.

They did. Suddenly a traitor was setting the terms of debate about the CIA's future.

Among those who noted Ames's soliloquy with interest was the then-chairman of the House of Representatives Permanent Select Committee on Intelligence, Dan Glickman, a genial Kansan who had become skeptical of the CIA's traditions of secrecy. A few hours after the speech went out over the news wires, Glickman wondered aloud about the issues Ames had raised. "What is the role of spying, what is the role of counterintelligence in the modern world?" he asked. "Does it make any difference at all? What's the human role in terms of the analysis and collection of intelligence, as well as the operations side? The Ames case allows us to ask these questions."

The questions threatened the existence of the CIA. For the critics of the Agency now included people of both the right and the left, old CIA spooks and young congressional staffers, the editorial boards of many of the nation's newspapers, the cultural elite of Hollywood, Pentagon generals, and State Department pashas. And the critique was devastating.

The debate Ames was seeking had started way back in 1975. As the worst of the Agency's cold war crimes had begun to be unveiled, some of its own people had broken ranks with resounding force, like river ice breaking up in a spring thaw. Ames said this had happened to him in slow motion over the years. He had joined the clandestine service in 1967 as a true believer, he said in a letter from prison, but "the fading of the justification for fun and adventure in the seventies was a very powerful factor in how I thought in 1985 and afterwards."

Many other men who professed to have loved the Agency in its glory were now bitter about their old flame. People like Tom Braden, a top CIA officer in the 1950s and later a syndicated newspaper columnist and bona fide member of the Washington establishment, came to believe that the Agency had become "a gargantuan monster . . . an establishment devoted to opposing the ideals we profess." He argued that it should be destroyed root and branch and its headquarters left standing empty as "our only national monument to the value that democracy places upon the recognition and correction of a mistake."

What had gone wrong? Power—"There was too much of it, and it was too easy to bring to bear," Braden wrote in 1975. Hubris—"An organization that does not have to answer for mistakes is certain to become arrogant." And there was what he called "the inside-outside syndrome"—or lying. Telling the truth was a practice reserved for the insider.

The gist of Ames's angry speech was that the lies told in the service of the CIA's mission had become one big lie. Was that true? Was the CIA past its prime, living off its reputation? Was it crucial to the nation's security? These were the hard questions that buzzed around Washington after Ames had said his piece.

Now that the Soviet Union was gone, how had the ten thousand or so case officers the CIA had sent up against the "evil empire" fared over the decades? What had they learned? As communism had crumbled in 1989, 1990, and 1991, what had the people they had recruited as sources contributed to America's understanding of what was past and passing and to come? Everyone knew the immense array of spies, satellites, and electronic eavesdropping stations over which the director of Central Intelligence presided had not seen the millions of people who were rising up to overthrow communism.

What about the CIA's analysts, the thousands of people paid to determine what was really going on behind the world's closed doors, in the bazaars of Islam, in the councils of the Chinese high command? "For a quarter of a century the CIA has been repeatedly wrong about the major political and economic questions entrusted to its analysts," argued Senator Daniel Patrick Moynihan of New York, a former vice chairman of the Senate Select Committee on Intelligence. What about on-the-spot intelligence? George Bush's White House had complained bitterly, back in the first days of the U.S. invasion of Panama, that the CIA's intelligence was worthless. They had been infuriated when the Agency's intelligence analysts had predicted that the leftist Sandinistas would win the 1990 elections in Nicaragua by 15 percentage points and the

Sandinistas had lost—by 15 percentage points. The list was long and depressing.

And what about covert action, the most powerful weapon in the CIA's arsenal? Once it had consumed half the Agency's budget, encompassing hundreds of programs around the globe: bribing politicians, buying elections, running guns to guerrillas, orchestrating public opinion. Now it had dwindled to a score of projects. There was a very good reason for that: few of its recent projects had stayed secret—witness the CIA's support for the Nicaraguan rebels fighting the Sandinistas—and those that had been revealed had often tarred the Agency's public image.

The traditional argument was that the CIA could not be judged like other agencies, that all its successes were secret and only its failures were trumpeted. Many of the several hundred people in Washington outside the Agency who knew its inner workings—including the members and the staffs of the congressional intelligence committees who in theory oversaw the CIA—were becoming skeptical of that tradition. Ever since 1991, Senator Moynihan had been arguing that the CIA's analytical functions should be given to the State Department, its paramilitary capabilities transferred to the Pentagon, spy catching left to the FBI, and the Agency itself given a decent burial. He had put those ideas into writing in an "End of the Cold War" bill. It never really had been meant as legislation but as a rhetorical device. After Ames's speech, even some conservatives started paying attention to Moynihan's proposal.

"One traitor like Ames should not in any way impugn the honor of people who have given their lives to the Agency and chosen a very difficult life of anonymity," Moynihan said a few days after Ames's attack. "The best things you do will never be known to anybody, and when you die they put a little gold star on the wall, but not your name. Ah, well, that was for its time. That time is past, and to persist is to ask for another Ames. The ideological wars are over. For the present generation in the Agency—there aren't many left who ever met a Communist—the dying of the ideology never sank in. They have yet to realize that nobody believes in this any longer."

In May, a week after Ames's speech, Senator John Warner, a Virginia Republican not known as a radical, told Woolsey to his face in an open hearing of the Senate intelligence committee that not one or two, but many senators would support Moynihan's bill if it were introduced. A few minutes later, Senator Dennis DeConcini, the chairman of the committee, exploded in anger at Woolsey for refusing to consider the committee's ideas on improving counterintelligence and spy catching.

"It's a disgrace, what's happened, and the American public is losing confidence in our intelligence," the senator said. "There is more and more mail coming to me and questions all the time. 'How much do we spend?' I can't say. 'Is it this much?' Well, that's what's been reported in the press. 'How can you spend that much on intelligence and have this kind of operation?' And 'Why doesn't somebody eliminate the CIA?, as Senator Moynihan says.' I mean, that's a real fear here. If you think for a moment that this is a passing feeling—"

In June, as the atmosphere of gloom and doom deepened both inside and outside the CIA, Woolsey went to work writing his own speech.

The Agency was taking its worst beating in a generation. Things had gotten to the point where people inside the CIA were talking to reporters about how dismal things were at headquarters. Recently retired officials were going on the record about the Agency's problems; even Richard Helms, the director of Central Intelligence from 1967 to 1973 and perhaps the staunchest living supporter of the Agency, was saying the place had no sense of mission. And the criticism from Congress was becoming intense. DeConcini and Representative Glickman, the chairman of the House intelligence committee, were calling the CIA "a cult." Damaging stories about the CIA that were only dimly related to Ames were appearing in the papers—stories about station chiefs being fired for thievery or drunken violence, about corruption and intellectual bankruptcy in the Agency's intelligence gathering—and Woolsey knew that more of this kind of thing was coming. He had to find a way to head it off.

On July 18, Woolsey strode into the basement auditorium of the Center for Strategic and International Studies, Washington's foremost traditionally conservative foreign affairs think tank, at his normal pace—as fast as a man can walk without breaking into a sprint. There he was on friendly ground and had an audience that could speak and understand his language. But he knew he had a much larger audience as well and an extraordinarily tricky message to deliver about the CIA.

From the time he had been sworn in as director of Central Intelligence, for more than a year before Ames was arrested, Woolsey had known all about the case, known that Ames had run free since 1985, known that when the news broke, the Agency would have to run a long gantlet of abuse and scorn. All that time, he had had to swallow his outrage and contain his dread. He had kept his silence even after the arrest, through the weeks of increasingly scathing news stories detailing the years of inaction and ineptitude, the vicious editorials, and the cruel cartoons lampooning the CIA. None of that had been fun or easy.

Now Woolsey had to speak out, diminish Ames, give voice to the anger and disgust he and his colleagues felt for the man, and try to seize control of the story. That could be done only by defining Ames and delimiting the debate the traitor had fueled.

Woolsey's speech was remarkable in many ways. He was trying to walk two tightropes at once. He had to buck up his demoralized troops while criticizing their work and their conduct, to show he was trying to change all that was wrong with the Agency while preserving all that was sound, explain its failures while singing its praises. Americans will tolerate spying if they think it is being done by honorable people; the infamy attached to Ames threatened to tar the entire Agency. Woolsey had to make sure the tar stuck to Ames and Ames alone. So he began by comparing him to the best-known and most-hated turncoat in American history, Benedict Arnold.

"For most of 1993 and early 1994, waiting for the case to be established against Ames was far from easy for me or for the handful of CIA and law enforcement officers and a few senior officials who were then aware of the Ames investigation," said Woolsey, anger simmering in his voice. "Ames is now trying to reinvent himself and will doubtless soon step into the media spotlight seeking to present himself as someone who just spontaneously gave the KGB a few names in a fit of absentmindedness, is a fan of Gorbachev's reforms and thus is a battler against the conservative direction of U.S. foreign policy in the 1980s, and as an objective and veteran commentator on the intelligence game. Ames deserves even less deference and respect for his credibility in this reinvention effort than would have been imbued to an earlier figure in American history.

"The man whose name has been synonymous with treason in this country for over two centuries was a far more modest traitor than Ames," he continued. "There are some important differences between him and Ames. And they are all in Benedict Arnold's favor."

The point was intended to be breathtaking. First, Woolsey had used the word treason, unspoken in public by the government up to that point. For centuries, under common law, treason had encompassed a wide variety of acts, from leading an insurrection to thinking about killing the king to having a love affair with the queen. The only punishment for a traitor had been death: in England, until 1870, a traitor had been hanged and, before dying, disemboweled. American law had evolved a little differently. First, it had defined treason as giving aid and comfort to an enemy. And second, at the time of Woolsey's speech, there was no death penalty for traitors—although Congress would pass one six weeks later, in large part due to Ames. So Ames had to be buried by the more modern and subtle means of silencing. Who would listen to a traitor more malignant than Benedict Arnold?

Actually, Ames was so much worse than Benedict Arnold that the comparison was "rather flattering," as Ames said in a letter from prison a few weeks later. Arnold had been a brilliant soldier for the American Revolution, twice seriously wounded in battle. In the first military engagement of an American fleet, he had beaten back a far superior British force. George Washington had placed him in command of Philadelphia in 1778. Yet he had grown embittered after his second trial and second acquittal on misconduct charges and by 1780 was plotting to surrender the fortress of West Point to a British general named Henry Clinton. Perhaps there was a point of comparison there, since Ames had been twice polygraphed and asked if he was a traitor, twice unstrapped from the machine and told to go about his business. There were other similarities: Arnold had been offered $20,000 for his treason, and he and his wife had not been averse to getting and spending it. But Arnold had been a major general who had done great things, and the CIA's public relations people kept insisting that Ames was a nobody who had done nothing of note for his country. In order to denigrate Ames, Woolsey was elevating him to the level of antihero, and the effect he had on his audience that day was nervous laughter, knitted brows, and quizzical expressions.

Had there been anyone like Ames in the annals of espionage? Alger Hiss, the State Department officer accused of spying for Moscow in the early 1950s? He had been convicted only of perjury, and he was still alive, as were the arguments over his case. Julius and Ethel Rosenberg, put to death for plotting to sell the secret of the atomic bomb to Moscow? Too raw a nerve, for Ames would not be executed, and the comparison would be taken as a suggestion that he should die for his crimes. None of the moneygrubbing villains arrested in 1985, the Year of the Spy, fit either; the blood on their hands, unlike that on Ames's, had been metaphorical. Woolsey's attempt to define him in the Agency's terms didn't work until he lifted a line from the federal prosecutor, Mark Hulkower, who had gone head to head with the spy in court: "Ames was and is a malignant betrayer of his country who killed a number of people who helped the United States and the West win the cold war," Woolsey said. "He killed them just as surely as if he pulled the trigger of a revolver put to their heads in the basement of the Lubyanka prison, the classic method of KGB execution. They—our agents in the cold war against the Soviet Union—risked their lives, helped keep you free, and died because this warped, murdering traitor wanted a bigger house and a Jaguar."

That got people's attention. Murder: that was something they could understand. What remained incomprehensible was how Ames could have gone undetected for so long. It was as if a district attorney had gone golfing every afternoon while a mass murderer ran loose in his city. Nor could Ames be explained away as an aberration; the inability of the CIA to deal with a traitor in its midst was a part of its cultural tradition of secrecy, arrogance, and denial.

Or so Woolsey said as he came to terms with what Ames meant to the CIA. No director of Central Intelligence ever had spoken of the culture of the Agency, much less criticized it openly, or talked about changing it as Woolsey did. What's more, he acknowledged that Ames had sparked the critique.

"Changes had to be made in the way we do business at the CIA and, indeed, in the culture of the CIA itself," he told his audience. "Ames's conviction has served as a catalyst to the necessary changes."

Woolsey's criticism focused on the CIA's Directorate of Operations. The D.O. *was* the CIA—or at least what remained of what was unique about the CIA. The operatives in the directorate knew it, and the secrecy that surrounded them and their work had always kept them shielded from outside influence. Now Woolsey was saying that it was time to make "important changes in that culture" and that changing the way the spies did business "may prove to be our most pressing need and our greatest challenge." The change he was promising had been brought about by the traitor.

"I've ordered a fundamental assessment of the entire structure and operations of the Directorate of Operations, a directorate which is on the front lines of espionage," Woolsey said. "The work's already begun. Two core groups have been established, a group of senior managers and simultaneously a larger group of midlevel officials, the future leaders of intelligence operations acting independently. Their task is to strip bare and to evaluate the directorate critically and to provide me directly with recommendations to make the fundamental changes that are needed." That would take years—if it ever came about. Woolsey said that, after he left the CIA, the changes would be enforced by a "senior accountability review board," whose members would include "distinguished individuals from outside the CIA and from outside the government," to watch over the Directorate of Operations.

Such boards had been created and destroyed for forty years, their criticism stamped "Top Secret," filed, and forgotten, and not one had made much of a difference. In 1956, at President Dwight D. Eisenhower's behest, two mandarins of the foreign policy establishment, David Bruce and Robert Lovett—one a prominent Foreign Service officer and the other a former Secretary of Defense, both friends and colleagues of the director of Central Intelligence, Allen Dulles— had been asked to report to the president on the CIA's Directorate of Operations. Their report remains classified to this day, although snippets have been discovered through the diligent work of a few historians granted exceptional access to presidential archives.

"We are sure," Bruce and Lovett reported, "that the supporters of the 1948 decision to launch this government on a political and psychological warfare program could not possibly have foreseen the ramifications of the operations which have resulted from it." The CIA's operations officers were intelligent but "politically immature" men without sufficient adult supervision "who must be doing something all the time to justify their reason for being." These officers, "busy, monied, and privileged" by virtue of their status at the CIA, had become a kind of secret society separate from the rest of the U.S. government. "The intrigue is fascinating—considerable self-satisfaction, sometimes with applause, derives from 'successes'—no charge is made for failures—and the whole business is very much simpler than collecting covert intelligence on the USSR through the usual CIA methods!" Wasn't the CIA "responsible in a great measure for stirring up the turmoil and raising the doubts about us in many other countries of the world today? What of the effects on our present alliances? What will happen tomorrow?"

These questions had never been answered. The powerful allure of secrecy, of thinking that you and you alone knew the truth, the insularity of an exclusive fraternity whose rules and codes and traditions no outsider could hope to understand—all of it remained.

Rick Ames was a member of the club, as his father had been before him. Woolsey knew it. He spoke of "a sense of trust and camaraderie within the fraternity that can smack of elitism and arrogance." The fraternity, he said, had become a place where "personnel problems tend to be passed along rather than dealt with," wherein "once you're initiated, you're considered a trusted member for life." And this eternal embrace was at the heart of "the culture of the system that failed to prevent or find Ames quickly."

Grand Delusion

Alone in jail, Ames still wanted to explain himself, to justify and rationalize the murders. He wanted to talk.

The interview room in the Alexandria city jail was as tiny as a cell, and the commotion of the jailhouse seeped under the steel doors. Ames was dressed like a car mechanic, in ridiculously ill-fitting coveralls and high-top sneakers. He started by remembering his first days at the CIA, his pleasure and pride at joining the fraternity.

He said he had loved the trappings of his work—the secrecy, the safe houses, the code names, and the classified briefings—but he had come to disdain the substance of it. He said he had become a traitor only when he had begun to realize that the work of the CIA amounted to an endless parade of meaningless secrets, that the whole thing was an elaborately routinized deception. And having lost his institutional loyalty to the Agency, he had shifted his allegiance to the KGB.

In the mid- to late 1970s, he said, he had begun to have his first fleeting thoughts about treason. He had had growing delusions of grandeur, a sense that he was in possession of a unique understanding of the inner workings of the cold war, deep insights into the way the Soviet Union really worked. Talking with Tomas Kolesnichenko, the *Pravda* correspondent who moonlighted as a playwright, and Arkady Shevchenko, the under secretary general of the United Nations who served the CIA as a defector-in-place, had given him the sense that he was possessed of a knowledge so powerful that it demanded drastic action.

"Call it arrogance, if you will, but I'd say, 'I know what's better. I know what's damaging, and I know what's not damaging, and I know what the Soviet Union is really all about, and I know what's best for foreign policy and national security.' And I do. Intellectually, I know not many people agree with me, and I don't expect them to, but I developed a kind of a sense that at least I know what I think. And I'm going to act on that."

Ames said his decision to aid the Soviets had begun with his sense that the CIA had triumphed over the KGB in the spy wars.

"Our penetration of the Soviet intelligence services was effective and long standing," he said. "We had cleaned their clock. Hands-down, total victory." The penetration of the KGB had reverberated throughout the highest levels of the Soviet leadership. The men who ran the nation had believed—wrongly, but with great conviction—that the CIA had infiltrated not only the state security system but every Soviet institution and every level of Soviet society. Their hysteria had mirrored the great fear of communism in the United States during the 1950s.

Ames said he had begun to think the world might be better off if the match were evened up. As he explained it, if the Soviet leadership knew that the CIA had not subverted all of Soviet society, it would realize that communism's profound

problems were self-inflicted. This was a magnificently byzantine idea, as well as a preposterous rationalization for betraying one's country. But it had not been the crucial factor in
Ames's decision to cross the boundary into treason.

Greed was.

"Money—money was the—money was the motivation,"
he said. "These other ideas and reasons were only enablers, if
you will. I mean, plenty of people need money. A lot of people throughout the Agency's history have stolen money from
the Agency and have done terrible things for money. Very few
have sold secrets to the KGB, and I think one of the reasons
is because many of them would have found there were a lot
of barriers in the way.

"For me, by 1985, some of those barriers weren't there any
more. I don't believe that I was affecting the security of this
country and the safety of its people. I did think that a lot of
the spy wars stuff was a kind of a bureaucratic game played
by the CIA and by the FBI and by the press. And not many
people in the Agency shared those views," he said.

Ames casually described how he had tried to keep his san-
ity during his nine years of treason. He said he had constructed walls inside his mind to try to segregate the KGB
side of his life from the CIA side. They were like two parts of
a binary chemical bomb; if one side touched the other, there
would be a fatal explosion.

"I adapted—in the sense of being able to deny things, to
avoid thinking about consequences," he said. "I see this in
other areas of my life in which I decide to do something, or
resolve to do something, and for some reason, I want to do it,
and I'm able to kind of close my mind off and not deal with
the consequences of it. I never spent a lot of time thinking
about my relationship with the KGB. When I would meet
them, when I would have personal meetings with the KGB

officers, say in Bogotá, when I left that meeting, at maybe two A.M., having had the better part of a bottle of vodka, I would have made a few notes about the communications planned for the next year. When I left that meeting, I just filed it in the back of my mind. File and forget. And I told the KGB. I worked that way, too. And it caused me problems. I mean, I would forget things."

He said that he had known deep down that if and when a serious investigation ever took shape, he would be done for. But he said he had never felt the hot breath of the hunters, never sensed that he was in the CIA's crosshairs. As the years passed, he said, he had successfully forced himself to become "totally unconscious" of the possibility that he would be caught and sentenced to life in prison.

"I deluded myself," he said.

"I didn't want to admit that this could be happening. I always found reasons not to engage in a serious sit-down and think: 'Where have things come to?' Had I done that, I might have seen what was coming. I did not. I shrank from it, I guess. Because had I come to the conclusion, it would have meant taking steps, untakebackable steps."

Such as defecting? Taking Rosario to the dacha by the river that the Russians had promised him?

"No. I hadn't thought that way, and I wasn't planning to do that. No. Well, it crossed my mind, but it was never a serious plan."

The CIA would not learn much from his case that would benefit their security in the future, Ames said. His conduct had been extraordinarily sloppy, and it was inconceivable that some future mole might repeat it. "It would be very, very naïve to expect other people who might be working for a foreign power to be as open with their money as I was," he said. "I didn't conceal my funds in any real way or set up numbered bank accounts. I sloshed my money around pretty good. Someone else in my position is very likely to be much more circumspect about where they put their money and what they do with it.

"In my case, the best way to put it would be that I felt that the perception of my having money would not fuel an investigation. And it didn't. Despite all the talk about high living, it wasn't really very high, you know. People assumed that my wife had a little money from her family in Colombia. And everybody lived in half-million-dollar houses. No one had asked someone in the Agency to count the Jags in the parking lot. There were a whole lot of them. So my feeling was that I was not aberrant. And that once an investigation had begun, once there was a serious look at me, virtually no measure I took would be proof against that investigation."

In retrospect, regarding the deaths of the men he had condemned by his betrayal, Ames regretted more than anything his lack of cold-bloodedness in his first dealings with the Soviets—and the KGB's lack of coolheadedness in killing the men he had sold them. "Had I known they were going to do that . . . I would have passed them out one by one"—in other words, parceled out the deadly information piecemeal, one traitor at a time, so as to better cover his tracks and give the KGB time to concoct foolproof cover stories for each of the disappearances.

Ames didn't need the benefit of hindsight to understand why he had stayed free for nine years. The real problem was the CIA itself, its immensity, its inability to police itself.

"If all you had was a small number of very high-value operations, you could watch it like a hawk," he said. "But this is what defeated them—the immense number of operations, many of them totally useless. You've got two or three or four thousand people running around doing espionage.

You can't monitor it. You can't control it. . . . The minute you get big, you get like the KGB, or you get like us."

When the jailhouse interview was over, Ames wanted to keep talking, and he telephoned from jail every few days throughout July 1994.

He was thrilled and fascinated by the fact that his critique of the CIA at his sentencing had been taken very seriously by politicians and pundits. "About all I can say is, if some of the issues that came up with me have a shock effect, at least offer people today something to chew on and lead people in the future to change things, I'll be happy," he said.

The United States in the cold war, and the CIA itself, the highest expression of the long twilight struggle, had been in the grip of its own myth, Ames said. But so had he—sufficiently deluded to link his own life with the KGB, that great instrument of repression. He gloried in the grandiose idea that he would not go down simply as the greatest American traitor of the cold war but as a man who had tried to pull down part of the CIA with him.

"It's a position that I don't at all shrink from," he said. "And I have a very private reason to be gratified by the fact that it worked out that way, and that's for my son. As he grows up, there'll be at least something that will appear more positive on the records than the most brutal facts of the case."

And given the brutal facts, given the way he thought and the way things turned out, shouldn't he have quit the Agency ten years before, when his bitterness had turned to betrayal?

There was a long silence on the end of the line, with the faint clanging and clamor of the jail in the background. Then Ames was crying, his composure crushed.

"My son would have his parents. . . . My wife would have a husband. . . . That just doesn't . . . that's . . . that's it." He hung up.

26

Endgame

The consequences came swiftly.

The Ames case effectively ended the long battle between the CIA and the FBI for control of counterintelligence. It was a total victory for the Bureau. The CIA's counterintelligence chief was dethroned, and an FBI agent was named in his place. Congress carried the ritual humiliation to deeper levels. The Intelligence Authorization Act of 1995 contained provisions that required the Agency to inform the FBI immediately when it suspected *any* loss of classified information. Next, the lawmakers handed the FBI a club it had long sought: the power to demand access to every employee and file it wanted to review. FBI Director Louis Freeh promoted the CIA's nemesis in the Ames case, Bear Bryant, from the Washington field office to head all intelligence matters for the FBI. John Lewis, Bryant's top counterintelligence deputy at the Washington field office, rose with Bryant, becoming his number two at the national security division. Les Wiser's career soared.

But the case damaged the lives of almost everyone it touched at the Central Intelligence Agency. It exposed the CIA to ridicule and humiliation. It blotted the records of good people who had served the United States in secret. And it wrote the epitaph for a dying world of secrecy and deception.

The affair destroyed the man who had vowed that he would change the Central Intelligence Agency. Jim Woolsey committed career suicide on the morning of September 28, 1994, when he called a dozen reporters up to the seventh floor of the CIA to hear his verdict on the CIA's conduct in the case.

Woolsey was nervous and bone tired, and his mood had not been improved by the lead story on the front page of *The New York Times* that morning. It said that Congress had concluded that the CIA was incapable of charting its own course and was creating an independent commission to remake the Agency—in effect, forcing the CIA to undergo something like a court-ordered bankruptcy reorganization. The consensus was that the Agency needed a total overhaul and that the Ames case was not an aberration but a core sample of the CIA.

Woolsey had ordered up three reports after Ames's arrest. The first had been a hodgepodge of suggestions for improving security at the CIA—the barn door creaking closed after the horses had fled. The second was a still-incomplete damage assessment—an attempt to figure out what Ames had handed the Russians and what impact his treason had had on the Agency. The third report had been requested by the House intelligence committee: an in-house investigation by the CIA's inspector general, Fred Hitz, a longtime covert operator and Ames's career-training classmate back in 1967. Woolsey had also asked Hitz for a list of all Ames's supervisors, the men who might be held accountable for the case. They would be frozen in their jobs, barred from awards or promotions, until their culpability was weighed.

Hitz and twelve investigators read through 45,000 pages of documents and interviewed 300 people over the spring and summer of 1994, then sat down together and argued over what it all meant. The report was now done, though it remained classified. It was by all accounts the single most embarrassing document ever compiled by the CIA.

It said the Agency had conducted a hopelessly flawed, impossibly slapdash, inexplicably low-key mole hunt, particularly in light of the fact that "essentially its entire cadre of Soviet sources" had been arrested and executed in 1985 and 1986. Hitz concluded that twenty-three people had been responsible: directors of Central Intelligence and their deputies, covert-operations directors, Soviet division chiefs, counterintelligence czars, security office heads—essentially every senior manager who had overseen Ames for nine years, including directors Bill Casey, William Webster, and Bob Gates.

Woolsey had absorbed the report. He said it showed the Ames case as "a systemic failure of the CIA—and most significantly, for the Directorate of Operations—a failure in management accountability, in judgment, in vigilance." Reading it, "one could almost conclude not only that no one was watching, but that no one cared."

There was one person who had cared: Paul Redmond, whom Woolsey described as "a voice crying out in the wilderness" for six years. He would be promoted to become a special assistant for counterintelligence. That was the only good news of the day.

Woolsey said eleven people bore responsibility for the case of Aldrich Ames. They would receive letters of reprimand. Of those, four were sharp scoldings that barred the recipients from taking on consulting contracts after they retired.

That was it. No one would be demoted or dismissed.

"Sorry," Woolsey said. "That's not my way. And in my judgment, that's not the American way and it's not the CIA's way."

He named no names, save one: Ted Price, his covert-operations chief, who had overseen Ames at the Counterintelligence Center three years earlier. No one at the CIA would disclose the identities of the others who had been disciplined.

The mild discipline contrasted sharply with his harsh words describing the depth of the Agency's failures. Woolsey knew that if he fired prominent people, protests of scapegoating would rise within the CIA. If he did not, he figured, some of his congressional overseers would howl, but the hue and cry would soon subside. So he called the failures sins of omission, placed stern letters in people's files, and faulted the culture of the CIA. Everyone was to blame, so no one was.

Woolsey presented his decision to the House intelligence committee in a closed-door session that afternoon. The chairman, Dan Glickman, said he told Woolsey: "The CIA was set up in the late 1940s to protect Americans against the Soviet Union. What's unbelievable is that the Ames case was the dagger in the heart of why the CIA was set up—and nobody took the case that seriously." Glickman then stuck in his own knife: "The question is whether the CIA has become no different from any other bureaucracy, if it has lost the vibrancy of its unique mission."

By the time the meeting broke up, Dennis DeConcini, the Senate intelligence commitee chairman who was about to retire, had his own assessment of Woolsey's letters of reprimand: "It's a very inadequate response to negligence in the biggest espionage case in the CIA's history. There's a huge problem here that you're not going to get at by leaving some of these people in place. It'll take dramatic reorganization to change the culture, the good old boys' club that protected this guy, promoted him, and gave him sensitive positions."

While Woolsey was off on Capitol Hill, furious gossip shot through the corridors of the CIA. Whom had Woolsey disciplined? Who had taken the rap?

Gradually the names emerged. Three of the nasty letters had gone to Clair George, the legendary director of covert operations; Gus Hathaway, the first chief of the Counterintelligence Center; and Alan Wolfe, Ames's station chief in Rome. The lesser reprimands had gone to two former covert-operations directors, Richard Stolz, now retired, and Tom Twetten, now the London station chief; Jack Lynch, who had run the Office of Security and now served as station chief in Israel; Jim Olsen, a former security office chief, now station chief in Mexico; the former deputy station chief in Rome, Jack Gower; and the former Soviet division chief, Burton Gerber. All had been severely criticized by the inspector general's report. Woolsey added another name to that list: the hapless polygraph operator who had breezily dismissed Ames and judged him an honest man back in 1986.

Of these ten men, only Price, Lynch, and Olsen still served in the Directorate of Operations. Everyone else had retired on a full pension, upward of $90,000 a year.

Woolsey issued a severe reprimand to only one man still on the payroll. The eleventh man: Milt Bearden, who was scheduled to retire two days later as station chief in Bonn and who had approved Ames's three-month appointment as Western Europe branch chief back in 1989.

The decision infuriated some of the barons at the CIA. The next day, Thursday, September 29, John MacGaffin, the number two man in the CIA's covert-operations directorate, and Frank Anderson, the chief of Near East operations, had a private talk about it. Without telling Woolsey or Price, they decided to present an award to Bearden on the unhappy occasion of his retirement. It took the form of an official thank-you for running the Afghan Task Force from 1986 to 1989 and smuggling more than a billion dollars' worth of weapons into Afghanistan in the biggest and most successful paramilitary operation the CIA had undertaken during the cold war. Anderson flew off to Bonn to present the award in person.

One week later, Woolsey was at his desk when his secretary buzzed him. Ted Price needed to talk to him—now. A few minutes later, Price entered and explained that two of his best people had run a covert operation on him. Woolsey was furious. He summoned MacGaffin and Anderson and summarily demoted them. You can't fire us, they said in so many words. We quit.

To add to the incompetence, malaise, backbiting, and managerial miasma at the Agency, insubordination was now reaching the highest levels. The award had been an act of defiance, triggered by Woolsey's failure to mete out discipline in a coherent way. MacGaffin and Anderson had widespread support throughout the Directorate of Operations, and Woolsey knew it. It did not go unnoticed that the punishments he meted out to them were more severe than any he had imposed in the matter of Aldrich Ames.

From that moment on, Woolsey was doomed. He was not going to change the culture of the CIA any more than a ship's captain can change the sea.

Sensing he was wounded, his enemies within the Agency went on the attack. Slurs against his character and his conduct circulated throughout the hallways and filtered into the general population of Washington. On the day after Christmas, he telephoned Bill Clinton, wrote a limp letter of resignation, videotaped his last speech to the men and women of the CIA, and went sailing in the Caribbean.

. . .

In retirement, Milt Bearden, who had done as much as any American to torment and weaken the KGB, worked on the manuscript of a novel in an isolated New Hampshire hamlet, contemplating a frozen lake framed by a picture window and looking back on the last great spy case of the cold war.

"One of the unintended consequences of the Ames case is that the people who think nothing has changed, that we need to go on as before, will lose," he said. "They will not be allowed to continue in their self-delusion. This case was the endgame. Ames is the end of all that."

. . .

On October 21, 1994, Rosario Ames went before Judge Claude M. Hilton in Alexandria to be sentenced. She steadfastly maintained that she should be viewed as her husband's victim and not as his accomplice. "Just as he lied and manipulated the CIA, he manipulated and lied to me," she said. Rosario saved her best argument for last. She pleaded that she be spared jail so that she could raise their five-year-old son: "I beg you, Your Honor, Paul needs me." Judge Hilton pronounced sentence upon her matter-of-factly: sixty-three months in jail, a sentence she is serving at the Federal Correctional Institution in Danbury, Connecticut.

. . .

The FBI's Rudy Guerin wrapped up the transcripts of his last prison interviews with Ames. He had debriefed Ames for close to a hundred hours during 1994, first at the Alexandria jail, then at the Allenwood federal penitentiary in Pennsylvania. The talks gave him a take on the case—not the great geostrategic picture, but a portrait of an ordinary man whose life had been shaped from childhood by the Central Intelligence Agency.

Several of the conversations stood out in Guerin's mind:

"I asked him one time, 'You and your dad—what did you talk about when you guys would be together?' You know, father-son relationship.

"He says, 'Communism. The KGB.'

" 'You and your dad would talk about this?'

" 'Yeah.'

" 'You never talked about, like, the Redskins game?'

" 'No, we really weren't into that.'

"To each his own," Guerin said, shaking his head. "But that's the upbringing he had."

The FBI man thought that fear and greed and the threat of loneliness were the forces that had driven Ames into the Soviet Embassy ten years ago. "I think Rick walked in in '85 because he was afraid of losing Rosario," Guerin said. "He wasn't thinking right. He was drinking. Rick never had a job in his life outside the Agency. He never had to dig a ditch or throw cases of Coke off a truck or pump gas. He never had to really sit down and go: 'I gotta figure this out.'

"I think her spending habits were bad from the get-go. When they moved in together in '84, she started running up bills. Rick took a loan out from the credit union at the Agency—a seven-, eight-thousand-dollar loan—trying to make ends meet.

"I think he was afraid. 'Rosario is obviously used to this kind of living, and if I don't give it to her, she'll leave me.' "

He said Ames had loved the life of a spy for the Soviets. "For the first time in Rick's life, he was accepted. He was part of the in crowd. He was one of the boys. He was always kind of a misfit in the Agency—as was his father. No one really took Rick seriously, and he knew that. But Rick has a high opinion of himself, and the reason people are not paying any attention to him is their mistake. It's nothing that he's done. He's never made real mistakes—in his mind. They don't heed what he said, and if they don't heed what he said, if they don't take seriously what he writes, they're wrong. They're just wrong.

"When he meets the KGB, they accept him immediately. He's got a rush. He's part of the A Team. . . . And he loves it. He finally was accepted. He finally was getting the recognition that he should have gotten from the Agency.

"I asked him one time, during one of the debriefings, I said to him, 'Rick, as we sit here right now, who do you feel more loyal to? The KGB or the CIA?' And he said, 'Oh, the KGB.' "

• • •

Ames spent part of his first few weeks in federal prison auditioning a parade of network correspondents, deciding to whom he would grant a television interview. The networks all sent their most glamorous female stars. At the end of her conversation with him, Connie Chung of CBS News asked Ames if she could give him a hug. She did, to the disgust of the FBI agents and CIA officers in the room.

But Ames rejected them all, choosing CNN instead, thinking its international outlets would allow him to communicate with the Russians. During the interview, he looked into the camera and said how much he admired and respected his former handlers. Perhaps he thought they would someday make a trade for him.

Devoted to an intelligence service that disappeared with the cold war, Ames sat in the hole—solitary confinement at the federal penitentiary in Allenwood. In a letter, he contemplated the idea that he would spend the rest of his life in solitary, and he resigned himself to it. It was as if he had gone to live in another country, one with its own culture and customs, and he would have to learn to live there, and to live with the idea that he would die there.

One small fact gave him satisfaction. The Central Intelligence Agency's damage assessment—its final attempt to evaluate and understand the meaning of his case and the extent of the destruction he had visited on the Agency—was in deep trouble. A full year after Ames was arrested, the intelligence officers working on the report were beginning to believe that they would never get to the bottom of the case.

The Agency could not rid itself of the idea that Ames was still hiding something enormous. It still placed its trust in the lie detector. And Ames had failed nearly every polygraph he had taken since his incarceration.

"I flunked all of it," he said. "There were three or four minor questions that were deemed inconclusive, and everything else was deception. So the CIA's worried that I'm still concealing relationships with the KGB before 1985 or withholding something big. They're agonizing over the damage assessment. They don't know how to cope with it. They think I'm sitting on some immense secret that I gave to the Soviets that I'm still concealing."

The CIA would never know the truth, and it would never be made free.

Acknowledgments and
a Note on Sources

We have tried to do something unusual in this book: to write a full account of an important chapter in the history of the CIA without quoting anonymous sources. Each interview reproduced in this book was on the record. Some sources demanded anonymity; their words were taken into account but not foisted on the reader with an unspoken request for blind faith in their credibility.

Aldrich Ames was interviewed privately, without the presence of CIA officials. Rosario Ames was interviewed at the Federal Correctional Institution in Danbury, Connecticut, without the presence of CIA officials, but because of her plea agreement with a federal court, a transcript of the interview was shown to the Agency to check if she had disclosed any classified information. No changes were made in her comments.

No government censorship constricted this book. We did not submit interview transcripts to the FBI for prepublication review or allow the CIA to interpose itself between us and our sources. In fact, many CIA officers ran the risk of official discipline to discuss the case with us. We thank them for their candor and, in some cases, their courage.

The Agency's public affairs officers also were helpful, within the strict limits placed upon them: thanks to the CIA's Kent Harrington, David Christian, and Mark Mansfield. At the Federal Bureau of Investigation, several officials, unaccustomed to on-the-record interviews, spent many hours talking with us about the case; they include Bob Bryant, John Lewis, Les Wiser, Rudy Guerin, Tim Caruso, and Jim Holt. To them we are grateful, and to John Collingwood, Mike Kortan, and Jennifer Spencer at FBI headquarters, who helped us arrange interviews.

A source list appears below. We want to thank each one of these people for taking time to talk with us.

Thanks also to our colleagues at the Washington bureau of *The New York Times* for their help and camaraderie; to Kathy Robbins and the staff of the Robbins Office and Joe Vallely of Flaming Star Productions; and especially to Robert Loomis, senior vice president of Random House, an extraordinary editor who turned our manuscript into a book.

We dedicate this book to our wives and families.

A List of Sources

We conducted interviews with, among others:

Aldrich Ames
Nancy Segebarth Ames, his first wife
Rosario Ames, his second wife

Former CIA Officials and Officers

Directors of Central Intelligence:
William Colby
Robert M. Gates
Richard Helms
Stansfield Turner
William Webster
R. James Woolsey

Clair E. George, chief, Directorate of Operations
Richard Stolz, chief, Directorate of Operations

Directorate of Operations officers:
Milt Bearden
Mark Blanchard
Duane "Dewey" Clarridge
Charles Cogan

Charles Emmling
Allan E. Goodman
William Hood
John Horton
Donald Jameson
George Kalaris
V. J. Maury
James McCargar
Angus Theurmer
Colin Thompson
Tom Polgar
David Whipple
F. Mark Wyatt
and seventeen others who wish to remain anonymous

FBI Officials and Agents

Robert M. "Bear" Bryant
Tim Caruso
Rudy Guerin
Jim Holt
John F. Lewis, Jr.
James Nolan
Les Wiser
and seven others who wish to remain anonymous

And:

Les Aspin, former Secretary of Defense
Plato Cacheris, attorney for Rick Ames
Tim Carlsgaard, former staff director, Senate intelligence committee
James Cassedy, former U.S.I.A. officer in Burma
Dennis DeConcini, former chairman, Senate intelligence committee
Richard Freeman, former student of Carleton Ames
Dan Glickman, former chairman, House intelligence committee
Oleg Gordievsky, former KGB officer
Oleg Kalugin, former KGB officer
Bob Kerrey, vice-chairman, Senate intelligence committee
Dr. and Mrs. B. H. Kettelkamp, residents of River Falls, Wisconsin
Robert McFarlane, former national security adviser
Michael Norman, University of Wisconsin at River Falls

Michael Nugent, neighbor of Rick and Rosario Ames
William E. Odom, former director, National Security Agency
Rita Sanford, town historian, River Falls, Wisconsin
L. Britt Snider, former counsel, Senate intelligence committee
Arlen Specter, chairman, Senate intelligence committee
Corbin B. Thompson, high school classmate of Rick Ames
Betsy Sue Trice, high school classmate of Rick Ames
Dick Viets, former U.S. ambassador
Chuck Wall, boyhood friend of Rick Ames
John Warner, former vice-chairman, Senate intelligence committee
Walker D. Wyman, school historian, University of Wisconsin at
    River Falls
Stephanie Zeman, librarian, University of Wisconsin at River Falls

We have also consulted the formal reports of the Senate and House intelligence committee on the Ames case. We thank James G. Hershberg, director of the Cold War International History Project at the Woodrow Wilson International Center for Scholars, and Vladislav Zubok of the National Security Archive, for providing the texts of Politburo meetings cited herein, first printed in the Project's *Bulletin*.

Index

TIM WEINER covers the CIA for *The New York Times*. The son of Herbert and Dora Weiner, professors at the University of California, Los Angeles, he was educated at Columbia University. He worked for *The Kansas City Times* and *The Philadelphia Inquirer,* where he won Pulitzer prizes for reporting. He is the author of *Blank Check: The Pentagon's Black Budget.* He is married to Kate Doyle, a foreign-policy analyst at the National Security Archive in Washington, D.C.

DAVID JOHNSTON covers the Justice Department and Federal law enforcement agencies for *The New York Times*. Since coming to the *Times* in 1987, he has had several reporting and editing assignments, including coverage of criminal trials arising from the Iran-contra affair. Before coming to the *Times,* Mr. Johnston covered national politics for the *San Francisco Examiner.* Born in Boston, he grew up in Florida and New York and attended Purdue University in Indiana.

NEIL A. LEWIS has worked for *The New York Times* since 1986, covering the State Department, the Justice Department, and the public school system in New York City. He has worked in Washington, Johannesburg, and London as a correspondent for Reuters. A native of New York City and a graduate of its public schools, he holds degrees from Union College and the Yale Law School, where he was a Ford Foundation Fellow. He is a general assignment correspondent in the Washington Bureau of the *Times* and writes a legal affairs column.

ABOUT THE TYPE

This book was set in Sabon, a typeface designed by the well-known German typographer Jan Tschichold (1902–74). Sabon's design is based upon the original letter forms of Claude Garamond and was created specifically to be used for three sources: foundry type for hand composition, Linotype, and Monotype. Tschichold named his typeface for the famous Frankfurt typefounder Jacques Sabon, who died in 1580.